010 702415

D1613295

This book is to be return~~ed on or before~~
the last date stamp~~ed below.~~ ⊃ ∪ ρ

26. SEP 81	14. MAR 84	
09. DEC 81.	10. JUL 84	05. FEB .85
27. JAN 82		FEB .85
ᵇₚ 26/2/82	08. AUG 84	
25. FEB 83	25. SEP 84	20. MAR 85
1. MAY 83	23. OCT 84	12. JUN 85
		20. JUL .85
	13. NOV 84	15. OCT
		13. MAY
		03. JUN

RENEWALS   *Please quote:* date of return, your ticket number
and computer label number for each item.

THE BASIS AND
ESSENTIALS OF
SPANISH

THE BASIS AND
ESSENTIALS OF
SPANISH

Containing all that must be known of
Grammar, Vocabulary and Idioms for
most everyday purposes by
CHARLES DUFF
Fourth edition, revised and partly rewritten

NELSON

THOMAS NELSON AND SONS LTD
36 Park Street London W1
P.O. Box 336 Apapa Lagos
P.O. Box 25012 Nairobi
P.O. Box 21149 Dar es Salaam
P.O. Box 2187 Accra
77 Coffee Street San Fernando Trinidad

THOMAS NELSON (AUSTRALIA) LTD
597 Little Collins Street Melbourne 3000

THOMAS NELSON AND SONS (SOUTH AFRICA) (PROPRIETARY) LTD
51 Commissioner Street Johannesburg

THOMAS NELSON AND SONS (CANADA) LTD
81 Curlew Drive Don Mills Ontario

THOMAS NELSON AND SONS
Copewood and Davis Streets Camden New Jersey 08103

First published 1933
This extensively revised edition published 1969

17 146064 2

Made and printed in Great Britain by
William Clowes and Sons, Limited, London and Beccles
for Thomas Nelson and Sons Ltd, 36 Park Street, London W1

PREFACE TO THIS EDITION

The Basis and Essentials of Spanish was first published in 1933; revised editions were published in 1936 and 1942. Those editions were reprinted many times, and the book proved to be 'very good and serviceable'—to quote Professor Walter Starkie—and to a large number of people. The main object of the book (and of all others in this series) always was and still is this: to provide those interested in the language with a minimal statement of grammar, which, when supplemented by a carefully chosen 'essential' vocabulary, would enable whosoever assimilated this material to deal with those requirements of everyday life which recur most frequently. The material offered in this new edition is an improvement on that of all previous editions, especially in the new 'Essential Vocabulary', which has been completely rewritten in the light of modern linguistics. It can be plainly stated that, whatever the purpose may be for which Spanish is studied, what is given in this book will always be of primary importance.

No person or body in any of the Spanish-speaking countries has yet compiled for the use of foreign learners a word-frequency list for *spoken* Spanish, though there is the *Word Frequency Dictionary** of the *written* language. I have often found this book useful in helping me to resolve difficulties when compiling my 'Essential Vocabulary', and I must acknowledge with gratitude the help it has been. But my main purpose here relates to spoken Spanish, on which my earlier vocabulary and the present entirely rewritten one is based. In the present one I have had to take into consideration many words required by the foreigner, especially the English-speaking visitor to a Spanish-speaking country. My own experience in using Spanish, which dates back many decades, and for years at times was a part of my day's work, has often been the decisive factor in the choice of a word or phrase. I have also,

---

* Helen S. Eaton, *An English–French–German–Spanish Word Frequency Dictionary*, Constable, London, 1961. The original edition was issued by the Committee on Modern Languages of the American Council of Education. Two other books which provide some useful guidance to the spoken language are: C. E. Eckersley and J. Picazo, *The Essential English–Spanish, Spanish–English Dictionary*, Longmans, Green, London 1953; and Hayward Keniston, *A Standard List of Spanish Words and Idioms*, Harrap, London, 1941.

when in doubt, consulted many Spanish-speaking friends of whom I would particularly wish to remember here the late José V. Barragán* (formerly Senior Lecturer in Spanish at Queen Mary College, University of London, and a Colombian by birth); Enrique Jarero (Lecturer in Colloquial Spanish at the University of Birmingham, by birth a Spaniard), and the late Casto Alonso (a Spaniard who for many years was a teacher and translator of great experience). Many words have been included among the 'Supplementary' words in the Essential Vocabulary for purely empirical reasons, failing the existence of a vocabulary of spoken Spanish based on tape-recordings in a wide field and a word-frequency study of the findings. All these factors demanded that the old vocabulary of this book should be replaced by a new one to meet modern requirements. It has not been found necessary to make any fundamental alterations in Part 1 (Grammar), though a few slips have been corrected and slight editorial amendments have been made in it.

This new edition should be of utility to almost any kind of visitor to a Spanish-speaking country, and also to every beginner who may ultimately wish to extend his or her Spanish studies. Previous editions were often used with success for private tuition, revision, and class work; and also by many people who taught themselves and used no other book. The present edition should better fulfil similar requirements. I have aimed to make the book a compact and practical repository of the fundamentals of the language, those parts which will always be required, and which are sufficient to enable whoever knows them to find expression and to understand Spanish for most everyday purposes.

Suggestions will always be welcomed, and should be addressed to the General Editorial Department, Thomas Nelson & Sons Ltd, 36 Park Street, Park Lane, London W.1

CHARLES DUFF

* Mr Barragán was also one of the four editors of Cassell's *Spanish–English, English–Spanish Dictionary*, perhaps the best of its kind now available.

CONTENTS

Preface to this edition, v

PART 1

THE BASIS OF GRAMMAR

Alphabet and pronunciation, 3

Spanish-American usage

Articles

The definite article, 8

The indefinite article, 9

Nouns

Gender, 11

Plural of nouns, 12

Adjectives

General rules, 14

Comparison, 15

The superlative, 16

Irregular comparison, 17

Position of the adjective, 17

Numbers

Cardinal numbers, 18

Ordinals, 19

Miscellaneous, 20

Different usage in Spanish, 20

Pronouns

Personal Pronouns, 22

Reflexive pronouns, 23

Use of personal and reflexive pronouns, 23

Four rules of position, 24

Pronouns with prepositions, 24

Relatives and interrogatives, 25

Demonstratives, 26
Possessive pronouns and adjectives, 27
Miscellaneous, 28

Verbs

Parts of the verb which must be known, 30
Formation of tenses, 31
What the Spanish tenses represent, 31
Auxiliary verbs **ser** and **haber**, 32
Inflexions of regular verbs, a table of, 34
Models for regular conjugations, 35
Orthographic changes, 35
The passive of verbs, 36
Reflexive verbs: **lavarse**, 37
The negative of verbs, 38
To use the verb interrogatively, 39
Impersonal verbs , 39
Ser and **estar**, 39
Subjunctive mood: for reference, 41
If, how to translate, 42
Irregular Verbs, 42
    1. First conjugation verbs in **-ar**, 42
    2. Second conjugation verbs in **-er**, 44
    3. Third conjugation verbs in **-ir**, 47
    4. Irregular past participles, 49

Conocer, saber, and poder

Some idiomatic usages of verbs, 50
Preposition **a** after a verb, 51
Prepositions and the infinitive, 52

Adverbs, 54

Prepositions, 56

Conjunctions, 60

Word building, etc., 61
Chiefly for Reference, 62

Idioms, 67

Forms of address and family names, 68

Correspondence, 71

PART 2

THE ESSENTIAL VOCABULARY

Abbreviations used in Part 2, 74

Preliminary to the Essential Vocabulary, 75
Hints on learning vocabulary,75

Days of the week, months, seasons, 76

Some common geographical names:
Countries, nationalities; places and names of
inhabitants, 77

Interrogatives, interjections and greetings, 77

**Extracts to illustrate the use and scope of the
Grammar and Vocabulary in this book**

1. *Madrid.* By Ricardo Saens Hayes, 79
2. From *La Prensa* of Buenos Aires, 81
3. El discurso de Don Quijote a los cabreros, 82

Alphabetical list of the Essential Vocabulary
Basic and supplementary words and phrases, 87
Weights and measures: money, 181

PART 1

THE BASIS OF GRAMMAR

NOTE FOR BEGINNERS

A foreign language cannot be acquired without work, but Spanish will be found easier than most by English-speaking beginners. The knowledge required for competence consists of (*a*) fundamental grammar; (*b*) a basic vocabulary plus a number of everyday idioms and phrases. All of this is economically given in this book: Part 1 is the minimum of grammar; the basic words and phrases are given in Part 2, which also contains a number of 'supplementary' words most of which will be required sooner or later by those who wish to achieve a greater range of expression and understanding. The vocabulary can be mastered piecemeal, beginning with not fewer than 10 words a day and rising to not more than 20 a day.

A general idea of the grammar is a first requirement. Not more than two pages (about an hour's work) should be attempted at one time. At first *some* grammar should be mastered every day, until the minimum for practical purposes is known fairly well. From that point onwards, the basic vocabulary comes next in importance.

If at all possible, a good speaker of Spanish should be found to help with pronunciation in the first stage. Then, listening to broadcast Spanish will train the ear to catch Spanish sounds.

For the rest, it is a matter of constant practice, constant revision of grammar, vocabulary and the phrases given in the Essential Vocabulary on pp. 87-181. Those who have a teacher, or a friend who knows Spanish and will help, make quicker progress than those who rely entirely on self-tuition. Many people have acquired a good knowledge of this language by self-tuition only.

ALPHABET AND PRONUNCIATION

The alphabet is the same as in English, but the Spanish Academy treats **CH, LL, RR,** and **Ñ** as additional letters; **W** is to be found only in words of foreign origin.

There is one 'graphic accent' (´) and it is used for two purposes: to indicate the syllable of a word that is to take the principal stress; and to mark a distinction between words that would otherwise be written exactly alike. Thus, in the word **difícil**, the **í** is stressed or accentuated; and **él** means *he*, while **el** without the 'graphic accent' means *the*.

The diæresis (¨) is used over **u** in **güe** and **güi** to indicate that each vowel is to be pronounced: **vergüenza** *shame*. The tilde (~) is used only over the letter **ñ**, to indicate that it is to be pronounced like English *ni* in such words as *onion, companion*: **Señor** *Mr, Sir*.

Each letter in the Spanish alphabet has one invariable sound, excepting **C** and **G**, which have two (as will be explained later).

ACCENTUATION OR STRESS

All words ending in a vowel, **N** or **S**, are accentuated or stressed on the last syllable but one. All words ending otherwise are stressed on the last syllable, unless there is a graphic accent (´) and then the vowel so accented is given the stress. Thus **dinero** *money*; **volumen** *volume*; **antes** *before* (dinER′o, volU′men, AN′tes). **La seguridad** *security*; **esperar** *to expect, hope* (seguriDAD′, esperAR′). **El Perú** *Peru*. **CÁdiz. El cÓnsul** *the consul*. **El paÍs** *the country*.

In these simple rules the student of Spanish has the complete solution of what is, in such languages as English and Russian, the problem of stress—one that is often of great difficulty.

VOWELS

A is pronounced midway between **a** in *that* and *father*.
E is pronounced like **a** in *ace*.
I is pronounced like **i** in *machine*.
O is pronounced like **o** in *order*.

U is pronounced like **u** in *rule*.

Y as a vowel is the same as **I**. As a consonant it is like English **Y**.

Vowel sounds are of very great importance in Spanish. As there are no double consonants (except **cc, ll, nn, rr** which, for pronunciation, represent single sounds) there are no very short vowels in the English or German sense, but only stressed or unstressed vowels. Every Spanish vowel sound is pure, clear, and well rounded—especially when it is stressed.

DIPHTHONGS AND TRIPHTHONGS

The two vowels **i** and **u** are used with other vowels to form diphthongs and triphthongs. Then, the vowel emphasised is the one other than the **i** or **u**:

Santia′go   pie′dra   trei′nta   fue′go   pue′rta   cua′nto

In all vowel compounds not made with **i** and **u**, each vowel must be pronounced with equal clarity: **real, aéreo** (four syllables). Pronounce Spanish **ai, ay** like *ah-ee* (spoken quickly), **hay**.

oi, oy	almost	like	oy in *boy*	hoy
ei, ey	,,	,,	ay-ee	ley
au	,,	,,	ah-oo, ow	pausa
ua	,,	,,	wah	cuanto
ue	,,	,,	wey	fuego
uo	,,	,,	oo-oh	continuo
ui, uy	,,	,,	oo-ee, wee	muy
uai, uay	,,	,,	wah-ee	Uruguay
uei, uey	,,	,,	oo-ay-ee	buey
ia	,,	,,	ee-ah	seria
io	,,	,,	ee-oh	acción
ie	,,	,,	ee-ay	piedra
iu	,,	,,	ee-oo	viudo

All other vowel compounds like the above follow the sounds of the simple vowels, in accordance with the rules given.

CONSONANTS

Unless mentioned below, consonants are pronounced as in English. Note well the following:

B and V are pronounced almost alike in the greater part of Spain (a less explosive sound than either letter in English, with the lips not quite closed). The beginner is advised to keep to the simple English **B** and **V** sounds until he can get a Spaniard to pronounce them for him.

C (1) before **e** and **i**, like English **th** in *thin* (**cinco** *five*); (2) otherwise it is like English **k** (**cura** *parish priest*).

CC is always followed by **i**. Then the first **c** is like **k**, the second like **th**: (**acción**, pr. **Akthiohn′**).

CU like **qu** in *quick* (**cuento** *a story*).

Ch like **ch** in *child* (**muchacho** *boy*).

D, a less distinct sound than English **d**, with a flavour of the **th** in *though* between vowels and at the end of a word: **ciudad** *city* (pr. **theeoodhadh**). Before **r** it is like the thick Irish sound heard in the Connaught pronunciation of words like *drink*, etc.

Note: At the end of a word **d** is often silent, for example in the word, **usted** *you* which is generally pronounced **oostay′**. This is common to the whole of Spanish-America; while even in some parts of Spain it is regarded as a slight affectation to pronounce **usted** otherwise than as indicated.

G (1) before **e** and **i**, like Scots **ch** in *loch* or German **ch** in *Bach*; (2) otherwise like hard **g** in *go* (**siglo** *century*). **General** *general*, pr. **heneral′**, with a strong **H** sound.

GU (1) before **e**, and **i**, like **g** in *go* (**guerra** *war*); (2) before **a** and **o**, like **gw** (**guante** *glove*).

GÜ, the **u** is given a diæresis to indicate that it is to be pronounced before **e** and **i** (**vergüenza** *shame*—pr. **vergooen′tha**).

H, always silent.

J, like Scots **ch** in *loch*, or German **ch** in *Bach*.

JU, before a vowel like a strongly aspirated English **wh** (**jueves** *Thursday*—pr. **Whay′ves**).

LL, like English **lli** in *million*.

NG, like English **ng** in *sing* (**domingo** *Sunday*).

Ñ, like English **ni** in *onion* (**Señor** *Mr, Sir*—pr. **Saynyohr**).

QU is always followed by **e** or **i** and sounds like **k** (**queso** *cheese*).

R is sounded more than in English and is strongly rolled at the beginning of a word and after **l, n, s** (**alrededor** *around*).

RR, a very strong **r** sound, with a fine roll about it (**perro** *dog*; **cerrar** *to shut, lock*). It is treated as a single letter.

S, usually hissed as in *sink*, but as in English **rose** before **b, d, g, l, m** and **n** (**esbozo** *sketch*; **desde** *from, since*; **rasgo** *feature*; **eslabón** *link*; **mismo** *same*; **asno** *ass*).

T, more distinct than in English.

X, as in English. In old Spanish it was pronounced like the modern Spanish J (Don Quixote, now written **Quijote**).

Z, like English **th** in *think* (**zapato** *shoe*).

SPANISH-AMERICAN USAGE

The pronunciation given above is Castilian which, in Spanish-America, is often regarded as Oxford (or British Broadcasting Corporation, Southern) English is regarded in the U.S.A. That is to say, it is considered to be affected. Let not the student forget that there can be only local arguments against following Castilian. Every Spanish-American country has its peculiarities of pronunciation; even in Spain there are many differences. It is, therefore, advisable for the beginner to keep to the rules given for standard Spanish. There are, however, a few points worthy of notice in regard to Spanish-American pronunciation: they may help the novice to avoid feeling overconscious of his Spanish-Spanish when speaking to Spanish-Americans.

C before **e** and **i** is everywhere in Spanish-America pronounced like English **ss.** (Thus, **cinco** is pronounced **sinco** instead of **thinco**, as in Spain.)

Z is always like English **ss. vez** *time*—pr. **vayss**

LL is pronounced like an English **yy** (**caballero, cabay'yero** *gentleman*. This applies to all Spanish-American countries, except in the River Plate countries, where **LL** is almost like an English **j**: **pollo** *chicken*, is there pronounced like English **pojo**.

Consonantal **Y** in the River Plate area is also like an English **j**: **yo** *I*—pr. **Jo.**

S: in Chile this is slurred, almost dropped entirely (**Usted**—pr. **oo'thay**—here the apostrophe represents a slight stop, or hesitation, where the **S** is dropped.

In such endings as **-ado**, the **d** is often silent: **colorado** *red*—pr. **colorao.**

Many other differences from Castilian pronunciation exist throughout Spanish-America, but the above are of most importance. There are also a few slight differences in orthography: **j** is often used instead of **g** before **e** and **i**—**jeneral** for **general**; **i** is often used for **y**—**hai** for **hay** *there is*, *there are*, and so on. But, apart from pronunciation and such very slight differences in orthography, Spanish is everywhere the same, and there is far less difference between the language as spoken in Spanish-America and Spain than there is between the English spoken in England and the U.S.A., apart from dialects. As might be expected, many native and old words are included in the Spanish-American vocabulary, and they are easily 'picked up' on the spot. From personal experience of all but a few of those countries, the author of this book can assure the beginner that, if he knows the material given here, he will rarely find himself embarrassed because of any difference of pronunciation or usage in the language. Chile may present a few problems. In Colombia and Peru very good Spanish is spoken, possibly the best on the Continent. In the River Plate area the language is soft and crooning. Nowhere is it harsh or ill-sounding.

WARNING!

The English equivalents for pronunciation given above are makeshifts. Strictly, every letter in Spanish and every combination of letters should be regarded as representing a sound or sounds distinct from any English sounds. Listen to Spanish records, wireless broadcasts, and follow the speaker, imitating exactly the pronunciation: this will give facility in making the sounds. Never be afraid of rolling the r's or pronouncing vowel sounds, especially those accented, with great clarity.

ARTICLES

The words *the* and *a* are called articles, the former the definite, the latter the indefinite article.

THE DEFINITE ARTICLE

For *the*, the Spanish equivalents are: **el** before a masculine noun, **la** before a feminine noun, **los** before a masculine noun in the plural, **las** before a feminine noun in the plural. Thus:

el muchacho *the boy*　　　**la muchacha** *the girl*
los muchachos *the boys*　　**las muchachas** *the girls*

When a feminine noun begins with either **a** or **ha** stressed, then the masculine article **el** is used for euphony. Thus: **el agua** *the water*; **el hacha** *the axe*. The plural would be **las aguas** *the waters*; **las hachas** *the axes*. Note that **la** is written in full (and not **l'** as in French) before all other nouns beginning with a vowel: **la ambición** *the ambition*.

There is a neuter article **lo**, but it has no plural. It is used before parts of speech other than nouns to make them nouns: **lo útil** *the useful* (**útil** is an adjective). Similarly: **lo difícil** *the difficult*; **lo dicho** *that which has been said* (**dicho** is past participle of the verb **decir** *to say*, see p. 48); **lo pasado** *the past*; **lo futuro** *the future*; **lo necesario** *the necessary*; **lo posible** *the possible*. The examples given should be memorised as they are of frequent occurrence.

The definite article is used in Spanish with a noun employed in a general sense, or when a noun is used to the fullest extent of its meaning. Thus: **El hombre es como Dios le hizo, y aún peor muchas veces** *Man is as God made him, and frequently even worse.** **El hombre es mortal** *Man is mortal.* **Los generales aman la gloria** *Generals love glory.* **La verdad, vale más que las riquezas** *Truth is worth more than riches.* Excepting as stated below, the usage is more or less the same as in English.

The article is used in Spanish:

1. for the hour: **La una (hora** understood) *One o'clock.* **Las dos, las diez (horas** understood) *Two, ten o'clock.*

* Cervantes

2. for the days of the week: **Abren los domingos a las diez y media** *They open on Sundays at 10.30.*

3. for the date of the month: **El 25 de setiembre** *On the 25th September.*

4. for the year: **El año 1984** *The year 1984.*

5. before titles: **El Rey Jorge V de Inglaterra** *King George V of England.* **El señor Martínez** *Mr Martínez.* The masterpiece of Cervantes is usually referred to as **El Quijote.**

6. before certain geographical names. The following should be noted, as they are frequently met: **El Brasil** *Brazil.* **El Canadá** *Canada.* **El Perú** *Peru.* **El Uruguay** *Uruguay.* There is generally a good reason for the use of the article in such cases. Thus: the city of **El Cuzco** in Peru is so called because of its Quechua name (**ccosco**) which means *the navel*—it was so named because it was the centre of the old Inca Empire. Note also: **El Río de la Plata** *the River Plate.* **La Coruña, La Mancha, La República Argentina** *the Argentine Republic.*

The article is often repeated before each noun: **El padre y la hija tienen una casa y un jardín** *The father and daughter have a house and garden.*

After the prepositions **a** *to* and **de** *of* the masculine singular of the definite article drops **e**, and is joined with the preposition. Thus: **al** *to the*; **del** *of the.* **Al padre** *to the father.* **Del hermano** *of the brother.* But: **a los padres** *to the fathers.* **De los hermanos** *of the brothers.*

Note:—The possessive case is expressed in Spanish by the preposition **de.** *The friend's name* becomes *The name of the friend*: **El nombre del amigo.** *My father's hat, the hat of my father*: **El sombrero de mi padre,** etc. One other use of **de** may conveniently be noted here. The material of which an object is made follows the name of the object, the two being connected by **de**: *a wooden chair* becomes in Spanish *a chair of wood*: **una silla de madera. Una casa de madera** *a wooden house.* And note: **El tonto de Pablo** *Silly Paul.*

THE INDEFINITE ARTICLE

The English indefinite article is expressed as follows:

Un before a masculine noun in the singular.

Una before a feminine noun in the singular.

Un and **una** have plural forms, **unos, unas,** meaning *some* or *few* in a rather vague sense:

un hombre *a man*	**una mujer** *a woman*
unos hombres *some men*	**unas mujeres** *a few women*

Generally the indefinite article is used in Spanish where it is used in English, but note the following exceptions.

Omit the article

1. When stating a nationality, rank, profession, or trade:

> **Soy capitán** *I am a captain*
> **Soy soldado** *I am a soldier*
> **Soy médico, abogado, ministro** *I am a doctor, lawyer, minister*
> **Soy inglés** *I am an Englishman*
> **Ella es española** *She is a Spaniard*

But use the article when there is an adjective following:

> **Es un médico muy bueno** (or, **Es muy buen médico**)

But: **El es un argentino de buena familia** *He is an Argentinian of good family*.

2. In proverbial expressions:

> **Amigo reconciliado, enemigo doblado** *A reconciled friend is a double enemy*
> **iglesia, o mar, o casa real** *the church, the sea, or the royal household* (referring to the three careers open to a seventeenth-century Spanish nobleman)

3. Before a noun in apposition:

> **Londres, capital de Inglaterra** *London, the capital of England*

Note: **antes de la comida** *before dinner*
        después del almuerzo *after breakfast*
        en la ciudad, iglesia, escuela *in town, church, school*
        Voy a la ciudad *I am going to town*

NOUNS

There are two genders for Spanish nouns: masculine and feminine.

GENDER

There is only one rule of gender which may be said to be without exceptions: that the names of men and male animals are masculine, and the names of women and female animals are feminine. Thus:

el padre *the father*	**la madre** *the mother*
el toro *the bull*	**la vaca** *the cow*

The safest rule for the student to follow is to learn the gender of each noun as it is met. Nevertheless, the following hints will serve as general indications of gender.

1. Nouns ending in **-E, -N, -R, -O, -L** (mnemonic *enrol*) are masculine. Also names of trees, days of the week, months, oceans, rivers, mountains,* and all other parts of speech used as nouns.
2. Nouns ending in **-A, -DAD, -IÓN, -TUD** (mnemonic *adadiontud*) are feminine. Also nouns in **-UMBRE, -EZ, -TAD,** and most names of cities and towns.

el sol *the sun*	(ending -l)
el cuerpo *the body*	(ending -o)
el cura *the priest*	(name of a man)
el diente *the tooth*	(-e)
el pan *the bread*	(-n)
el calor *the heat*	(-r)
la cabeza *the head*	(-a)
la cantidad *quantity*	(-dad)
la virtud *virtue*	(-tud)
la condición *condition*	(-ión)
la costumbre *custom*	(-umbre)
la timidez *timidity*	(-ez)
la mitad *half*	(-ad)

* But note **Sierra Nevada, las Montañas Rocosas.**

The word **el arte** *the art*, should be noted. It is masculine in the singular and feminine in the plural:

las bellas artes *the fine arts*

Never forget gender. The word **Majestad** *majesty*, is feminine, for example, so we say: **Su Majestad el rey** *His Majesty the king*; and **Su Majestad la reina** *Her Majesty the queen*. **Un ángel** is masculine, so we say: **La muchacha es un ángel.**

-o is a characteristic masculine ending and **-a** is a characteristic feminine ending. But do not forget the first rule of all—that names of men are masculine and names of women are feminine. Learn also:

el día *the day*
el programa *the programme*
el idioma *the language*
el sistema *the system*
el sud *the south*
la sal *the salt*
la flor *the flower*
la labor *the work*
la calle *the street*
la mano *the hand*

All these exceptions are frequently recurring words and not academic curiosities.

El guía *the guide*, is the man who acts as a guide; **la guía** is inanimate —a *guide book*. **El ayuda** is *the assistant*; **la ayuda** is *assistance, aid*.

The feminine of many nouns, especially those of relationship, is formed by changing the ending **-O** into **-A** or by adding **-A** when the ending is a consonant:

el hijo *the son*   **la hija** *the daughter*
el gato *tomcat*   **la gata** *she-cat*

By means of this simple change hundreds of words can be added to one's vocabulary. Other feminine endings for nouns are: **-esa, -isa, -ina.** And **macho** means *male* and **hembra** *female*. So we say, if we wish to emphasise gender: **El pájaro es hembra** *The bird is a female (or a hen)*.

PLURAL OF NOUNS

Add **-s** to:

1. Nouns ending in an unstressed vowel:

el padre, los padres

2. Nouns ending in stressed **e, o,** or **u**:

> **el café, los cafés   el pie, los pies**
> **el landó, los landós   el tisú, los tisús**

Exception: **el calicó, los calicóes**

Add **-es** to:

1. Nouns ending in a consonant (except those of more than one syllable ending in **-es** or **-is**):

> **el jardín, los jardines   el mes, los meses**

But: **el lunes, los lunes   la dosis, las dosis**

2. Nouns ending in **z**, after changing the **z** to **c**:

> **la vez, las veces**

3. Nouns ending in stressed **a** or **i**:

> **el bajá, los bajaes   el rubí, los rubíes**

Exceptions: **el papá, los papás   la mamá, las mamás   el sofá, los sofás**

Family names generally remain unchanged in the plural:

> **Martínez, los Martínez**

Stress is not affected when the plural is formed: **el árbol** *the tree* **los árboles; el joven** *the young man* **los jóvenes.** In this last word it is necessary to write the accent, for otherwise **jovenes** would, in accordance with the rules of pronunciation, be wrongly pronounced **joven'es.** Similarly **el cañón** *the gun*, drops the graphic accent in the plural, which is **los cañones.**

ADJECTIVES

In Spanish the adjective agrees in gender and number with the noun and usually follows it. The same rule applies whether there is one or more adjectives qualifying the noun.

Most adjectives end in **-o** in the masculine, **-a** in the feminine, and **-s** in the plural. Thus: **rico** (masculine singular), **rica** (feminine singular), **ricos** (masculine plural), **ricas** (feminine plural).

A Spanish adjective can stand alone and be used as a noun. Thus **un rico** *a rich man*, **una rica** *a rich woman*; **(los) ricos** *(the) rich (men)* and *the rich* in general. **(Las) ricas** *(the) rich women*. In full these would be:

un hombre rico *a rich man*	**una mujer rica** *a rich woman*
hombres ricos *rich men*	**mujeres ricas** *rich women*

Adjectives ending in a consonant or in any vowel except **-o** do not change to form the feminine. Adjectives ending in **-án, -ón, -or** add **-a** to form the feminine. Thus:

un hombre triste *a sad man*
una mujer triste *a sad woman*
una cosa útil *a useful thing*
una muchacha holgazana *a lazy girl* (**holgazán** *masculine*)

But adjectives of nationality ending in a consonant form their feminine by adding **-a**:

un caballero inglés *an English gentleman*
una señora inglesa *an English lady*

Adjectives of nationality are used to indicate the language or native of the country concerned. Thus:

el inglés *Englishman*
la francesa *Frenchwoman*

Adjectives follow the same rules as nouns to form the plural (now see pp. 12–13 and revise the rules given):

los hombres tristes *the sad men*
las cosas útiles *the useful things*

Invariable as regards gender are:

> **mayor** *greater*   **menor** *lesser, smaller*
> **mejor** *better*   **peor** *worse*

And the following, which have the same meaning in English:

> **superior, inferior, exterior, interior**

Irregularities

When **grande** indicates importance or is used for impressiveness, and not for mere physical size, it drops the **-de** and is placed before the noun:

> **un gran amigo** *a great friend*
> **un amigo grande** *a big (tall) friend*
> **un gran poeta** *a great poet*

Santo *holy* becomes **San** when used as a title. **San Pedro, San Juan** *St Peter, St John*. For euphony it is written in full before **Do** or **To**. **Santo Domingo** *St Dominic*; **Santo Tomás** *St Thomas*.

The following drop **-o** when placed before a masculine singular noun:

> **alguno** *some*   **bueno** *good*
> **malo** *bad*   **ninguno** *no one*
> **primero** *first*   **uno** *one*
> **tercero** *third*

Although these adjectives may be placed after, they are generally placed before the noun:

> **un buen amigo** *a good friend*
> **el mal tiempo** *the bad weather*
> **ningún padre** *no father*
> **el primer día de julio** *the first day of July*

COMPARISON

1. Superiority:

(1)	(2)	(3)
más	(adjective)	que *more . . . than*
más	hermoso	que
more	*beautiful*	*than*

2. Inferiority:

menos	(adjective)	**que** *les . . . than*
menos	**feo**	**que**
less	*ugly*	*than*

In affirmative (but not in negative) sentences use **de** instead of **que** *than* before numerals:

Tengo más de tres	*I have more than three*
menos de seis	*less than six*

But: **no tengo más que tres** (negative sentence)

3. Equality:

(1)	(2)	(3)
tan	(adjective)	**como** *as . . . as*
tan	**pobre**	**como**
as	*poor*	*as*

Tan before a noun becomes **tanto**, which is variable:

Yo tengo tanto dinero como Vd. *I have as much money as you*

When **tanto** follows a verb (that is, when there is no adjective, noun, or adverb) and is used in an absolute sense it is followed by **cuanto**:

Tengo tanto cuanto quiero *I have as much as I want*

But: **Tengo tanto dinero como él** *I have as much money as he*

THE SUPERLATIVE

The word **muy** *very*; the ending **-ísimo**; and **más**, **menos**, with the article are the three ways of forming the superlative in Spanish. The ending **-ísimo** (feminine, **-ísima**) is both beautiful and expressive; but, as its usage is full of pitfalls both of grammar and style, it should be avoided by the tyro. **Muy** is a most useful word and is of even more frequent occurrence in Spanish than *very* is in English. The words **el más** *the most*, and **el menos** *the least* are frequently used to form the superlative and then the article comes first, then the noun, then **más** (or **menos**), and then the adjective:

el hombre más inteligente	*the most intelligent man*
la mujer menos fea	*the least ugly woman*

Take the sentence: *John is patient, Charles is more patient, but*

Robert is the most patient. This may be translated: **Juan es paciente, Carlos es más paciente, pero Roberto es el más paciente.**

Instead of **el más paciente**, we could say either **muy paciente** or **pacientísimo.** Or, **Carlos es pacientísimo y Roberto es el más paciente.** Thus, the Spanish superlative does *not* correspond exactly to the English. For emphasis **del mundo** *in the world*, may be placed after a superlative: **La mujer más fea del mundo** *the ugliest woman (in the world).*

IRREGULAR COMPARISON

bueno *good*	**mejor** *better*	**el (la) mejor** *the best*
malo *bad*	**peor** *worse*	**el (la) peor** *the worst*
grande *great*	**mayor** *greater*	**el (la) mayor** *the greatest*
pequeño *small*	**menor** *smaller*	**el (la) menor** *the smallest*

Grande and **pequeño** also have regular comparatives: **más grande, más pequeño.** However, these forms are more usual when size is referred to. **Mayor** and **menor**, when applied to persons, mean *older* and *younger*:

> **él es más grande que yo** *he is bigger than me*
> **él es mayor que yo** *he is older than me*

POSITION OF THE ADJECTIVE

As a general rule the adjective follows the noun, almost invariably when it denotes nationality, size, shape, colour, weight, or any quality of distinction or importance. When in doubt put it after. Also for emphasis: *My new hat*, emphasis on *new*: **Mi sombrero nuevo.**

But when the quality is a vague general one and is not peculiar to the case in question, the adjective may come before the noun. *My new hat* (no emphasis on the *new*): **Mi nuevo sombrero.**

> **el pobre muchacho** *the poor boy* (i.e. wretched)
> **el muchacho pobre** *the poor boy* (the one without money)

Beyond the above rules the beginner ought not to venture. He will best learn where to place the adjective by reading and hearing Spanish.

For Demonstrative Adjectives, see page 26.

NUMBERS

CARDINAL NUMBERS

1	uno, una	*21*	veinte y uno, una*
2	dos	*22*	veinte y dos
3	tres	*23*	veinte y tres
4	cuatro	*24*	veinte y cuatro
5	cinco	*25*	veinte y cinco
6	seis	*26*	veinte y seis
7	siete	*27*	veinte y siete
8	ocho	*28*	veinte y ocho
9	nueve	*29*	veinte y nueve
10	diez	*30*	treinta
11	once	*31*	treinta y uno,* etc.
12	doce	*40*	cuarenta
13	trece	*50*	cincuenta
14	catorce	*60*	sesenta
15	quince	*70*	setenta
16	diez y seis*	*80*	ochenta
17	diez y siete	*90*	noventa
18	diez y ocho	*100*	ciento, cien
19	diez y nueve	*101*	ciento uno
20	veinte	*200*	doscientos, -as

300 trescientos (-as)   *400* cuatrocientos   *500* quinientos   *600* seiscientos   *700* setecientos   *800* ochocientos   *900* novecientos   *1,000* mil   *100,000* cien mil   *1,000,000* un millón

Uno becomes **un** or **una** if a noun follows:

un caballo *a* or *one horse*

Ciento changes to **cientos, cientas** to agree with the noun following:

cuatrocientas mujeres

* In Spanish America (and sometimes in Spain also) it is customary to write these compounds as one word: **dieciséis, diecisiete, veintiuno, veintidós, treintaiuno,** etc.

When **ciento** comes immediately before a noun or **mil** *a thousand* it drops the final syllable:

> **cien hombres** *100 men*   **cien mil pesos** *100,000 pesos*

Uno is not used before **ciento** and **mil**:

> **mil doscientos** *1200*   **ciento cincuenta** *150*

Above nine hundred count by thousands, with the odd hundreds following:

> **mil novecientos treinta y tres** *1933*

ORDINALS

primero *first*	**segundo** *second*	**tercero** *third*
cuarto *fourth*	**quinto** *fifth*	**sexto** *sixth*
séptimo *seventh*	**octavo** *eighth*	**noveno** or **nono** *ninth*
décimo *tenth*		

They are abbreviated thus: $1°$, $2°$, $3°$, $4°$, $5°$, $6°$, $7°$, $8°$, $9°$, $10°$.

There is no need to learn more than *1–10* at this stage. The ordinal numbers above ten are generally replaced by cardinals, except in old, dignified, or ironical style. Thus we say:

> **el siglo veinte** *the twentieth century*
> **la página diez y nueve** *the nineteenth page* (or *page nineteen*) as in English

Ordinals should be regarded as adjectives, agreeing in gender and number with the noun or nouns which follow:

> **los primeros días** *the first days*
> **la segunda clase** *second class*

Primero and **tercero** drop the **-o** before a noun masculine singular:

> **el primer hombre** *the first man*
> **el tercer año** *the third year*

Also when separated from their noun by an adjective only:

> **el primer buen día** *the first good day*

But not when other parts of speech come between:

> **el primero** (or **tercero**) **de mis amigos** *the first (third) of my friends*

MISCELLANEOUS

una vez *once*
dos veces *twice*
tres veces, cuatro veces, etc.
doble, triple *double, triple*
cuádruplo *quadruple*
la mitad *the half* (n)
medio *half* (adj)
una hora y media *an hour and a half*
un tercio *one-third*
un cuarto *one-quarter*
un par *a couple*
la decena *half a score*
una docena *a dozen*
una veintena *a score*
un centenar *a hundred*
un millar *a thousand*
más o menos *more or less*
cosa de *about, approximately*

o cosa así *or thereabouts*
ocho días *a week*
quince días *a fortnight*
¿Cuántos años tiene Vd.? *How old
   are you?*
Tengo veinte años *I am 20 years old*
a la edad de *at the age of*
¿Qué hora es? *What time is it?*
Es la una *It is one o'clock*
Es la una y media *1.30*
Son las dos *It is two o'clock*
Son las dos y media *2.30*
Son las dos y cinco *Five past two*
Las dos y cuarto *2.15*
Las tres menos cuarto *2.45*
Son cerca de las tres *It is almost
   three o'clock*

DIFFERENT USAGE IN SPANISH

It is important to remember that age is expressed by **tener** and time by **ser**, as in the examples given above (which should be thoroughly mastered). Use ordinals for kings, popes, etc., up to ten; and cardinals after ten: **Felipe segundo** *Philip II*. **Pío nono** *Pius the ninth*. **Alfonso trece** *Alfonso XIII*.

El primero de julio *the first of July*. **El 2 de julio**. As these two examples show, days of the month are expressed by cardinal numbers, excepting the first. In dating letters it is customary to leave out the article: **Madrid, 7 de abril de 1984**. **Vendrá el día veinte** *He will come on the 20th*. **El día veinticuatro de agosto** *On the 24th of August*. To ask the date, say: **¿A cuántos estamos hoy?** Reply: **A once** *It is the eleventh*. **¿Qué fecha será mañana?** *What will the date be tomorrow?* Reply: **El cinco, seis**, etc.

On Monday, Tuesday, etc., is expressed simply by the words **el lunes, martes**, etc. **Vendré el lunes** *I will come on Monday*.

The verb **DAR** *to give* is used for the striking of the hour. **Ha dado la una** *It has struck one*. **Han dado las dos** *It has struck two*. *Next* in expressions of time is translated by **que viene** *which is coming*: **La semana que viene** *next week*. **El mes que viene** *next month*. For days of the week, use **próximo**: **el próximo lunes** *next Monday* (or **el lunes** próximo). **El año que viene. La semana pasada** *last week*. **El año pasado** *last year*.

Measurement: Use **TENER** followed by the noun or adjective of dimension followed by **de**. Thus **Esta casa tiene 90 pies de largo y 50 de ancho** *This house is 90 feet long by 50 wide*. **La casa tiene 80 pies de alto** *the house is 80 feet high*. **Alto** *high*. **Largo** *long*. **Ancho** *broad, wide*. **Profundo** *deep* (also **hondo**). **Grueso** *thick*.

PRONOUNS

TABLE OF PERSONAL PRONOUNS

Subject	Indirect object	Direct object	Reflexive	Prepositional
yo *I*	me *(to) me*	me *me*	me *myself*	(a) mí *to me*
tú *thou*	te *(to) thee*	te *thee*	te *thyself*	ti *to thee*
él *he*	le *(to) him*	le *him*	se *himself*	él *to him*
ella *she*	le *(to) her*	la *her*	se *herself*	ella *to her*
	le *(to) it*	lo *it** (m) la *it* (f)	se *itself*	
usted *you*	le *(to) you*	le *you* (m) la *you* (f)	se *yourself*	usted *to you*
nosotros *we* (m)	nos *(to) us*	nos *us*	nos *ourselves*	(a) nosotros *to us*
nosotras *we* (f)	nos *(to)us*	nos *us*	nos *ourselves*	nosotras *to us*
vosotros *you* (m)	os *(to) you*	os *you*	os *yourselves*	vosotros *to you*
vosotras *you* (f)	os *(to) you*	os *you*	os *yourselves*	vosotras *to you*
ellos *they* (m)	les *(to) them*	los *them* (m)	se *themselves*	ellos *to them*
ellas *they* (f)	les *(to) them*	las *them* (f)	se *themselves*	ellas *to them*
ustedes *you*	les *(to) you*	los *you* (m) las *you* (f)	se *yourselves*	ustedes *to you*

Subject pronouns answer the question *Who acted?* Direct object pronouns answer *Who* or *what was the direct or primary recipient of the action?* Indirect object pronouns answer for the *indirect or secondary recipient of the action.* In the sentence *I will give it to him, I* is subject; *it* is direct object; *(to) him* is indirect object. Reflexive pronouns are used with reflexive verbs (see pp. 37–38). The prepositional pronouns are used after a preposition: **a mí** *to me*; **a él** *to him*; **por ella** *by her*.

Never forget Spanish genders. English *it* may be in Spanish **él** or **ella**. These, however, are not expressed as the subject of a sentence. Thus: **Aquí está mi casa. Es muy cómoda** *Here is my house. It is very comfortable.* A neuter pronoun **ello** *it*, also exists in Spanish: **Ello†podrá ser verdad, pero no lo creo** *It may be true, but I do not believe it.* **No tenemos evidencia de ello** *We have no evidence of it.*

In the Table the use of **tú** and **vosotros** can be learnt later (see p. 68). **Usted**, pl. **ustedes**, are the polite, everyday forms for *you* in singular and plural. *Usted* (=*your grace*, see p. 68) always takes third person singular verb, **ustedes** third person plural verb.

* **Lo** is also used to mean *him*.

† **Ello** can be omitted, i.e. taken for granted. This is much more usual in conversation.

REFLEXIVE PRONOUNS

Reflexive pronouns are used when a person (or thing) does something to himself, herself (or itself): *I wash myself. He hides himself. Myself* and *himself* are reflexive pronouns. The Spanish reflexive pronouns are:

me	*myself*	**te**	*thyself*
nos	*ourselves*	**os**	*yourselves*

And now we come to a word which must be watched because of its manifold meanings. Se is the third person reflexive pronoun for all genders, singular and plural, and for **Vd.**, and its plural **Vds.** Thus:

> *himself, herself, itself, oneself* ⎫
> *themselves* (all genders) ⎪ translate by **se**
> *yourself* ⎪
> *yourselves* ⎭

> **El se llama** *He calls himself*
> **Ella se engaña** *She deceives herself*
> **Ellos se conocen** *They know themselves*
> **Vd. se admira** *You admire yourself*
> **Vds. se levantan** *You get up* (pl)

Reflexive verbs are common in Spanish, hence these reflexive pronouns are in great demand (see p. 37).

USE OF PERSONAL AND REFLEXIVE PRONOUNS

As will be seen later, the Spanish verb is inflected for changes of person (see p. 34), and therefore it is not always necessary to use a subject personal pronoun with it. **Tengo** can only mean *I have*, and **estoy** can only mean *I am*. So it is unnecessary to say **yo tengo, yo estoy**—unless for emphasis. But **tiene**, the third person singular of the present tense, may mean *he, she,* or *it has,* or *you have* (**Vd.**). It is therefore advisable to put a pronoun with it, unless there can be no doubt as to its meaning.

Object and reflexive pronouns precede the verb except: (1) the infinitive and the present participle, with which they are joined, and (2) the imperative affirmative, with which they are also joined.

> **tenerlo** *to have it*   **teniéndolo** *having it*
> **¡Tómalo!** *Take it!*
> **lavarse las manos** *to wash one's hands*

FOUR RULES OF POSITION

1. When two object pronouns are required—direct and indirect—as in the sentence, *He gives it to me,* the order of the object pronouns in Spanish is the reverse of the English order. Thus,

(1) (2)
English: *He gives it to me*
(2) (1)
Spanish: **El me lo da**

2. **Se** in all its meanings precedes any other object pronoun or pronouns. **Se lo diré** *I will tell it to him.*
3. **Te** and **Os** precede all pronouns except **Se**. **Te lo diré** *I will tell it to thee.*
4. **Le, lo, la, les, los, las** take the last place before the verb: **Yo se lo doy** *I give it to him.*

PRONOUNS WITH PREPOSITIONS

Certain pronouns when preceded by a preposition change their form slightly: **me** becomes **mí**, **te** becomes **ti**, and **se** becomes **sí**. The preposition **con** *with* makes **conmigo, contigo,** and **consigo** for *with me, with thee, with him, her, it, them, etc.* Thus:

para mí *for me*   **con nosotros, nosotras** *with us*
sin ti *without thee*   **por ellos** *by them*
con él *with him*   **a ella** *to her*

If the person has already been designated, always use **sí** instead of **él, ella, ellos, ellas, Vd., Vds.**

Ellos hablan de sí *They are speaking of themselves*

When two object pronouns are in the third person, then in order to avoid repetition of the letter **l**, the first is changed to **se**. Instead of saying **Le lo di** *I gave it to him*, we must say, **Se lo di**. Similarly, **Dígaselo** *Tell it to him*

When there is ambiguity or doubt, then it is advisable to add **a él, a Vd.**, etc. **Se lo avisaré a Vd.** *I will let you know about it (tell it to you)*

Examples of the use of pronouns:

Vd. me habla *You speak to me*
Hablo de mí *I speak of myself*
Yo le he hablado *I have spoken to her*

Yo les digo *I tell them*
Les escribiré *I will write to them*
Los tengo *I have them*
Me parece probable *It seems to me probable*
El me ha comprado las manzanas *He has bought the apples from me*
Yo me he ofrecido a él como amigo *I have offered myself to him as a friend*
Le digo a Vd. *I tell you* (emphatic)
¿Se ha lavado Vd. las manos? *Have you washed your hands?*

Mismo. The word **mismo** means *same* and also *self.* It agrees with and may be placed after any personal pronoun for emphasis. **Yo mismo** *I myself.* **Nosotros mismos** *We ourselves.* **Ellas mismas** *They themselves* (f). **Ella misma** *She herself.* It should not be confused with reflexives.

Lo is often used as an equivalent for *so, one, it,* in such sentences as:

El está enfermo, pero no lo parece *He is ill, but does not appear so*
O es médico, o va a serlo *Either he is a doctor, or he is going to be one*

RELATIVES AND INTERROGATIVES

A relative pronoun is one which connects the noun or pronoun to which it refers with the part of the sentence which follows. Thus: *The man whom I know. The house that Jack built. Whom* and *that* are relatives.

The relative pronouns must always be expressed in Spanish, and are:

> **quien** *who*   **el cual** *which*
> **que** *that*   **cuyo** *whose*   **cuanto** *as much*

Que is invariable. All the other relatives are variable and follow the same rules for inflexions as adjectives. Thus:

> quien, quienes
> el cual, la cual, los cuales, las cuales
> cuyo, cuya, cuyos, cuyas

Que may refer either to persons or things. **Quien** refers only to persons:

El hombre que viene es mi amigo *The man who comes is my friend*
Quien viene es mi amigo *He who comes is my friend*

El cual is used for persons and things, and is a more accurate relative than **que** or **quien**. It is generally used after a preposition:

> **Han llegado mis dos hermanos, con los cuales Vd. debe tratar** *My two brothers have arrived, with whom you must deal*

Cuyo is the possessive, and may be used with persons or things:

> **El padre cuyos hijos están aquí** *The father whose sons are here*
> **La llave cuya pérdida me ha costado tanto** *The key of which the loss has cost me so much*

The above relatives are used as interrogatives* but then they must be written with the graphic accent:

> **¿Quién?** *Who?* **¿Cuál?** *Which, which one* (of several)?
> **¿Qué?** *What?* **¿Cuánto?** *How much?*
> **¿Quién está hablando?** *Who is speaking?*
> **¿A quién habló Vd.?** *To whom did you speak?*
> **¿Qué le falta?** *What are you short of?*
> **¿Cuál quiere?** *Which does he want?*
> **¿Cuáles son sus ideas?** *What are your ideas?*
> **¿De quién es esta casa?** *Whose is this house?*
> **¿Cuánto dinero tiene él?** *How much money has he?*

Qué and **cuánto** (**cuán** before adjectives) are used in exclamations:

> **¡Qué muchacha tan hermosa!** *What a beautiful girl?*
> **¡Cuán rico es!** *How rich he is!*
> **¡Cuántas veces!** *How often . . . !*

DEMONSTRATIVES

Without accent the following are adjectives, with accent they are pronouns:

	singular		plural		
	masc	fem	masc	fem	
this	este	esta	estos	estas	present or nearby
that	ese	esa	esos	esas	a little way off
that	aquel	aquella	aquellos	aquellas	remote

> **Este libro que yo tengo** *This book which I have* (hold)
> **Ese libro que Vd. tiene** *That book which you have*
> **Aquel libro que él tiene** *That book* (over there) *which he has*
> **Aquella muchacha** *That girl*

* Except **cuyo**, which is not used interrogatively in modern Spanish.

With accent in all forms **éste, ése, aquél** are used as pronouns which can stand alone, and then mean *this one, that one, that (remote) one.* Thus:

> **Este libro y aquél** *This book and that one (over there)*
> **Esa mujer y aquélla** *That woman (a little way off) and the one over there (remote)*

The forms **esto, eso, aquello** are used for neuter *it, this* (thing, matter):

> **¿Quién ha dicho eso?** *Who (has) said that (or it or so)?*
> **eso no importa** *That doesn't matter*
> **eso es** *That's it (so)*

As adjectives these words agree with their noun, as pronouns with their antecedent.

POSSESSIVE PRONOUNS AND ADJECTIVES

Adjectives	Pronouns	
mi (pl **mis**) *my*	**mío** (**mía, míos, mías**) *mine*	
tu (**tus**) *thy*	**tuyo** *thine*	
su (**sus**) *his, her, its*	**suyo** *his, hers, its*	
nuestro (-a, -os, -as) *our*	**nuestro** *our*	-a, -os, -as
vuestro (-a, -os, -as) *your*	**vuestro** *your*	
su (**sus**) *their*	**suyo** *their*	

Su, sus, and **suyo,** it should not be forgotten, are also used as possessive adjectives and pronouns corresponding to **Vd., Vds.** But in case of ambiguity, it is better to use **de Vd., de Vds., de él, de ella,** etc.

The possessive adjectives (or adjectival pronouns) **mi, tu, su, nuestro, vuestro, su,** and their plurals are generally placed before the noun. The forms **mío, tuyo,** etc., may be placed after for emphasis, with an article before the noun. Thus:

> **mi padre** *my father*
> **el sombrero mío** *my hat*

Mío, tuyo, suyo are also true pronouns—that is, they may replace nouns:

> **el mío** *mine*   **el suyo** *his, hers*
> **Este sombrero es mío** *That hat is mine*

Note:—Possessive adjectives and pronouns in Spanish agree in gender and number with the object possessed:

> **mis sombreros** *my hats*
> **Esos sombreros son míos** *Those hats are mine*
> **Las plumas son suyas** *The pens are his, hers*
> **Las plumas son de él** *The pens are his*
> **mi querido amigo** *my dear friend* (masc)
> **querida amiga mía** *my dear friend* (fem)
> **El es buen amigo mío** *He is my good friend*
> **Ella es buena amiga mía** *She is my good friend*

MISCELLANEOUS

A number of very useful words are like adjectives and pronouns in that they can be used either as adjectives with a noun, or as pronouns instead of a noun or nouns.

> **todo, -a, -os, -as** *all, every one*
> **mucho, -a, -os, -as** *much, many*
> **poco, -a -os, -as** *few, little*
> **entero, -a, -os, -as** *whole, entire*
> **solo, -a, -os, -as** *alone*
> **único, -a, -os, -as** *unique, only*
> and the invariable word **cada** *each*

Examples:

> **Toda la semana** *All the week*
> **Todo el día** *All the day*
> **Lo he visto todo** *I saw all of it*
> **Lo haré todo** *I will do it all*
> **Todo lo que he hecho** *All that I have done*
> **Vds. todos** *All of you*
> **Todos ellos, Ellas todas** *All of them*
> **Es la verdad, todo** *It is the truth, all of it*
> **Vinieron todos** *They all came*
> **Todo el mundo** *Everybody*
>
> **Con mucho gusto** *With much pleasure*
> **Mucho** is the word for *very* with verbs
> **Me gusta mucho** *I like it very much*
> **Tiene mucha suerte, ¿no es verdad?** *He is very lucky, is he not?*
> **Mucha** *Very*

Un poco de leche *A little milk*
Hay poca luz en esta casa *There is little light in this house*
¿Tiene Vd. mucho dinero? *Have you much money?*
No, Señor, muy poco *No, Sir, very little*

Estoy solo* *I am alone*
Yo sólo *I only*
mi hermano único *my only brother*
mi hermano sólo *my brother alone*

Una cajita para cada veinte huevos *A little box for each score of eggs*
cada uno de mis hermanos *each one of my brothers*
la noche entera or toda la noche *all the night*
una semana entera *a whole week*

Note also the following:

otro *other*	alguno *some*
ambos *both*	varios *several*
propio *own, very own*	cierto *a certain*

All these are variable: **otro, otra, otros, otras,** etc.

él, la, lo, los, las demás *the rest, the others*
tal (tales) *such*   semejante *similar*

Alguna cosa and **algo** (something), **ninguna cosa, nada** (nothing),
are interchangeable.

No me gusta ninguna cosa *Nothing pleases me*
Nada me gusta *Nothing pleases me*

alguien *someone, somebody*
nadie *no one, nobody*

All these words recur frequently, and must be known.

* **Sólo** is sometimes used instead of **solamente** the adverb. But note that it is then written with an accent. **Sólo tengo un cigarrillo** *I have only one cigarette.*

VERBS

———◆———

Compared with the verbs of some other European languages those of Spanish are fairly straightforward. It is unnecessary to know all the parts of even the regular verbs, unless the student aims to become an expert translator. As for the 900 irregular verbs, only about 100 recur frequently, and of these only the most useful parts will be given. It is, however, necessary for the student to realise at the outset that there is not a line in the treatment of the verb given in these pages which he can afford to neglect. What is given must be known thoroughly—so thoroughly that the part of a verb required comes without hesitation to the mind.

PARTS OF THE VERB WHICH MUST BE KNOWN

1. The infinitive, i.e. 'that part of a verb which names the action, without reference to any doer, and is therefore not limited by person or by number'. Thus: **comprar** *to buy*; **vender** *to sell*; **vivir** *to live*.

2. The present tense, which represents the English forms *I —*, *I do —*, *I am —ing*. Thus: **Yo compro** *I buy, I do buy*, or, *I am buying*.

3. The past tense definite, which corresponds to the English simple past, or, *I did —*. Thus: **Yo compré** *I bought*, or, *I did buy*.

4. The future tense simple, which represents the English *I shall —*. Thus: **Yo compraré** *I shall buy*.

5. The past participle, which is used to form compound tenses, and often as an adjective. Thus: **Yo he comprado** *I have bought*.

The infinitive of all Spanish verbs has one of the three endings: **-ar, -er,** or **-ir.** Thus: **comprar** *to buy*; **vender** *to sell*; **vivir** *to live*. All verbs ending in **-ar** are conjugated similarly to **comprar**; all in **-er** similarly to **vender**; all in **-ir** similarly to **vivir**. Those which do not follow the models of these verbs are called 'irregular', and their essential parts will be found on pp. 42–49.

FORMATION OF TENSES

For the purposes of reference a complete table of the inflexions of all regular verbs is given on p. 34.

Every part of a regular verb can be formed from this table, the auxiliaries being used for compound tenses.

To form any tense, simply add the inflexions in the Table to the 'stem' of the verb. This 'stem' is found by removing the infinitive ending. Thus **compr-**, **vend-**, **viv-**, are the stems of **comprar**, **vender**, and **vivir**. In the future indicative and conditional, the endings in the Table are added to the full infinitive.

Examples:

The present of **comprar** is:

compro, compras, compra, compramos, compráis, compran

The future of **vender** is:

venderé, venderás, venderá, etc.

The past definite of **vivir** is:

viví, viviste, vivió, etc.

The conditional would be:

compraría, etc.

The imperfect tenses of the three are:

compraba, vendía, vivía, etc.

Important note: Pronouns (subject) may be omitted where the inflexion of a verb clearly indicates the person. The pronoun should, however, always be used for emphasis.

It will be noticed that, excepting the infinitive and the two forms built upon it (future and conditional), the inflexions of -er and -ir verbs differ only in the 1st and 2nd persons plural indicative present and in 2nd person singular of the imperative.

WHAT THE VARIOUS SPANISH TENSES REPRESENT IN ENGLISH

Let us take the verb **hablar**, a regular verb, and, in the first person of each tense, the translation into an English equivalent would be:

Infinitive: **hablar** *to speak*
Present participle: **hablando** *speaking*
Past participle: **hablado** *spoken*

Indicative—

> Present tense: **hablo** *I speak*
> Imperfect: **hablaba** *I was speaking*
> Past definite: **hablé** *I did speak, I spoke*
> Future: **hablaré** *I shall speak*
> Conditional: **hablaría** *I should speak*
> Imperative: **habla (tú)** *speak thou!* **hablad (vosotros)**

Subjunctive—

> Present: **que hable** *that I speak*
> Imperfect: **que hablase** *that I spoke*
> Future: **que hablare** *that I shall speak*

Compound tenses—

> Perfect: **(Yo) he hablado** *I have spoken*
> 1st Pluperfect: **había hablado** *I had spoken*
> 2nd Pluperfect: **hube hablado** *I had spoken*
> Future perfect: **habré hablado** *I shall have spoken*
> Past conditional: **habría hablado** *I should have spoken*

And similarly, the subjunctive:

> Perfect: **que yo haya hablado** *that I have spoken*
> Pluperfect: **que hubiere hablado** *that I had spoken*
> Future: **que hubiere hablado** *that I shall have spoken*
> Conditional: **que hubiera hablado** *that I should have spoken*

Note: Neither the table of inflexions on p. 34 nor the above need be memorised at this stage. The somewhat extended treatment is given so that when the student reaches the reading stage, he may be able to return here for guidance. It is, all the same, advisable to read through these pages until the general principles are grasped. Once grasped, they are easily memorised.

AUXILIARY VERBS

The two verbs **ser** *to be*, and **haber** *to have*, are called auxiliaries, because they are used not only to express 'to have' and 'to be' but also to form compound tenses and the passive of all verbs.* Hence, they are of great importance. They are both irregular.

> Infinitive: **ser** *to be*
> Present participle: **siendo** *being*
> Past participle: **sido** *been*

* See page 45 for **tener** *to possess*.

Present tense	Imperfect tense
Yo soy *I am*	**era** *I was*
tú eres *thou art*	**eras** *thou wast*
él, ella, es *he, she, it is*	**era** *he, she, it was*
nosotros, -as, somos *we are*	**éramos** *we were*
vosotros, -as, sois *you are*	**erais** *you were*
ellos, -as, son *they are*	**eran** *they were*

Past definite	Future
fui *I was*	**seré** *I shall be*
fuiste	**serás**
fue	**será**
fuimos	**seremos**
fuisteis	**seréis**
fueron	**serán**

Conditional	Present subjunctive
sería *I should be*	**(que) yo sea** *(that) I be*
serías	**seas**
sería	**sea**
seríamos	**seamos**
seríais	**seáis**
serían	**sean**

Infinitive: **haber** *to have*
Present participle: **habiendo** *having*
Past participle: **habido** *had*

Present tense	Imperfect
he *I have*	**había** *I used to have*
has	**habías**
ha	**había**
hemos	**habíamos**
habéis	**habíais**
han	**habían**

Past definite	Future
hube *I had, did have*	**habré** *I shall have*
hubiste	**habrás**
hubo	**habrá**
hubimos	**habremos**
hubisteis	**habréis**
hubieron	**habrán**

Conditional	Present subjunctive
habría, -ías, etc., *I should*	**haya, -as, -a** *that I have*
have	**hayamos, -áis, -an**

For impersonal use, see page 39 and **haber** in the Essential
Vocabulary, Part 2, page 125.

TABLE OF INFLEXIONS OF REGULAR VERBS

Infinitives
- 1st conjugation: **-ar (comprar)**
- 2nd conjugation: **-er (vender)**
- 3rd conjugation: **-ir (vivir)**

Present participles
1. **-ando**
2. **-iendo**
3. **-iendo**

Past participles
1. **-ado**
2. **-ido**
3. **-ido**

Indicative

Present tense
1. **-o, -as, -a; -amos, -áis, -an**
2. **-o, -es, -e; -emos, -éis, -en**
3. **-o, -es, -e; -imos, -ís, -en**

Imperfect
1.   **-aba, -abas, -aba; -ábamos, -abais, -aban**
2 and 3. **-ía, -ías, -ía; -íamos, -íais, -ían**

Past definite
1.   **-é, -aste, -ó; -amos, -asteis, -aron**
2 and 3. **-í, -iste, -ió; -imos, -isteis, -ieron**

Future, all conjugations: **-é, -ás, -á; -emos, -éis, -án**

Conditional, all conjugations: **-ía, -ías, -ía; -íamos, -íais, -ían**

Imperative

1. **-a, -e; -emos, -ad, -en**
2. **-e, -a; -amos, -ed, -an**
3. **-e, -a; -amos, -id, -an**

The subjunctive

Present subj
1. **-e, -es, -e; -emos, -éis, -en**
2 and 3. **-a, -as, -a; -amos, -áis, -an**

Imp subj
1. **-ara, -aras, -ara; -áramos, -arais, -aran**
     -ase, -ases, -ase; -ásemos, -aseis, -asen
2 and 3. **-iera, -ieras, -iera, -iéramos, -ierais, -ieran**
     -iese, -ieses, -iese; -iésemos, -ieseis, -iesen

Future subj
1. **-are, -ares, -are; -áremos, -areis, -aren**
2 and 3. **-iere, -ieres, -iere; -iéremos, -iereis, -ieren**

MODELS FOR THE REGULAR CONJUGATIONS

Infinitives:

comprar *to buy*   **vender** *to sell*   **vivir** *to live**

Present participles:

comprando *buying*   **vendiendo** *selling*   **viviendo** *living*

Past participles:

comprado *bought*   **vendido** *sold*   **vivido** *lived*

Present tense:

1. **Compro, compras, compra, compramos, compráis, compran** *I buy, thou buyest, he buys,* etc.
2. **Vendo, vendes, vende, vendemos, vendéis, venden**
3. **Vivo, vives, vive, vivimos, vivís, viven**

Imperfect:

1. **Compraba,** etc. *I was buying.*
2. **Vendía,** etc. *I was selling.*
3. **Vivía,** *I was living.*

Past definite:

1. **Compré, compraste, compró, compramos, comprasteis, compraron**
2. **Vendí,** etc.
3. **Viví,** etc.

Future:

1. **Compraré, -ás, -á, -émos, -éis, -án**
2. **Venderé,** etc.
3. **Viviré,** etc.

A compound verb, regular or irregular, follows the conjugation of the parent verb.

ORTHOGRAPHIC CHANGES

With the exception of the irregular verbs noted below, the tenses of all the verbs given on pp. 87–180 may be formed in accordance with the rules stated. There are, however, certain orthographic changes

* Compare throughout with the Table on p. 34.

which take place in the formation of parts of certain regular verbs, notably:

1. Verbs ending in **-car** change the **c** into **qu** before an **e**. Thus:

> **tocar** *to touch*   **yo toqué** *I touched*

2. Similarly, verbs ending in **-gar** take **u** after **g** when an **e** follows. Thus:

> **pagar** *to pay*   **yo pagué** *I paid*   **que él pague** *let him pay*

3. Verbs ending in **-zar**, change **z** into **c** before **e**. Thus:

> **gozar** *to enjoy*   **yo gocé** *I enjoyed*

4. Verbs ending **-cer**, **-cir**, preceded by a consonant change **c** to **z** before **a** or **o**. Thus:

> **vencer** *to conquer*   **venzo** *I conquer*

5. But verbs ending in **-cer**, **-cir**, preceded by a vowel take in a **z** before the **c** when followed by **a** or **o**. Thus:

> **lucir** *to shine*   **luzco** *I shine*

6. Verbs ending in **-ger**, **-gir** change **g** into **j** before **a** or **o**. Thus:

> **escoger** *to select*   **escojo** *I select*

7. Verbs ending in **-eer**, change the **i** of an ending into **y** when it occurs between two vowels and when unstressed. Thus:

> **creer** *to believe*   **creyendo** (not **creiendo**) *believing*

8. Verbs ending in **-guir**, **-quir**, drop the **u** before **a** or **o**. Thus:

> **distinguir** *to distinguish*   **distingo** *I distinguish*

Note: The above changes are, strictly speaking, not irregularities. They are for the purpose of preserving the sound of the stem as it is pronounced in the infinitive; or for euphony, as in (5).

THE PASSIVE OF VERBS

The passive is formed by using the auxiliary **ser** with the present participle of the verb of which the passive is required. Thus:

> **yo soy querido, él es querido** *I am loved, he is loved*

The participle agrees with the subject of the sentence. Thus:

> **ella es querida** *she is loved*
> **ellos son queridos, ellas son queridas** *they are loved* (m & f)

When it is necessary to use a compound tense of the auxiliary **ser** before another past participle, then the past participle of **ser** remains invariable, while the past participle of the other (i.e. transitive) verb agrees in gender and number with its subject noun. Thus:

> **ella ha sido querida** *she has been loved*
> **ellos han sido queridos** *they have been loved*

The reflexive form (see below) is frequently used for the English passive:

> **eso se hará pronto** *that will quickly be done*

REFLEXIVE VERBS

A verb is called reflexive (1) when its action is both performed and suffered by the subject, and (2) when two pronouns are used instead of one in conjugation. In English comparatively few verbs are reflexive, but there are many in Spanish, and they are not necessarily translated by the English reflexive. Thus: **lavarse** *to wash oneself*, is a reflexive verb in both languages, but **equivocarse** *to make a mistake* is reflexive in Spanish only.

Present tense of **lavarse** *to wash oneself*

yo me lavo *I wash myself*	nosotros ⎱	nos	
tú te lavas	nosotras ⎰	lavamos	
él ⎱		vosotros ⎱	os laváis
ella ⎬ se lava		vosotras ⎰	
Vd. ⎰			

ellos, ellas, Vds. se lavan

And so on, throughout all other tenses.

In a compound tense, the order is (1) subject pronoun, (2) reflexive pronoun, (3) auxiliary, (4) past participle. Thus:

> **yo me he lavado** *I have washed myself*

Note: Do not confuse the word **mismo** *same, self* with the reflexive.
The reflexive form is more often used as an equivalent of the English

passive than the true passive form given earlier. But this chiefly applies to the third person, thus:

> **Se dice que es médico** *It is said that he is a doctor*
> **No se explica cómo ha aprendido el castellano** *It is not explained how he learnt Spanish*
> **No se sabe la fecha** *The date is not known*
> **Eso se comprenderá fácilmente** *That will easily be understood*
> **¿Qué se debe hacer?** *What is to be done?*
> **Se habla inglés** *English spoken*
> **¿Se permite hacer eso?** *May that be done?*
> **Se necesita un mozo** *A waiter is wanted*
> **Se ruega a los Sres pasajeros ...** *Passengers are requested ...*
> **¿Cómo se llama Vd.?** *What are you called? (What is your name?)*
> **Se habló de todo** *Everything was discussed*
> **Los diarios se venden en todos los kioskos** *Newspapers are sold at all the kiosks*

THE NEGATIVE OF VERBS

To form the negative of any verb, put the word **no** *not* before the verb or auxiliary:

> **Yo no compro** *I do not buy*
> **No he comprado** *I have not bought*

The negative precedes all personal pronouns except the subject:

> **Yo no tengo dinero** *I have no money*
> **No lo he conseguido** *I have not obtained it*

Other negatives are:

> **nadie** *nobody*   **nada** *nothing*   **nunca** *never*
> **no** (verb) **más que** *not more than ...*
> **No tardo más tiempo que el necesario** *I take only what time is necessary* (literally: *I do not take more time than the necessary*)
> **nada más, nada menos** *no more, no less*
> **ni ... tampoco** *neither*
> **ni yo tampoco** *nor I either*
> **no ... ni** *not ... nor*
> **No compro el libro, ni tengo tiempo para leerlo** *I do not (wish to) buy the book, nor have I time to read it*
> **No tengo ni dinero ni géneros** *I have neither money nor goods*
> **no ... ni siquiera ...,** *not even ...*
> **No le conozco ni siquiera de vista** *I do not know him even by sight*
> **No ... nadie, no ... ninguno, No he visto a nadie** *I have not seen anybody*
> **No hay ninguna casa** *There is no house*

The negative imperative follows the same rules as the simple negative:

> **No haga eso** *Do not do that*
> **No toque esto** *Do not touch this*

TO USE THE VERB INTERROGATIVELY

Place the subject pronoun or noun after the verb to ask a question. Thus:

> **¿Tengo yo?** *Have I?*
> **¿Tiene Vd.?** *Have you?*
> **¿Es bueno el muchacho?** *Is the boy good?*

In Spanish it is very common to ask a question merely by modulating the voice, and without changing the construction of a direct statement:

> **¿El padre va a venir?** *Will the father come?*

The inverted note of interrogation or exclamation (¿ ¡) is placed at the beginning of a Spanish sentence to inform the reader in advance of the necessity for modulation. **¡Bueno!** *Good!*

IMPERSONAL VERBS

The verb **haber** is used impersonally for *there . . . to be. There is, there are* is expressed by an irregular form **hay**. Other useful forms are: **había** *there was, there were.* **Hubo** *there was, there were* (definite or historical past). **Habrá** *there will be.* **Habría** *there would be.*
Note also:

amanece *day is breaking*	**anochece** *night falls*
hiela *it is freezing*	**llueve** *it is raining*
relampaguea *it is lightening*	**truena** *it is thundering*
ventea *the wind blows*	**basta** *it is sufficient*
parece *it seems*	**importa** *it matters*
conviene *it suits*	**es de esperar** *it is to be hoped*
es lástima *it is a pity*	**es necesario** *it is necessary*
está claro *it is clear*	

SER AND ESTAR

There are two verbs in Spanish for the English *to be.* **Ser** has already

4—B.E.S.

been conjugated as an auxiliary. **Estar** will be found among the irregular verbs below. There is a fundamental difference between the meaning of **ser** and **estar**, the usage of which often puzzles foreigners. And yet, apart from subtleties in style (with which the foreigner need seldom be concerned unless he attempts to translate literature), this difference can be tabulated:

ser	estar
1. Represents permanency or the essential: **Yo soy pálido** *I am by nature pale.*	Represents the temporary or accidental: **Yo estoy pálido** *I am pale—just at this moment.*
2. Expresses origin, nationality, ownership, or material. **Yo soy de Londres. Yo soy inglés. El perro es de mi hermano. La mesa es de madera.** *I am from London. I am an Englishman. The dog is my brother's. The table is of wood.*	Expresses location: **Madrid está en España y mi hermano está ahí** *Madrid is in Spain and my brother is there.*
3. A profession, or a calling: **Yo soy cónsul** *I am a consul.*	But not if it is transitory. **Estoy ahora de cónsul aquí** *I am (acting as) consul here.*
4. With **bueno** and **malo**, refers to character: **Mi padre es bueno** *My father is a good man.*	With **bueno** and **malo**, refers to health: **Mi padre está malo** *My father is ill, a sick man.*
5. Is the true auxiliary: **Yo soy querido** *I am loved.* N.B.—All passives are formed with it.	Follows generally the meaning of the original Latin word 'stare' to stand, from which it is derived. Hence we say, **Estoy hablando** *I am speaking.* N.B.—The continuous present is always formed with it.
6. Is used to translate the impersonal *it*: **Es tarde, temprano** *It is late, early.* And in the phrase: **¿No es verdad?** *Is it not so?* Also for time: **Es la una, son las dos.***	But we say: **Está claro** *It is clear.*

The above are fairly safe rules and cover most cases. But they are by no means exhaustive or impregnable. The correct use of **ser** and **estar** is undoubtedly difficult to master: having memorised the above rules the student should for a long time look closely at the usage of **ser** and **estar** whenever he meets these words in reading. He will learn to distinguish between **soy borracho** and **estoy borracho**, and to realise

* See p. 20.

that the latter is less serious than the former. So, for some time, beware of **ser** and **estar**!

SUBJUNCTIVE MOOD: FOR REFERENCE

Unfortunately for the English student, it is not possible to avoid the subjunctive in Spanish—it is in everyday use. The indicative tenses are used to state certainties in principal clauses and in direct questions; they can stand by themselves. The subjunctive tenses are always subjoined to a main clause or indirect statement or some uncertainty. There are general principles, and a rough guide to subjunctive usage. See Table on p. 34.

General Indications: After desire, uncertainty, emotion, indirect statement or indirect question the subjunctive mood is usually employed.* Also after relative pronouns and certain conjunctions.

1. Desire (including command, request, suggestion, permission, approval, and disapproval):

> **Le ruego a Vd. que se vaya** *I beg you to go away*
> **¡Viva el rey, la república!** *Long live the King, the Republic!*

2. Uncertainty, emotion (includes entreaty, surprise, fear, denial):

> **Temo que se lo diga a él** *I fear that (lest) he may tell it to him*
> **Extraño mucho que Vd. no lo haya hecho** *I am greatly surprised that you have not done it*

3. Indirect statements or questions:

> **Dijo que ellos hablaran†** (or **hablasen**) **en la tienda** *He said that they should converse in the shop*
> **¿Cree Vd. que mi hermano se alegre mucho de eso?** *Do you believe that my brother is very delighted about that?*

4. After a relative:

> **Quiero un amigo que hable castellano** *I wish to have* (or, *I want*) *a friend who speaks Spanish*

* This is a general working rule which may be qualified thus: In subordinate clauses referring to a different subject from that of the principal clauses, then after desire, etc. **Deseo que Vd. estudie** *I want you to study*. Otherwise use infinitive: **Deseo estudiar** *I want (myself) to study*.

† It will be noticed that in the Table of Inflexions, two forms for the imperfect are given. The first (**-ara, -iera**) is used as a conditional subjunctive, corresponding approximately to the English, *that I should*. Thus: **que yo hablara** *that I should speak*. The second (**-ase, -iese**) is the imperfect subjunctive proper: **que yo hablase** *that I spoke*.

Si Vd. quiere un libro español cuyo estilo sea bueno, yo se lo prestaré *If you require a Spanish book of which the style is good, I will lend you one**

The subjunctive is also used after compounds of **-quiera** *ever* (**quienquiera** *whoever*; **dondequiera** *wherever*; **cuandoquiera** *whenever*; **comoquiera** *however*; **cualquiera** *whatever, whichever*).

quienquiera que sea *whoever he may be*, etc.

5. After certain conjunctions, etc.
For list, see p. 60.

en caso que		*in case he arrives*
no obstante que	**llegue**	*notwithstanding his arrival*
aunque		*although he arrives*

The subjunctive is also used after impersonal verbs (see p. 39).

Es menester que venga *It is necessary for him to come*

IF, HOW TO TRANSLATE

The translation of this word into Spanish needs care. The present indicative can be used for most cases:

Si tengo tiempo le escribiré *If I have time, I shall write to you*

For a straightforward conditional *if*, etc., use the Spanish imperfect subjunctive:

Si él tuviese tiempo, sin duda habría escrito *If he had time, no doubt he would have written*

When *if* is equivalent to *whether*, use the conditional indicative in Spanish:

No sabía si él podría venir *I did not know if (whether) he would be able to come*

IRREGULAR VERBS
First conjugation verbs in -ar

The most important group of verbs in this conjugation are very slightly irregular. They merely change the **-e-** of the stem into **-ie-** when the stress is moved from the last syllable (in the infinitive) to the one

* Note that the antecedent is indefinite.

before it with the various inflexions. For example, take the verb
cerrar *to shut*. This becomes **cierro** in the present indicative first
person, the **-ie-** syllable being the one stressed. But the first person
plural is **cerramos**, because the accent in this word is on the **-a-** and not
on the **-e-**. The full conjugation of the present indicative is:

cierro, cierras, cierra, cerramos, cerráis, cierran

And the present subjunctive:

cierre, cierres, cierre, cerremos, cerréis, cierren

The imperative is:

cierre (Vd.) *shut*	**que él cierre** *let him shut*
cerremos *let us shut*	**cierren (Vds.)** *shut* (polite plural)

The rest of the verb is regular

cerré *I shut* (past definite)   **cerraba** *I was shutting*
cerraré *I shall shut*

Essential verbs like **cerrar** are:

calentar *to warm*	**comenzar** *to begin*
confesar *to confess*	**despertar** *to awake*
empezar *to begin*	**gobernar** *to govern*
helar *to freeze*	**manifestar** *to manifest*
negar *to deny*	**nevar** *to snow*
pensar *to think*	**plegar** *to fold*
quebrar *to break*	**recomendar** *to recommend*
sentarse *to seat oneself*	

Similarly there is another group in which the **-o-** of the stem changes
to **-ue-** with the change of stress. **Costar** *to cost*:

Present indicative:

cuesto, cuestas, cuesta, costamos, costáis, cuestan

Present subjunctive:

cueste, cuestes, cueste, costemos, costéis, cuesten

Essential verbs conjugated like **costar** are:

acordar *to agree*	**acostarse** *to lie down* (*go to bed*)
almorzar *to breakfast*	**colgar** *to hang*
concordar *to agree*	**consolar** *to comfort*
contar *to count, relate*	**encontrar** *to meet*
forzar *to force*	**probar** *to prove*
recordar *to remind, to remember*	**renovar** *to renew*

rogar *to pray, beg*	**sonar** *to sound*
soñar *to dream*	**tronar** *to thunder*
volar *to fly*	

Compounds of these verbs are similarly conjugated.

Jugar *to play* changes the **-u-** into **-ue-** in a similar manner:

juego, juegas, juega, jugamos, jugáis, juegan

Andar *to walk* has an irregular past definite:

anduve, anduviste, anduvo, anduvimos, anduvisteis, anduvieron

Excepting the little used imperfect, future, and conditional of the subjunctive, it is otherwise regular. Thus:

ando *I go*   **andaré** *I shall go*, etc.

Dar *to give*. This important verb is conjugated as follows:

Present indicative: **doy, das, da, damos, dais, dan**
Past definite: **di, diste, dio, dimos, disteis, dieron**
Otherwise it is regular: **daré** *I shall give*   **dado** *given*, etc.

Estar *to be* in a temporary sense (see p. 40):

estando, estado

Present indicative: **estoy, estás, está, estamos, estáis, están**
Past definite: **estuve, estuviste, estuvo, estuvimos, estuvisteis, estuvieron**
Future: **estaré, -ás, -á,** etc.
Present subjunctive: **esté, estés, esté, estémos, estéis, estén**

Otherwise regular.

Second conjugation verbs in -er

The most important group of verbs in this conjugation ends in **-acer, -ecer, -ocer** (excepting **hacer** *to do*, and **cocer** *to cook*) and are conjugated like **conocer** *to know*:

Present indicative: **conozco, conoces, conoce, conocemos, conocéis, conocen**
Present subjunctive: **conozca, conozcas, conozca, conozcamos, conozcáis, conozcan**

They are otherwise regular: **conocí** *I knew*; **conoceré**, etc.

The verb **lucir** *to shine* of the third conjugation, is congujated similarly: **luzco** *I shine*; **luces, luce,** etc.

Present subjunctive: **luzca,** etc. (see p. 36, etc.)

Hacer *to make or do* is as follows:

Present participle: **haciendo** *doing*
Past participle: **hecho** *done*
Present indicative: **hago** *I do*; **haces, hace, hacemos, hacéis, hacen**
Present subjunctive: **haga, hagas, haga, hagamos, hagáis, hagan**
Imperative: **haga (Vd.)** pl **hagan (haz tú** *do thou*)
Past definite: **hice, hiciste, hizo, hicimos, hicisteis, hicieron**
Future: **haré, -ás, -á, -emos, -éis, -án**

Compounds of **hacer** are similarly conjugated: **deshacer** *to undo*; **rehacer** *to redo, do again*; and **satisfacer** *to satisfy* (**satisfecho** *satisfied*, the most common part).

Entender *to understand*

Present indicative: **entiendo, entiendes, entiende, entendemos, entendéis, entienden**
Present subjunctive: **entienda,** etc.

Like **entender** are: **defender** *to defend*; **perder** *to lose*; **pierdo, pierdes, pierde,** etc.

Tener *to have, hold, possess* always translates English *to have* except when used as an auxiliary. **Teniendo, tenido.**

Present indicative: **tengo, tienes, tiene, tenemos, tenéis, tienen**
Past definite: **tuve, tuviste, tuvo, tuvimos, tuvisteis, tuvieron**
Future: **tendré, -ás, -á, -emos, -éis, -án**
Present subjunctive: **tenga, -as, -a, -amos, -áis, -an**
Imperative: **ten, tenga (Vd.), tened, tengan (Vds.)**

There is a group of **-er** verbs conjugated similarly to **costar** (see p. 43). For example: **absolver** *to absolve*; **absuelvo** *I absolve*.

Present subjunctive: **absuelva,** etc.
Imperative: **absuelva, absuelvan (Vd. and Vds.)**

Such are: **cocer** *to cook*; **doler** *to ache*; **llover** *to rain*; **morder** *to bite*; **mover** *to move*; **oler*** *to smell*; **resolver** *to resolve*; **soler** *to be accustomed*; **torcer** *to twist*; **volver** *to return*. And all the compounds of these verbs.

* The present (rarely used) is **huelo, -es, -e,** etc.

Caer *to fall*; **caigo** *I fall*. Otherwise regular: **caes, cae,** etc. And its compounds: **decaer** *to decay*; **recaer** *to fall again*.

Poder *to be able*; **pudiendo** *being able*; **podido** past participle.

Present Indicative: **puedo, puedes, puede, podemos, podéis, pueden**
Past definite: **pude,*** etc.

Future: **podré,** etc.

Poner *to put*.

Past participle: **puesto** *put*
Past definite: **puse**
Present indicative: **pongo, pones, pone, ponemos, ponéis, ponen**

Querer *to wish, like*.

Present indicative: **quiero, quieres, quiere, queremos, queréis, quieren**
Past definite: **quise, quisiste, quiso, quisimos, quisisteis, quisieron**
Future: **querré,** etc.
Present subjunctive: **quiera,** etc.
Conditional: **querría,** etc.

Saber *to know*; **sabiendo** *knowing*; **sabido** *known*.

Present indicative: **sé, sabes, sabe, sabemos, sabéis, saben**
Future: **sabré,** etc.
Past definite: **supe, supiste, supo, supimos, supisteis, supieron**
Present subjunctive: **sepa,** etc.

Traer *to bring, carry*.

Past participle: **traído**
Present indicative: **traigo** *I carry*; **traes, trae, traemos, traéis, traen**
Past definite: **traje, trajiste, trajo, trajimos, trajisteis, trajeron**
Future: **traeré,** etc.

Similarly, the compounds: **atraer** *to attract*; **contraer** *to contract*; **distraer** *to distract*.

Valer *to be worth*.

Present indicative: **valgo, vales, vale, valemos, valéis, valen**
Present subjunctive: **valga,** etc.
Past definite: **valí**
Future: **valdré**
Conditional: **valdría**

Similarly: **equivaler** *to be of equal value*, and **prevaler** *to prevail*. Also the **-ir** verb **salir** *to go out of*; **salgo, sales, sale,** etc.

Future: **saldré,** etc.

* Pude, pudiste, pudo, pudimos, pudisteis, pudieron.

Ver *to see.*

Past participle: **visto** *seen*
Present: **veo, ves, ve, vemos, veis, ven**
Imperfect: **veía**
Present subjunctive: **vea,** etc.
Past definite: **vi, viste, vio, vimos, visteis, vieron**
Future: **veré,** etc.

Compounds: **prever** *to foresee*; **rever** *to review.*
For impersonal verb *caber*, see Vocabulary, p. 97.

Third conjugation verbs in -ir

There is a group of verbs ending **-ucir**, similar to the **-cer** verbs in **-er. Conducir** *to conduct, lead*; **conduciendo, conducido.**

Present indicative: **conduzco, conduces, conduce, conducimos, conducís, conducen**
Past definite: **conduje, condujiste, condujo, condujimos, condujisteis, condujeron**
Future: **conduciré,** etc.
Present subjunctive: **conduzca, -uzcas, uzca, uzcamos, -uzcáis, -uzcan**

Similar to **conducir** are: **deducir** *to deduct, infer*; **producir** *produce*; **reducir** *reduce*; **traducir** *translate*; and **lucir** *shine* (see p. 45).

Sentir *to feel, to be sorry*; **sintiendo, sentido.**

Present indicative: **siento, sientes, siente, sentimos, sentís, sienten**
Past definite: **sentí, -iste, sintió, sentimos, sentisteis, sintieron**
Future: **sentiré, -ás, -á,** etc.
Present subjunctive: **sienta, -as,** etc.

Verbs conjugated like **sentir** are: **advertir** *advise*; **convertir** *to convert*; **mentir** *to lie*; **preferir** *to prefer.* And their compounds.

Dormir *to sleep*; **durmiendo, dormido.**

Present indicative: **duermo, duermes, duerme, dormimos, dormís, duermen**
Past definite: **dormí, dormiste, durmió, dormimos, dormisteis, durmieron**
Future: **dormiré,** etc.
Present subjunctive: **duerma, -as,** etc.; **durmamos, durmáis, duerman**

Morir *to die*; **muriendo.**

Past participle: **muerto**
Present indicative: **muero, mueres, muere, morimos, morís, mueren**
Past definite: **morí,** etc. like **dormí**

pedir *to ask*; **pidiendo, pedido**.

Present indicative: **pido, pides, pide, pedimos, pedís, piden**
Past definite   **pedí, pediste, pidió, pedimos, pedisteis, pidieron**
Future: **pediré**, etc.
Present subjunctive: **pida, pidas**, etc.

And its compounds: **despedir** *dismiss*; **impedir** *prevent*. Also: **reir**
to laugh; **seguir** *to follow*; **servir** *to serve*; **vestir** *to clothe*. And compounds of these verbs.

Venir *to come*; **viniendo, venido**.

Present indicative: **vengo, vienes, viene, venimos, venís, vienen**
Past definite: **vine, viniste, vino, vinimos, vinisteis, vinieron**
Future: **vendré, -ás, -á**, etc.
Present subjunctive: **venga, vengas**, etc.

And its compounds: **contravenir** *contravene*; **intervenir** *to intervene*, etc., **convenir** *to agree*

Decir *to say, tell*; **diciendo, dicho**.

Present indicative: **digo, dices, dice, decimos, decís, dicen**
Past definite: **dije, dijiste, dijo, dijimos, dijisteis, dijeron**
Future: **diré**, etc.
Present subjunctive: **diga, digas, diga**, etc.

Also: **bendecir** *to bless*; **maldecir** *to curse*; but these have regular futures.

Oir *to hear*; **oyendo, oído**.

Present indicative: **oigo, oyes, oye, oímos, oís, oyen**
Past definite: **oí, oiste, oyó, oímos, oísteis, oyeron**
Future: **oiré**, etc.
Present subjunctive: **oiga, oigas**, etc.

Salir *to go out, set out, leave*; **saliendo, salido**.

Present indicative: **salgo, sales, sale, salimos, salís, salen**
Past definite: **salí, saliste, salió, salimos, salisteis, salieron**
Future: **saldré, -as, -á**, etc.
Present subjunctive: **salga, -salgas**, etc.

Ir *to go*; **yendo, ido**.

Present indicative: **voy, vas, va, vamos, vais, van**
Past definite: **fui, fuiste, fue, fuimos, fuisteis, fueron**
Future: **iré, -ás, -á, -emos, -éis, irán**
Imperfect: **iba, ibas, iba, íbamos, íbais, iban**

Present subjunctive: **vaya, vayas, vaya, vayamos, vayáis, vayan**
Imperative: **ve, vaya (Vd.), vamos, id, vayan**

Note: On p. 44 will be found **andar** *to go, to walk*. The difference between the use of **andar** and **ir** is that the former has in it an indication of undefined movement—that of animals, clocks, machines, and inanimate objects generally. **Ir** means a definite movement in a specific direction. Thus:

Mi reloj no anda bien *My watch does not go well*
Este caballo anda despacio *This horse goes slowly*
But: **Voy a la casa** *I am going home (to the house)*

The imperative **¡Vamos!** is a common interjection which means: *Let us come* (or *go*) and also to express surprise, disbelief, and sometimes even contempt. After hearing a tall story, one may say: **¡Vamos!**

Irregular past participles

abrir *to open*; **abierto** *opened*
cubrir *to cover*; **cubierto**
escribir *to write*; **escrito**
imprimir *to print*; **impreso** (**impresos** *printed matter*)
volver *to turn*; **vuelto**
concluir* *to conclude*; **concluso**
incluir* *to include*; **incluso**
juntar* *to join*; **junto**
romper *to break*; **roto**
torcer* *to twist*; **torcido** or **tuerto**
freir* *to fry*; **frito**
decir *to say, tell*; **dicho**
hacer *to do, make*; **hecho**

CONOCER, SABER, AND PODER

Saber is used for knowledge or understanding of a fact or subject, and demands intellectual ability.

¿Sabe Vd. francés? *Do you know French?*

Conocer is used for acquaintanceship or superficial knowledge.

¿Conoce Vd. al francés? *Do you know the Frenchman?*

* These verbs have also regular past participles in common use.

Poder is used for purely physical ability. Thus:

> **Yo no sé leer** *I do not know how to read*
> **Yo no puedo leer** *I cannot read* (because I am blind)
> **Yo no conozco ese camino** *I do not know that road* (because I have never travelled it)

SOME IDIOMATIC USAGES OF VERBS

> **¿Qué quiere decir eso?** *What does that mean?*
> **Yo siento el frío** *I feel the cold*
> **Siento mucho que . . .** *I am very sorry that . . .*
> **Yo estoy de pie** *I am standing up*
> **ponerse en pie** *to stand up* (the action)
> **ir a pie** *to walk* (on foot)
> **ir en automóvil** *to go by car*
> **Vale más hacer eso** *It is better to do that*

Oir means *to hear* any noise. **Entender** means *to hear* with intelligence or understanding.

> **Yo entiendo el castellano** *I understand Spanish*

Hacer is used before other verbs in the sense of *to cause* or *to make*. **Hacer saber** *to make known*. (Note that the infinitive is used after it.) **Hacer falta** means *to be short of*. **Le hace falta a Vd** *you are short of*. Two verbs **dar** and **echar** (*to throw*) form many idioms:

> **dar un paseo, una vuelta** *to take a walk*
> **dar voces** *to shout*
> **dar guerra** *to wage war*
> **dar una carcajada** *to burst into laughter* (*explode*)

Echar is a dreadful verb (look at the dictionary and you will realise what I mean). The simple meaning is *to throw*, but it can mean all sorts of things. Remember the following:

> **echar carnes** *to grow fat*
> **echar las cartas** *to deal the cards*
> **echar llave a la puerta** *to lock the door*
> **No me echarán de menos cuando muera** *They will not miss me when I die*
> **Echo de ver que Vd. está cansado** *I notice that you are tired*
> **Me eché a llorar** *I burst into tears* (*I began to weep*)
> **Lo echará a perder** *He will spoil it*

The verb **doler** *to pain, ache,* is used as follows:

    Me duele la cabeza, la mano *My head, hand, aches*
    Me duelen los pies *My feet ache**

    Dejar means *to leave, allow, permit.* **Déjale solo** *leave him alone (by himself).* **Dejar de** means *to cease from,* or *to fail to.* **No dejaré de escribir** *I shall not fail to write.* **Deje Vd. de hablar** *Stop talking.*

    Deber before another verb expresses a duty. **Debo venir** *I must come.* **Tener que** is even stronger. **Tengo que venir** *I must come.*

THE PREPOSITION 'A' AFTER A VERB

The preposition **a** *to* is used in Spanish in most cases where it would be used in English. It is also often used where no preposition would be used in English, and as this usage is extremely common in Spanish it must be mastered.

    Rule: Where the *direct* object of an *active* verb is a person or persons, the preposition **a** must precede such a direct object:

    No conozco a Fernández *I do not know Fernández*
    No comprendo a mi amigo *I do not understand my friend*
    Yo he llamado al padre *I have called the father*
    Mi amigo quiso ver a sus hijos *My friend wished to see his sons*

    Two important inferences from the above rule are (1) that **a** is required before proper names of persons in all circumstances, and (2) before demonstrative, interrogative, relative, and indefinite pronouns when they represent the *object*.

    No hallo a ninguno *I do not find anybody*
    No he visto a nadie *I have not seen anybody*

    Sometimes **a** is used when the direct object is not a person but some *familiar* or intelligent animal:

    He visto al gato en la habitación *I saw the cat in the room*

    The two verbs **tener** and **querer** are exceptions to the above rules and do not take **a** before their direct objects, unless used in their specialised meanings of *to hold* and *to love.* Thus: **Tengo un amigo** *I have a friend.* **Tengo una hermana** *I have a sister.* But: **Tengo al caballo** *I am holding the horse.* **Tengo a mi amigo** *I am holding my friend* (or *relying on him).* **Quiero una camarera** *I want a waitress, stewardess.*

---

    * The philosopher Unamuno said in 1933, 'Me duele España, me duele la república ...'

Quiero a una camarera *I like (love) a waitress*. It will be seen from the last example that one must be careful to use **a** correctly with **querer** or embarrassing misunderstandings may arise.

PREPOSITIONS AND THE INFINITIVE

1. The preposition **para** *for* followed by an infinitive indicates purpose, *in order to*:

> **Necesito una pluma para escribir** *I require a pen to write*

2. Generally the English *to* before an infinitive is translated by **de**:

> **No tengo tiempo de hacer esto** *I have not time to do this*

3. But a few common verbs when followed by other verbs take the preposition **a**. These are:

empezar *to begin*	**invitar, convidar** *to invite*
enseñar *to teach*	**aprender** *to learn*
persuadir *to persuade*	

Thus:

> **Empiezo a hablar** *I begin to speak*
> **El me ha enseñado a hablar inglés** *He has taught me to speak English*

4. As a rule verbs of motion take the preposition **a**. **Andar, ir, salir, venir, volver,** and the regular verb **correr** *to run*.

5. No preposition is required after verbs used impersonally.

6. There is a list of verbs which do not take any preposition when followed by another infinitive. They are as follows:

acostumbrar *to accustom*	**parecer** *to seem*
agradar *to gratify*	**pensar** *to think*
deber *to owe* (duty)	**permitir** *to permit*
dejar *to allow*	**poder** *to be able*
desear *to wish*	**preferir** *to prefer*
esperar *to hope*	**prometer** *to promise*
gustar *to like*	**saber** *to know*
hacer *to make*	**sentir** *to feel*
importar *to matter*	**ser lástima** *to be a pity*
intentar *to intend*	**servirse** *to be pleased*
mandar *to order*	**soler** *to be wont to*
necesitar *to want*	**temer** *to fear*
ofrecer *to offer*	**valer más** *to be better*
oir *to hear*	**ver** *to see*

Examples:

> **Sírvase cerrar la puerta** *Please shut the door*
> **Es lástima hacer eso** *It is a pity to do that*
> **Prefiero irme** *I prefer to go (out of this)*
> **Debo escribir una carta** *I must write a letter*
> **No puedo comprender una palabra** *I cannot understand a word*
> **Deseo hablarles** *I wish to speak to them*

Note: The above list of verbs should be memorised. With it and the preceding five general rules the student will seldom be at a loss to use the Spanish verbs fairly correctly in so far as using them with a preposition is concerned. This is one of the real difficulties of Spanish, the full scope of which will be appreciated in reading: and mastered only by continual attention. Outside the few rules given one can only say: Follow the usage of the best authors and speakers!

ADVERBS

Four simple rules enable one to form all the adverbs or adverbial expressions ever likely to be required.

1. Add -**mente** to the feminine of all adjectives ending in **o**.
2. Add -**mente** to the masculine of all adjectives which have no separate form for the feminine.
3. Use the phrase **de una manera** . . . followed by the adjective in the feminine. (Literally: *in a . . . manner*.)
4. Use **con** *with* followed by the noun.

Examples of 1: **industrioso** *industrious*. Adverb: **industriosamente** *industriously*; **caro** *dear*; **caramente** *dearly*; **público** *public*; **públicamente** *publicly*.

Examples of 2. **útil, útilmente** *useful, usefully*; **fácil, fácilmente** *easy, easily*.

Examples of 3: **de una manera industriosa** *in an industrious manner*; **de una manera muy clara** *in a very clear manner*.

Examples of 4: **con facilidad** *with facility*; **con claridad** *with clarity*; **con industria** *with industry*.

When several adverbs ending in -**mente** would follow one another it is customary to add the -**mente** only to the final one:

Habla clara, fácil y rápidamente *He speaks clearly, easily, and rapidly*

Adverbs formed with -**mente** retain, each part, its original accentuation: **públicamente, perfectamente** *publicly, perfectly*. **Orgullosamente** *proudly*.

Another useful phrase is **de un modo** to vary **de una manera** (it means almost the same thing):

de un modo valiente *in a valiant manner*

As in English, an adverb may qualify an adjective:

Ella es extraordinariamente hermosa *She is extraordinarily beautiful*

The Spanish adverb follows the simple verb or the past participle in compound tenses and precedes an adjective or a direct object noun:

> **Hablo bien** *I speak well*
> **He hablado bien** *I have spoken well*
> **Hablo bien inglés** *I speak English well*

Adverbs follow the same rules as adjectives to form the comparative and superlative (see pp. 15–16): **fácilmente, más fácilmente, lo más fácilmente** *easily, more easily, most easily*; **claramente, más claramente, lo más claramente** or **muy claramente**.

In the Essential Vocabulary on pp. 87–181, only a few adverbs ending in **-mente** are included. These are so given because they are in everyday use and should be memorised.

PREPOSITIONS

The grammar of the Spanish language is, on the whole, straight-forward and logical, following a number of rules and principles which can be enunciated with reasonable certainty. But when we come to the prepositions we encounter difficulties which are not merely so to the foreign student but to the cultured native speaker or writer. So careful a scholar as my friend Baldomero Sanin Cano says in his *Grammar**:
'There are no precise or general rules in Spanish for the use of the prepositions ... assiduous practice following the best usage is the only way to master this section of Spanish grammar ... good writers often differ as to what is the best usage.' In other words, mastery of the prepositions comes only by care and experience.

A *to, at*: its basic meaning is the point to which anything reaches or tends, and hence it is used to indicate *direction* both in regard to place and time.

> **Voy a la casa** *I go to the house*
> **A la derecha, a la izquierda** *to the right, left*
> **De calle a calle** *from street to street*
> **a pie, a mano** *on foot, by hand*

It is used for the manner of doing something, for the instrument with which something is done, for the price, rate, and resemblance, and for many expressions of time. After verbs of depriving it corresponds to English *from*. Memorise the following:

> **Sentarse a la mesa** *to sit down to table*
> **a mediodía, a medianoche** *at midday, midnight*
> **a la llegada, salida** *on arrival, departure*
> **a ojos vistas** *visibly*
> **¿A cuánto se vende?** *At how much does it sell?*
> **A cinco pesetas el metro** *At five pesetas the metre*
> **A la española, inglesa** *In the Spanish, English manner (style)*
> **uno a uno, dos a dos** *one by one, two by two*
> **Poco a poco** *little by little*
> **Quité al marinero su sombrero** *I took away from the sailor his hat*
> **a bordo de un vapor** *on board a steamer*

* An Elementary Spanish Grammar, by B. Sanin Cano (Oxford, 1918).

See also p. 51 for **a** after certain verbs and p. 51 for its use with a personal object. (A is the most confusing preposition; compared with it the others are not difficult.)

De *of, from*: the basic meaning is direction from some thing, place, time, or condition. Also used for the material of which something is made, for ownership or relation of a part to a whole, the use for which something is intended. Thus:

> **Del Río de La Plata hasta el Brasil** *From the River Plate to Brazil*
> **Don Quijote de la Mancha, Dulcinea del Toboso, De vez en cuando** *From time to time*
> **Una silla de madera** *A wooden armchair*
> **Las obras de Pérez de Ayala** *The works of Pérez de Ayala*
> **La corrida de toros** *The bull-fight*
> **La cabeza del perro** *The dog's head*
> **Un caballo de caza** *A horse for hunting*
> **Vengo de Madrid** *I come (or am) from Madrid*
> **Hablo de memoria** *I speak from memory*
> **¡Pobre de mí!** *Poor me!*

De is also frequently used after a superlative to translate English *in*:

> **Río Janeiro es la ciudad más populosa del Brasil** *Rio de Janeiro is the most populous city in Brazil*

Con *with*: primary meaning, accompaniment. Also: instrumentality, association, addition.

> **Llego con mi hermano** *I arrive with my brother*
> **Lo hago con mis propias manos** *I do it with my own hands*
> **Café con leche** *white coffee (café au lait)*

It sometimes means *nevertheless*:

> **con todo eso** *for all that*
> **Es rico, con todo no le quiero mucho** *He is rich, yet I don't like him*

Desde *from*: is used for *since* when applied to time

> **desde que le vi la semana pasada** *since I saw him last week*
> **desde Londres hasta Liverpool** *from London to Liverpool*

En *in*: is used for time, place, and manner.

> **Cuando le vi en Córdoba el verano pasado hablaba en serio** *When I saw him in Cordoba last summer he spoke in earnest*

It is used with a present participle to denote an action immediately preceding another action:

> **En llegando a casa le quité la espada** *The moment I reached home I took his sword from him*

Hasta means *until, up to.* **Hacia** means *in the direction of.*

> **desde Buenos Aires hasta Mendoza** *from Buenos Aires right up to Mendoza*
>
> **hasta mañana** *until tomorrow*

Hasta luego, literally, *until soon,* is a very common expression meaning *Au revoir, and I hope we'll soon meet again.*

> **Hasta la vista** *Until we see each other again*
> **Hacia el Norte hay una tempestad** *In the North there is a storm*
> **Hacia allí está el parlamento** *In that direction is parliament*

Por and **para** both are freely translated by *for*, but in Spanish their meaning is more definite. **Para** is used for direction, motion towards, goal or end to be served. Thus:

> **Hay que trabajar para comer** *One must work in order to eat*
> **el vapor para Valparaíso** *the steamer for Valparaiso*
> **para eso** *for all that*

Por is used when referring to an equivalent, or in return for:

> **Me dio su libro por el mío** *He gave me his book for (in exchange for) mine*

It also denotes length of time, in the neighbourhood of a place or through one, manner and motive:

> **Estaré de viaje por un año** *I shall be travelling for (during) a year*
> **El aeroplano pasa por París a las ocho** *The aeroplane passes Paris at eight o'clock*

Note also:

> **Lo hizo por ignorancia** *He did it from ignorance*
> **pasar por la calle** *to walk along the street*
> **Lo hago por fuerza** *I do it by force (strength)*
> **Vendió el caballo por cien pesetas** *He sold the horse for one hundred pesetas*
> **Me ausento de Lima por un mes** *I am (shall be) absent from Lima for a month*
> **mañana por la mañana** *tomorrow morning*
> **¡Por Dios!** *Good gracious!*

Voy por pan *I am going (to fetch) bread*
por lo que dice *to judge from what he says*
por grande que sea *however big it may be*
por ahora *for the time being*
por lo que a mí hace *in so far as I am concerned*

Según *according to.* **Según las circunstancias** *according to circumstances.* This is the only preposition which can be used by itself. **¿Cuándo llegará Vd?** *When will you arrive?* **Según** *That will depend.* And note:

según se ve *as can be seen (on the face of it)*

Sobre *on, upon*:

sobre la mesa *on the table*
Escribo sobre Derecho *I write about law*
Hemos hablado sobre las cosas del día *We have spoken about current affairs*
Tomo sobre mí mucho trabajo *I take much work upon myself*

CONJUNCTIONS

The principal Spanish conjunctions are:

Pero, mas, sino, equivalent to English *but.*
O *or.* This becomes **u** before words beginning **o** or **ho.**
Y *and.* This becomes **e** before words beginning **i** or **hi.** (Except **hie.**)
Ni *nor, neither;* **si** *if, whether;* **que** *that.*

General usage corresponds approximately to that in English, and only **que** and **sino** need be singled out for special attention. Remember that **sino** consists of **si** *if,* and **no** *not.* If we present an alternative in a sentence which contains words which show that a negative answer is expected, then the English word *but* is translated by **sino.** Also when the first clause in a sentence is negative. Thus:

No le he visto a él, sino a su hermano *I have not seen him, but his brother*
¿Cuándo deberemos ir sino ahora? *When shall we go if not now?*

If a verb follows in the second clause, then **pero** is used:

No le he visto a él, pero he visto a su hermano *I have not seen him, but I have seen his brother*
No tengo sino un sombrero *I have only one hat*
No lo sabía sino de memoria *I only knew it by memory*
No he estado en España, sino dos semanas *I have been in Spain only two weeks*

The conjunction **que** must always be used in Spanish, even where it may be omitted in English. Thus, sentences such as 'I think he is a good man', 'I believe it will rain', 'John replied he did not know', etc., must be rendered, 'I believe *that* it will rain', 'John replied *that* . . .', etc.: **Creo que va a llover** (or **lloverá**). **Contestó Juan que no conocía,** etc.

WORD BUILDING, ETC.

———

In Spanish and English there are many thousands of words which have a common parentage in Latin, and they tend to resemble one another. It is hardly necessary to have to be told that **futuro** means *future*. At the same time, in the early stage of learning, it is as well to be able to recognise certain endings in Spanish which are frequently equivalents for English endings. Of these the commonest are:

1. Nouns:

English ending	Spanish ending	Gender
-age	**-aje,** as in **personaje**	m
-ct	**-cto,** as in **conducto**	m
-ism	**-ismo,** as in **comunismo**	m
-ment	**-mento,** as in **parlamento**	m
-cy or *-ce*	**-cia,** as in **abundancia**	f
-ion	**-ión,** as in **religión**	f
-tion	**-ción,** as in **acción**	f
-tude	**-tud,** as in **multitud**	f
-ty	**-dad,** as in **falsedad**	f

2. Adjectives:

-ate	**-ado,** as in **duplicado**	
-acious	**-az,** as in **sagaz, tenaz**	
-arious⎫ *-ary*⎭	**-ario,** as in **precario, contrario**	

3. Verbs:

-ize	**-izar,** as in **civilizar**
-ate	**-ar,** as in **fumigar**
-fy	**-ficar,** as in **fortificar**

When an English word with the ending in the first column above has to be translated into Spanish, it is nearly always safe to do so by adding the endings in the second column, making at the same time whatever orthographic changes may be necessary. The only double

letters in Spanish are **cc, oo, ee, ll, nn,** and **rr.** The most useful orthographic changes to remember are:

English	Becomes in Spanish
qu	**cu consecuencia**
th	**t teatro**
ph	**f filología**
ch	**c** (or **qu** before **e** and **i**), **carácter, característico**
s, initial	**es- estricto**
y	**i simpatía**

CHIEFLY FOR REFERENCE

The capacity of Spanish for making new words by adding new syllables
is one of the principal characteristics and beauties of the language, but
it is a difficulty for the foreigner as well as being an encouragement. It
is proposed here to treat only a few general principles, more as
examples of what can be done than as an effort to exhaust the subject
(for which a treatise would be required). The syllables added to
Spanish words in order to change their meaning are (1) the Augmentatives which increase or intensify the meaning of the original
word; (2) the Diminutives which act in a contrary sense; and (3) a
number of what may conveniently be called Derivative Suffixes. There
are also a number of Prefixes but, as they are nearly all common to
both English and Spanish, they are for practical purposes self-
explanatory.

Augmentatives

The endings **-on, -azo, -ote, -ajo, -acho, -ucho** add to the original
meaning (size, degree, quality) and may modify it by a still further
addition of clumsiness, grotesqueness, or some other quality to
excite either admiration or contempt.

-ón, -ona, merely increase the original meaning in regard to size.
Thus: **cuchara** *a spoon*; **cucharón** *a ladle.* **Soltero** *a bachelor*; **solterón**
a 'crusted' bachelor.

-azo, -aza, is also a simple augmentative. **Hombre** *man*; **hombrazo**
a big man.

-ote, -ota, is an augmentative usually in a depreciative sense. **Feo**
ugly; **feote** *extremely* or *frightfully ugly.* **Una feota** *a 'fright'.*

-ajo adds a strong element of contempt to the original meaning. Thus: **Latín** *Latin*; **Latinajo** *Latin jargon, dog-Latin.*

-acho, -ucho, are depreciative but not exactly contemptuous. Thus: **vino** *wine*; **vinacho** *a very poor wine.* **Casa** *a house*; **casucha** *hovel.*

-uco, -uca, is used in a few cases instead of **-ucho, -ucha,** but it may have in it an element of strong contempt when used for men or women. **Casa** *house*; **casuca** *a shanty.* Note the following: **fraile** *friar*; **frailuco** *a poor friar.* **Hermano** *brother*; **hermanuco** *a poor member of a religious brotherhood.*

Diminutives

-ito, -ico, -illo, -uelo, -ete. To these are sometimes added still further diminutives:

-ito	-cito	-ecito	-ececito ⎫
-ico	-cico	-ecico	-ececico ⎪
-illo	-cillo	-ecillo	-ececillo ⎬ rare
-uelo	-zuelo	-ezuelo	-ecezuelo ⎭
-ete	-cete	-ecete	..

The above table is given for reference, as some of these endings are rarely used and have meanings too subtle to be safely employed by the foreigner. Indeed, the foreigner who dares to employ any of the above excepting **-ito, -cito,** and perhaps **-ecito** may be courting real bodily danger! This will become apparent in considering the meanings of the diminutives, which are given below for reference and to assist in understanding Spanish:

1. **-ito, -cito, -ecito, -ececito,** indicate smallness to which is added a sense of endearment, prettiness, pleasantness, etc. They may sometimes be found to give a flavour of irony, especially with names of prominent men. **Viejo** *old man*; **viejito** *little old man*; **viejecito** *nice little old man.* These endings may be added to baptismal names of persons to indicate affection, and to almost any other words, with a pleasantly intensifying effect. Thus: **Miguelito** *Mike.* **Dieguito** *Jimmie.* **Juanito** *Jack.* **Voy ahora mismito** *I'm going this very second.* **Prontito** *very soon.* **Juntito** *near by, close.* **Lejitos** *some distance away.* **Enseguidita** *immediately.* **Hablo un poquito el español** *I speak Spanish just a little* (**un poquito** *a very little*).
2. **-ico, -cico, -ecico,** have the same meanings as (1) but more frequently contain an element of sarcasm.
3. **-illo** decreases size and takes away from quality—objectively and

without either malice or love. **Cigarro** *cigar*, **cigarrillo** *cigarette*. **Chico** *small*; **los chiquillos** *the little children*.

4. **-uelo**, etc. This generally belittles with contempt. **Pintor** *a painter, artist*; **pintorzuelo** *a dauber*.

5. **-ete**, etc. Often depreciates as well as decreases size or quality. **Burla** *joke, trick*; **burleta** *a nasty trick*.

Four other diminutives of less importance will sometimes be met: **-ejo, -ín, -ino, iño.** The first is contemptuous, the others dialect.

Two points will be observed in connection with both augmentatives and diminutives: the last vowel of an original word is dropped before the ending is added; and there may be a slight orthographic change in the original. Thus: **bueno** *good*; **bonazo** *good big fellow*. **Chico, chiquillo. Pedazo** *piece*; **pedacito. Lengua** *tongue, language*; **lengüecita.** It will be appreciated that these last are our old friends, the orthographic changes made to preserve the original sound when an inflexion is added.

Derivative suffixes

This is, again, a subject upon which a considerable treatise might usefully be written. Here we can only deal with a few of the suffixes, merely to indicate the extraordinary flexibility and richness of Spanish, and as an illustration of a few of the general principles involved. The suffixes chosen for this purpose are of fairly frequent occurrence.

-ada expresses the capacity or duration of what is denoted by the original noun. **Cuchara** *spoon*; **cucharada** *spoonful*. **Mano** *hand*; **manada** *handful*. Also indicates a class or collection: **caballo** *horse*; **cabalgada** *cavalcade*. And it denotes the stroke given with an instrument: **cuchillo** *knife*; **cuchillada** *cut, gash*.

-ada, -ida. These past participle endings indicate the completed action. **La entrada** *the entrance*. **La salida** *the departure*. **La llegada** *the arrival*. **La venida** *the coming*.

-ero: indicates the person who is in charge of something, or responsible for an action. **Cabra** *goat*; **cabrero** *goatherd*. **Escudo** *shield*; **escudero** *shield-bearer, squire*. **Rancho** *ranch*; **ranchero** *ranch-owner*. **Toro** *bull*; **torero** *bull-fighter*.

-ero also denotes the place or article for containing something: **Sal** *salt*; **salero** *salt-cellar*. **Azúcar** *sugar*; **azucarero** *sugar-bowl*. And it denotes a dealer: **cuchillo** *knife*; **cuchillero** *cutler*. **Libro** *book*; **librero** *bookseller*. **Zapato** *shoe*; **zapatero** *shoemaker*.

-ía: denotes the place of business or the actual trade or business of the person: **libro** *book*; **librería** *bookseller's shop* (also *the business of bookselling*). **Reloj** *watch, clock*; **relojería** *clock-trade, clock or watch shop*. **Zapatería** *shoe-shop, shoe-trade*. This ending forms abstract nouns from adjectives: **cortés** *courteous*; **cortesía** *courtesy*. **Bizarro** in Spanish means *gallant, high-minded*; **bizarría** *gallantry*. **Mejor** *better*; **mejoría** *betterment*.

-ero and **-ía** are the two endings which the beginner will find most useful, especially if he intends to travel in Spanish-speaking countries. The following list of derivative suffixes may be memorised at leisure, and treated at this stage as for reference only:

-ador, -edor, -idor: the person who performs the action of the verb. **Beber, bebedor.**

-aje: corresponds to English *-age* in such words as **pilotaje** *pilotage*; **carreta, carretaje** *cart, cartage*.

-anza: forms abstract or verbal nouns. **Matar** *to kill*; **matanza** *killing, slaughter*.

-ar: denotes a collection. **Manzano** *apple tree*; **manzanar** *apple orchard*.

-ario: often corresponds to English ending *-ee*. **Consignar** *to consign*; **consignatario** *consignee*. **Concesionario** *grantee*, the person to whom a concession is made.

-azgo: the office, function or jurisdiction of the person indicated in the original noun. **Almirante** *admiral*; **almirantazgo** *admiralty*. **Hermano** *brother*; **hermanazgo** *fraternity*

-azo: blow, stroke, or wound. **Bala** *bullet*; **balazo** *bullet wound*. **Zapato** *shoe*; **zapatazo** *kick*, or *blow with a shoe*.

-dero: place. **Fondear** *anchor*; **fondeadero** *anchorage*. **Matar** *to kill*. **matadero** *slaughter-house*. Also forms adjectives from verbs: **casar** *to marry*; **casadero** *marriageable*.

-dizo: fitness, capability, susceptibility. **Beber** *to drink*; **bebedizo** *fit to drink*.

-dumbre: forms abstract nouns from adjectives. **Mucho** *much*; **la muchedumbre** *multiple, crowd*. **Cierto,** *certain*; **certidumbre** *certainty*.

-ear: forms verbs from nouns, and makes verbs frequentative. **Ventana** *window*; **ventanear** *to be continuously looking out of a window*. **Borracho** *drunk*; **borrachear** *to be drunk very often*. **-ear** verbs form nouns in **-eo. Rodear** *to go round*; **rodeo** *a round-up* (in Spanish America, *a tournament*).

-edo, eda: the place where something grows. **Viña** *vineyard*; **viñedo** *vine district*. **Arbol** *tree*; **arboleda** *grove*.

-era: similar to **-ero**. **Tabaco,** *tobacco*; **tabaquera** *pouch*.

-ez, -eza, -iento, -ino, -izo, -oso, -udo, -uno: all these form adjectives and nouns that are generally recognisable from the original word.

-mento, -miento: form nouns from verbs. **Nacer** *to be born*; **nacimiento** *birth*. **Casar** *to marry*; **casamiento** *marriage*.

-ón: forms adjectives from nouns and verbs, with a meaning which has something of the augmentative in it. **Burlar** *to joke*; **burlón** (adj), *jocular, waggish*.

The student is advised not to regard the equivalents given for all these derivative suffixes as strictly accurate. They give but a general indication of the meaning, which sometimes varies in accordance with usage—always the final arbiter in all such matters. To give some indication of the richness of Spanish, the word **tierra** *land* and its derivatives are quoted by an authority who gives sixty-one other words formed from it. Thus: **terreno** *ground*; **terráceo** *made of earth*; **terradillo** *small terrace*; **terrín** *peasant*; **terroncillo** *small clod*; **terraje** *rent of land*; **aterraje** *drifting ashore*; **desterrado** *exile, outcast*; **desenterrador** *body-snatcher*, etc., etc. If we add a number of possible inflexions to these words (feminines, diminutives, augmentatives, etc.) the list could be extended to the neighbourhood of two hundred words —all deriving from this one word **tierra**. The student will (wisely) conclude from this that if it is a comparatively straightforward business to get a working knowledge of Spanish, such as will carry him through life for most practical purposes, to know it thoroughly is quite another matter. This warning is uttered so that the learner may not be misled by the simplicity of the grammar into believing that it is always an easy language. It is nothing of the sort!

IDIOMS

An idiom is a turn of phrase peculiar to a language. Thus, when we say in Spanish **dar un paseo** *to take a walk*, this is an idiom. The most important idiomatic expressions have been mentioned already under the different parts of speech, as in Spanish most of the idioms are peculiarities of usage rather than completely different phrases, as in French. Many others will be found in the Essential Vocabulary.

Examples:

Tengo que irme	I must go
tener hambre, sueño, miedo, vergüenza, sed	to be hungry, sleepy, afraid, ashamed, thirsty
tener razón, no tener razón	to be right, wrong, etc.
Tengo 30 años	I am 30
Tengo frío, calor	I am cold, hot
Tenga Vd. la bondad de decirme	Be so good as to tell me
¿Qué quiere Vd. decir?	What do you mean?
¿Qué tiempo hace?	What is the weather like?
Hace frío, calor	It is cold, hot
Haga por venir	Try to come
Hace una semana, un año	A week, a year ago
¿Qué hay?	What is the matter?
No hay de qué	'Not at all' in reply to 'Thank you', etc.
¿Cuántos años tiene Vd.?	How old are you?
No se sabe	It is not known

See also p. 50, 'Some Idiomatic Usages of Verbs'.

FORMS OF ADDRESS AND FAMILY NAMES IN SPANISH

Spanish-speaking peoples are more formal and polite than we are in forms of address. Nothing strikes the visitor to Spain more forcibly than the dignity and courtesy with which two peasants will speak to one another, and this courtesy permeates society. The same may be said of Spanish-America. Hence, it is of the utmost importance for the foreigner to make himself familiar with usage and custom; and he should dó so fairly early in his studies. English 'bluntness' should be avoided, as it is merely regarded as a lack of delicacy.

USTED, TÚ, AND VOSOTROS

The word **Usted** (generally written **V.** or **Vd.**, plural **Ustedes**, written **VV.** or **Vds.***) is the general equivalent for the English word *you* and it is the form of address which should always be used by the foreigner in addressing adults. **Usted** is a contraction of **Vuestra merced** (pl **Vuestras mercedes**) meaning *Your Grace*, and therefore requires the verb to be in the third person: **¿Tiene Vd. un fósforo?** *Have you a match?* When the abbreviation is met in writing it should always be read in the full form **Usted**, just as in English we read Mr and Dr as Mister or Doctor, etc.

Tú, thou, is used between relations, intimate friends, in addressing children, the Deity, animals; and also in speaking to servants, or by officers speaking to privates, etc. It does not always imply a sense of superiority on the part of the speaker. **Vosotros** is the plural of **tú**, and is the form used by public speakers, preachers, or to address two or more people to whom **tú** would apply.

The word **Vd.** should be used frequently in conversation, at least once in each sentence; but, having used it once, there is seldom any need to repeat it in the same sentence:

> **Vd. tiene un sombrero, pero no tiene zapatos** *You have a hat, but you have no shoes*

* It is also written **Vmd., Vmds., Ud., Uds.**

It should also be used to clarify or emphasise:

Le digo a Vd. que no tiene razón *I tell you that you are not right*

Sí and **se** are nominative and accusative reflectives for **Usted**:

Delante de sí *Before you*
Vd. se casó *You got married* (see p. 23).

EQUIVALENTS FOR MR, SIR, ETC

Mr and *Sir* are expressed by **Señor** and **Caballero**, the latter being a little more formal than the former. **Señor** may have in it an indication of respect (as when a servant speaks to the head of a house or a guest). Also, **Señor** is used only with surnames: **Señor Fernández** (or **El Señor Fernández**). **Caballero** is used between equals. Furthermore, **caballero** is probably more widely employed in Spanish-America than in Spain. **Don** and **Doña** (*Mr Mrs*) are peculiar to Spanish and are used only with Christian names: **Don Carlos, Doña María**. **Don** may be preceded by **Señor** and **Doña** by **Señora** (*Mrs*) or **Señorita** (*Miss*). **Señor Don Carlos, Señora Doña María**. Thus, a gentleman named **Carlos Fernández** may be addressed as follows:

Señor Don (or **D.**) **Carlos Fernández.**
Señor Fernández. Don Carlos Fernández.
  Or **Don Carlos.**
And spoken of as **El Señor Fernández.**

Similarly: **Señora de Larrañaga,* Señora Doña María de Larrañaga, Doña María de Larrañaga,** or **Doña María.**

FAMILY NAMES

Let us imagine that **Sr. D. Carlos Fernández** marries **Sra. Doña María Larrañaga.** If they wrote their names in full they might be as follows: **Señor Don Carlos Fernández y Castro** (**Fernández** would then represent his father's name and **Castro** his mother's) and **Sra. Doña María Larrañaga y Villegas.** The children would take the family names of both parents, and be called **Fernández y Larrañaga.** The principal names of the son might thus be **Juan Fernández.**

This use of family names is common and accounts for the long names sometimes to be met in Spanish. The names of estates were

* In Spanish-America the **de** is generally omitted.

often added to family names. Basque names are often formidable: **Señor Don Guillermo Echagaray de Guipúzcoa y Urritucoichea**.

Señorito is used for *Master*, and is only used by servants or with the article—**el señorito** *the young gentleman*. **Señorita** is used for English *Miss*. **Señor** is used for *Lord* and **Señora** (in **Nuestra Señora**) for *Our Lady* (meaning the Virgin Mary). Note also: **Don Fulano de tal** *Mr So-and-so* (*Monsieur un tel* in French).

In speaking directly to a person always use **Señor, Señora**, etc., '**Buenos días, Señor**', '**Buenas tardes, Señor Doctor**'. (**Señor Profesor**, etc.) And in Spanish-America say: ¿'**Cómo está Vd., caballero?**'

Note: **El Presidente Alcalá Zamora** *President Alcalá Zamora*; **El General Martínez Anido** *General M.A.*; **El Padre Fernando** *Father Fernando*; **El rey Felipe II** *King Philip II*; **La Señora Fortuna** *Dame Fortune*; **Es un verdadero caballero** *He is a true gentleman*; **Mi señora** (or **esposa**) *My wife*. **Mi señor** means *my master*, and not *my husband*, which would be **mi marido**.

One can be very polite and say **Señor caballero**. But remember that **caballero** is never used with a name—only alone or with **señor**.

CORRESPONDENCE IN SPANISH

The date is written thus: **26 de setiembre de 1984. 1° de enero de 1985.** (The first of the month always **El primero.** Other days simply the number.)

A formal opening: **Muy Señor mío. Muy Señores míos. Muy Señores nuestros** (the latter when writing from a firm to a firm). **Muy Señora mía. Distinguida Señorita.**

A moderately familiar opening: **Muy estimado Señor Fernández,** or **Muy Señor mío y amigo.** Or, **Distinguido amigo.**

A familiar opening: **Mi querido amigo. Querido amigo. Querido Fernández.**

A formal ending to a gentleman: **S.S.S.** and then, immediately above the signature, **Q.B.S.M.** (**Su seguro servidor, que besa su mano** *Your obedient servant, who kisses your hand.*)

A formal ending to a lady: the same, with **Q.B.S.P.** (**que besa sus pies**).

A moderately familiar ending: **Se repite de Vd.** (if there has been previous correspondence), and then, above the signature, **Afmo. atento y S.S.** If no previous correspondence: **Se ofrece a V. . . .**

A familiar ending: **Saluda a Vd. muy atentamente, su afmo. amigo.** Or, **Le saluda su buen amigo.** (Or, **Le abraza su buen amigo.**)*

It is usual for one correspondent to refer to another's letter as **la estimada de Vd.**

In Spanish-America the **Q.B.S.M.** is omitted, and the expressions **Su atento servidor, su seguro servidor,** or **Su muy atento y seguro servidor** are used alone.

* Very familiar.

PART 2

THE ESSENTIAL VOCABULARY

ABBREVIATIONS USED IN PART 2

abbr	abbreviation	Kg	Kilogramo(s)
adj	adjective	Km	kilómetro(s)
adv	adverb	l	litro(s)
c	céntimo(s)	m	masculine
	centavo(s)	neut	neuter
cm	centímetros	obj	object(ive)
cond	conditional tense	p.p.	past participle
conj.	conjunction	pers	personal
excl	exclamation	pop	popular speech
coll	colloquial	prp	preposition
f	feminine	pron	pronoun
gr	gramo(s)	pts	pesetas
hect	hectare	rel	relative
impers	impersonal	sb	somebody
indef	indefinite	sth	something
inf	infinitive	SA	South America(n)
inter	interrogative	Sp	Spain, Spanish
intr	intransitive	SpA	Spanish America(-n)
inv	invariable	tr	transitive

Basic words in the Vocabulary are in capitals. Words not in capitals are supplementary.

PRELIMINARY TO THE ESSENTIAL VOCABULARY

——◆——

The Essential Vocabulary of Spanish consists of words which may for convenience of learning be classified as follows:

1. Numeral words and expressions—given on pp. 18–19 of Part 1. The cardinal and ordinal numerals are omitted from the Vocabulary on pp. 87–181.
2. Days of the week, months of the year and seasons, all of frequent recurrence, are given on p. 76 for learning. These are also omitted from the Vocabulary on pp. 87–181.
3. A limited number of geographical names and adjectives of nationality given on p. 77 for learning. Also omitted from the Vocabulary on pp. 87–181.
4. A limited number of very common and useful everyday expressions, given on p. 67 for memorising at an early stage.
5. The pronouns given on pp. 22–23 of Part I *all* have to be memorised at an early stage and in their various forms. The subject forms of these words are included in the basic vocabulary on pages 87–181 in bold type.
6. Basic Words and Supplementary Words: These are all listed in the Essential Vocabulary on pp. 87–181.

The basic words are printed in capitals. All other words may be considered as useful supplementary words to those that are basic.

HINTS ON LEARNING VOCABULARY

Obviously the beginner should try to master first things first, and, for a time—that is, until p. 41 of Part 1, just before the subjunctive has been reached—one should first concentrate on grammar, plus those words required to show how it works. From that point onwards it is desirable to concentrate on the basic words given in bold type in the Vocabulary.

Know all words both ways: **el hombre**=(*the*) *man*: (*the*) *man*=**el hombre**. Say the Spanish word aloud when memorising it. Always learn the correct article with each noun. (Every noun in the vocabulary is marked (m) or (f) to indicate gender, which must never be overlooked.)

At first do not attempt to memorise more than ten new words daily. A large number of Spanish words greatly resemble their equivalent in English—see pp. 61–62 for word building, which will be a great help. After a few weeks some English-speaking learners can memorise as many as 20 new words daily; at this rate the Basic Vocabulary can be assimilated in a matter of weeks.

Visualisation: It is important to become accustomed to the idea of thinking in Spanish. A beginning can be made with the numbers. When you see the numeral *6*, think of **seis**; when you see *20*, think of **veinte**, and so on. You can even do little sums in Spanish. Thus *6 y 4 son diez*; and so on. When you meet the noun **la casa**, think of a *house*, picturing a house in your mind as you repeat aloud the Spanish noun and its proper article. When you meet the word **correr**, think of running. In this way **correr** will be assimilated with the idea of *running*; and so on. This is the early stage of learning to think in Spanish, the key to ultimate fluency in the language. The rest is a matter of practice in speaking with Spaniards or Spanish-Americans, for which no opportunity should be missed. Listening to radio broadcasts in Spanish, even when you do not always understand the words, gets the novice accustomed to hearing the sounds. Pronunciation is best learnt from hearing the sounds and imitating them.

DAYS OF THE WEEK, MONTHS, SEASONS

el domingo *Sunday*	**el martes** *Tuesday*	**el jueves** *Thursday*
lunes *Monday*	**miércoles** *Wednesday*	**viernes** *Friday*
	sábado *Saturday*	

(All months are masculine)

enero *January*	**mayo** *May*	**septiembre*** *September*
febrero *February*	**junio** *June*	**octubre** *October*
marzo *March*	**julio** *July*	**noviembre** *November*
abril *April*	**agosto** *August*	**diciembre** *December*
	la primavera *spring*	**el otoño** *autumn*
	el verano *summer*	**el invierno** *winter*

* Sometimes written *setiembre*.

SOME COMMON GEOGRAPHICAL NAMES

Name of country	Adj. of nationality	Name of place	Inhabitant & adj.
Inglaterra *England*	**inglés** *Englishman English*	**Andalucía**	**andaluz,** -a m & f
		Galicia	**gallego,** -a
España *Spain*	**español**$\{$*Spaniard Spanish*$\}$ m	**Madrid**	**madrileño,** -a
		Cataluña	**catalán,** -a
Francia *France*	**francés**$\{$*Frenchman French*$\}$	**Sevilla**	**sevillano,** -a
		Cádiz	**gaditano,** -a
Italia *Italy*	**italiano** *Italian*	**Buenos Aires**	**porteño,** -a
Alemania *Germany*	**alemán** *German*		
Portugal *Portugal*	**portugués** *Portuguese*		
Rusia *Russia*	**ruso** *Russian*		
Los Estados Unidos *U.S.A.*	**norteamericano** *(North) American*		
El Brasil *Brazil*	**brasileño** *Brazilian*		
El Perú *Peru*	**peruano** *Peruvian*		
Méjico *Mexico*	**mexicano** *Mexican*		
Chile *Chile*	**chileno** *Chilian*		
la Argentina *Argentine Rep.*	**argentino** *Argentine (-nian)*		
Panamá *Panama*	**panameño** *Panamanian*		
El Uruguay *Uruguay***	**uruguayo** *Uruguayan*		
Venezuela *Venezuela*	**venezolano** *Venezuelan*		
Guatemala *Guatemala*	**guatemalteco** *Guatemalan*		

Note: The names of inhabitants often differ from the place-name, and care must be taken with this. Vizcaya = *Biscay* (= the Basque country): **vizcaíno** = *a Biscayan* (= *Basque*, also **vasco**, adj **vascongado**).

Adjs of nationality form their feminines in the normal way by adding **-a**: Similarly their nouns: **un inglés** = *an Englishman*; **una inglesa** = *an Englishwoman*.

INTERROGATIVES

¿**Quién(-es)**? *Who?*
¿**Cuál (-es)**? *Which?*
¿**Cuánto (-a, -os, -as)**? *How much? How many?*
¿**Cuándo**? *When?*
¿**Dónde**? *Where?*
¿**Adónde**? *Whither?*
¿**Cómo**? *How?*
¿**Por qué**? *Why?*
¿**Qué cosa . . .**? $\}$ *What?*
¿**Qué**?

INTERJECTIONS

¡**Hola**! *Hello!*
¡**Ole**! *Well done!*
¡**Otra vez**! *Encore! Again!*
¡**Caramba**! *Heavens!*
¡**Vamos**! *Well, now!*
¡**Vaya**! $\{$ *Go on! (Tell that to the*
¡**Anda**! $\}$ *marines!)*
¡**Bravo**! *Bravo!*
¡**Cuidado**! *Be careful! Look out!*
¡**Pare**! ¡**Alto**! *Stop! Halt!*
¡**Calla**! *Silence! Shut up!*

* Also **La República Oriental del Uruguay,** and the inhabitant **un oriental.**

¡Dios! ⎧ Do not mean '*My*
¡Por Dios! ⎨ *God!*' but merely
¡Dios mío! ⎩ '*Good gracious!*'
¡Oiga! *Listen!*
¡Ay de mí! *Alas for me!* etc.
¡Hombre! Very common in all Spanish-speaking countries, and often used to punctuate sentences. Means *My dear fellow,* etc. Used alone it may express astonishment.
¡Adelante! *Come in!* etc. etc.

GREETINGS, ETC.

¿Qué tal? Familiar and friendly way of saying ¿Cómo está Vd.? *How are you?*
Buenos días, Buenas tardes, Buenas noches *Good morning, evening, night*
Hasta luego *Until we meet*
Hasta la vista *Au revoir*
Hasta mañana *Until tomorrow*
¡Adiós! *Good-bye!*
¡Vaya Vd. con Dios! *May it go well with you. Farewell!*
¡Buen viaje! *May you have a good voyage!*
¡Buen provecho! ¡Buen apetito! *May it benefit you! May you have a good appetite!* (said at meal-times)
¡Salud! *Good health!*

EXTRACTS TO ILLUSTRATE THE USE
AND SCOPE OF THE VOCABULARY
AND GRAMMAR

1. MADRID

Hemos recorrido Madrid en las opuestas direcciones que
We went round Madrid in directions opposite to those

marcan sus cuatro puntos cardinales, despacio, con paso mesurado
marked by its four cardinal points, slowly, with unhurried step

y ojo atento, sin la menor inquietud que pudiera amenguar
and attentive eye, without the least hustle that might diminish

nuestras impresiones. Tuvimos la buena ventura de llegar con
our impressions. We had the good luck to arrive during

unos días de sol primaveral que invitaban a las excursiones por
some days of Spring sunshine which invited excursions through

los barrios lejanos y por los alrededores. El sol que aquí
outlying districts and suburbs. The sunshine which here

reina déjase sentir con ardores de país tropical y el cielo es
reigns can be felt with (the) ardours of a tropical country and the sky is

tan azul y deslumbrante como los cielos de América. Inquirimos:
as blue and dazzling as that of (South) America. We enquire:

— ¿Siempre hace este sol en Madrid?
— Is there always sun(shine) like this in Madrid?

— Cuando sale el sol brilla y calienta que da gusto—se nos contesta.
— When the sun comes out it shines and warms so as to give pleasure—we are told.

— ¿Y nunca hace frío? ¿Nunca soplan vientos huracanados?
— And it is never cold? Are there never hurricanes?

— Rara vez, muy poco—se nos vuelve a contestar.
— Rarely, very little—they answer (again).

No dudamos ya de que nos hallamos en un país de clima
We doubt no more that we are in a country with a

80 *The Essential Vocabulary*

benigno, y nos echamos a andar por las aceras de sol en busca de
benign climate, so we set about walking along the sunny paths seeking

sensaciones.* Cuando cae el día regresamos al hotel, no sólo para
sensations. When day falls we return to the hotel, not only for

reposarnos, sino también para catalogar las sensaciones. Luego,
rest, but also to catalogue the sensations. *Soon,*

al tomar la pluma y con el apremio de concretar un juicio, tratamos
on taking the pen and intent upon fixing a judgment, we endeavour

de hacerlo de esta manera: Madrid es una ciudad agradable,
to do it as follows: Madrid is a pleasant city,

bulliciosa, alegre; alegre y confiada, como se ha dado en llamarla.
lively, cheerful; cheerful and confident, as it has (so) often been called.

La ciudad de viejo aspecto ha desaparecido para ceder su
The city (in its) old aspect has disappeared to yield

lugar a una metrópoli modernísima, con edificios de discutible
place to a most modern metropolis, with buildings of disputable

arquitectura que han sido construidos en un abrir y cerrar de
architecture which have been built in a trice (or *in the twinkling of an eye*)

ojos, por obra y gracia del cemento armado. La piedra ha sido
by work and grace of reinforced cement. Stone has been

relegada. Estamos hoy, indudablemente, en la edad del ladrillo
banished. We are, today, undoubtedly, in the age of brick

y el hormigón. Con todo, lo que se pudiera objetar sobre
and concrete. For all that, one may be opposed to the

la desigualdad de los estilos arquitectónicos, Madrid realiza
inequality of architectonic styles, Madrid represents

el tipo de ciudad municipal—como lo entienden y practican
the type of municipal city—such as is understood and practised by

los alemanes—escrupulosamente limpia y abierta al sol y al aire.
the Germans—scrupulously clean and open to the sun and to the air.†

Note: In the above and other extracts, given to illustrate the flexibility and scope of the instrument provided, it will be observed that the difficulties of grammar and vocabulary are few. An occasional reference to a dictionary will get the student over those for which a solution has not been provided in the preceding pages. Occasionally ideas rather than words may cause hesitation.

* Impressions.
† This extract is taken with acknowledgments from *España: Meditaciones y Andanzas*, by the Argentine writer, Ricardo Saenz Hayes. (Buenos Aires, 1927.)

2. FROM *LA PRENSA* OF BUENOS AIRES

The Modern Theatre

Are we nearing the end of the phase of theatrical spectacle? It would appear so. Once again those responsible for our entertainment have underestimated our intelligence, and must revise their ideas. The purely commercial theatre is failing in many countries and, I think, must fail in all. The Art Theatre will take its place. This has already happened in Russia, and there are definite indications of the same tendency in the United States and other countries.

The arts are the ideal paraphrase of life and, so far as the theatre is concerned, the more closely we adhere to it the more convincing and successful the theatre will be. Today the relation of art to life may be difficult to define, but only on the rarest occasions is it even moderately fulfilled in the theatre; and it can never be fulfilled by overwhelming life with external and ingenious mechanics. The modern theatre has damned itself by obscuring the true function of the dramatist, by reducing the actor to a mere marionette, by failing to provide wisdom instead of knowledge, and by omitting to give human answers to human problems.

By this I do not mean that salvation can be reached merely by abolishing mise-en-scène *or by returning to the bare or naturalistic state of our forefathers. Not at all. An artistic revaluation of values has already begun and, in the minds of the very*

El teatro moderno

¿Nos hallamos cerca del fin de la fase del espectáculo teatral? Así lo parecería. Una vez más, aquéllos que tienen la responsabilidad de proporcionarnos deleite no han estimado bien nuestra inteligencia y deben revisar sus ideas. El teatro puramente comercial está en decadencia en muchos países y, en mi opinión, debe caer en todos. El teatro de arte lo reemplazará. Esto ha ocurrido ya en Rusia, y existen indicaciones definidas de la misma tendencia en los Estados Unidos y en otras naciones.

Las artes constituyen la paráfrasis ideal de la vida, y en lo que respecta al teatro, cuanto más nos ciñamos a ella más convincente será y más éxitos alcanzará el teatro. Hoy puede ser difícil definir la relación del arte con la vida, pero sólo en muy raras ocasiones se encuentra esta relación, aun moderadamente realizada en el teatro; y jamás podrá ser realizada mediante la supeditación de la vida a procedimientos mecánicos externos e ingeniosos. El teatro moderno ha hecho su condenación al oscurecer la verdadera función del dramaturgo por la reducción del actor a un simple fantoche, dejando de proveer sabiduría en vez de conocimiento, y omitiendo dar soluciones humanas a los problemas humanos.

No quiero significar con esto que pueda conseguirse la salvación con sólo abolir la 'mise-en-scène' o volviendo al escenario desnudo o naturalista de nuestros antepasados. De ninguna manera. Ha comenzado ya una revaluación artística de

few true artists of the theatre, is progressing. It may ultimately mean a utilisation of all the riches of mechanical effects and externals now available, with others besides. But the centre, the dominating influence must be emotional and intellectual interplay of ideas and characters, based upon a logic of human values that is genuine and never false.

The work of the producer should be akin to that of a doctor or midwife at an accouchement. All his skill and care is required, but he must not do too much or he will kill either patient or baby—the dramatist and his play. In other words, the creative dramatist must be nursed and encouraged. The small theatre must be his home for some time—until a wider public has been educated to appreciate his worth. Then the theatre will flourish as in Greece. I am optimist enough to believe that this will happen, perhaps in the course of our own lifetime.

valores, y esta revaluación progresa en las mentes de los muy pocos verdaderos artistas del teatro. Ello podrá significar, en último término, una utilización de todas las riquezas de efectos externos y mecánicos de que hoy se dispone, acompañadas de otras. Pero el centro, la influencia dominante debe ser de interjuego emocional e intelectual de ideas y caracteres, basada sobre una lógica de valores humanos que es genuina y nunca falsa.

La tarea del productor debe ser análoga a la de un médico o una obstétrica en su trabajo. Se requiere toda su habilidad y cuidado, pero no debe poner demasiado de su parte, porque, de lo contrario, matará a la paciente o a la criatura; o sea, al dramaturgo y su obra. En otras palabras, se debe criar y alentar al dramaturgo creador. El teatro humilde debe ser su hogar durante algún tiempo, hasta que haya sido educada una mayor masa de público para que pueda apreciar su valor. El teatro florecerá entonces como en Grecia. Soy yo bastante optimista para creer que esto sucederá quizá en el trascurso de nuestra propia vida.

Note: The above extract from *La Prensa* of 21 August 1932 is taken, with acknowledgements and thanks to the editor, from an article by Charles Duff on the subject of 'The Modern Theatre'.

3. EL DISCURSO DE DON QUIJOTE A LOS CABREROS*
Don Quixote's Speech to the Goatherds

Después que Don Quijote hubo bien satisfecho su estómago, tomó
After (that) Don Quixote had well satisfied his stomach, he took

* My translation attempts to follow the Spanish word for word, but cannot give an idea of the beauty and roll of this magnificent passage. No translator has yet done it justice.—C.D.

un puño de bellotas en la mano, y mirándolas atentamente, soltó
a handful of acorns (in his hand), and looking attentively at them, gave

la voz a semejantes razones: 'Dichosa edad y siglos dichosos
utterance in this fashion: 'Happy age and happy centuries (were)

aquéllos a quien los antiguos pusieron nombre de dorados; y no
those upon which the ancients bestowed (the) name of golden; and not

porque en ellos el oro, que en esta nuestra edad de hierro tanto
because in them gold, which in this iron age of ours is so greatly

se estima, se alcanzase en aquella venturosa sin fatiga alguna,
esteemed, could be obtained in that fortunate (period) without any toil,

sino porque entonces los que en ella vivían ignoraban estas dos
but because those who lived then did not know these two

palabras de "tuyo" y "mío". Eran en aquella santa edad todas las
words "mine" and "thine". In that blessed age were all

cosas comunes: a nadie le era necesario, para alcanzar su ordinario
things (in) common: to nobody was it necessary, in order to win his daily

sustento, tomar otro trabajo que alzar la mano, y alcanzarle
sustenance, to engage in any work save to extend his hand and take it

de las robustas encinas, que liberalmente les estaban convidando
from the stout oaks, which were liberally inviting

con su dulce y sazonado fruto. Las claras fuentes y corrientes ríos
with their sweet and mellow fruit. The clear fountains and running streams

en magnífica abundancia sabrosas y trasparentes aguas les ofrecían
offered in magnificent abundance delicious and limpid waters.

   'En las quiebras de las peñas y en lo hueco de los árboles
   'In the clefts of (the) rocks and in the hollow of (the) trees

formaban su república las solícitas y discretas abejas, ofreciendo
did the careful and sagacious bees make their republic, offering

a cualquiera mano sin interés alguno la fértil cosecha de su
to every hand without any interest the fertile harvest of their

dulcísimo trabajo. Los valientes alcornoques despedían de sí, sin
sweetest labour. The mighty cork-trees divested themselves, without

otro artificio que el de su cortesía, sus anchas y livianas cortezas,
any other art (but), that of their own courtesy, of their broad light barks,

con que se comenzaron a cubrir las casas sobre rústicas estacas,
with which men began to roof (the) houses (built) on rude stakes,

sustentadas no más que para defensa de las inclemencias del cielo.
supported only as a defence against the inclemency of heaven.

'Todo era paz entonces, todo amistad, todo concordia: aun
'*All was peace then, all friendship, all concord: as yet*

no se había atrevido la pesada reja del corvo arado a abrir ni
there was no attempt by the heavy curved ploughshare to (break) open or

visitar las entrañas piadosas de nuestra primera madre, que ella
disturb the tender bowels of our first mother, who

sin ser forzada ofrecía por todas las partes de su fértil y espacioso
without constraint yielded from every part of her fertile and spacious

seno lo que pudiese hartar, sustentar y deleitar a los hijos
bosom all that could fill, sustain and delight the children

que entonces la poseían. Entonces sí que andaban las simples y
who then possessed her. Then (verily) roamed the simple and

hermosas zagalejas de valle en valle y de otero en otero, en trenza
beautiful shepherdesses from vale to vale and hill to hill, tresses flowing

y en cabello, sin más vestidos de aquéllos que eran menester para
and braided, (and) with no other garments but those needful to

cubrir honestamente lo que la honestidad quiere y ha querido
cover modestly what modesty requires and has required

siempre que se cubra; y no eran sus adornos de los que ahora
always to be covered; nor were their ornaments like those now

se usan, a quien la púrpura de Tiro y la por tantos modos martirizada
used, which (the) purple of Tyre and (the) much tortured

seda encarecen, sino de algunas hojas de verdes lampazos
silk set off, but (only) a few green dock leaves

y yedra entretejidas, con lo que quizá iban tan pomposas y compuestas
and ivy intertwined, wherewith possibly they strutted as bravely and composed

como van ahora nuestras cortesanas con las raras y peregrinas
as do now our courtesans with the rare and far-fetched

invenciones que la curiosidad ociosa les ha mostrado.
artifices which idle curiosity has taught them.

'Entonces se decoraban los concetos amorosos del alma simple y
'*Then were clothed the amorous conceits of the soul simply and*

sencillamente del mismo modo y manera que ella los concebía, sin
innocently in the same mode and manner as they were conceived, nor

buscar artificioso rodeo de palabras para encarecerlos. No había
sought (they) by artificial subterfuge of words to enhance them. There was no

la fraude, el engaño ni la malicia mezcládose con la verdad y llaneza.
fraud, or deceit, or malice mingled with truth and straightforwardness.

'**La justicia se estaba en sus propios términos, sin que la osasen**
'*Justice was kept within her own bounds, nor dared to*

turbar ni ofender los del favor y los del interés, que tanto
disturb or assail her either favour or interest, which so greatly

ahora la menoscaban, turban y persiguen. La ley del encaje aun
now impair, pervert, and importune her. Arbitrary law had as yet

no se había sentado en el entendimiento del juez, porque entonces
not possessed the understanding of the judge, for then

no había qué juzgar ni quién fuese juzgado. Las doncellas y la
there was nothing and nobody to be judged. Maidens and

honestidad andaban, como tengo dicho por donde quiera, solas y
modesty wandered, as I have said, where they willed, alone and

señeras, sin temor que la ajena desenvoltura y lascivo intento
unattended, without fear that strangers' licence and lewd intent

las menoscabasen y su perdición nacía de su gusto y propia voluntad.
molest them, and their undoing was born of their pleasure and their own will.

'**Y ahora en estos nuestros detestables siglos no está segura**
'*And now in these hateful times of ours no one is*

ninguna, aunque la oculte y cierre otro nuevo laberinto como el
safe, even if hidden and closed (away) by some new labyrinth like that

de Creta; porque allí por los resquicios o por el aire, con el celo
of Crete; because there through chinks or through the air, with the zeal

de la maldita solicitud, se les entra la amorosa pestilencia, y les
of accursed importunity, will enter (the) amorous pestilence, and

hace dar con todo su recogimiento al traste. Para cuya seguridad,
make them yield in spite of all (their) seclusion. For their safety,

andando más los tiempos y creciendo más la malicia, se instituyó
as time progressed and wickedness increased, was instituted

la orden de los caballeros andantes para defender las doncellas,
the order of knights-errant to defend maidens,

amparar las viudas, y socorrer a los huérfanos y a los
protect widows, and succour orphans and the

menesterosos. De esta órden soy yo, hermanos cabreros, a quien
needy. Of this order am I, brother(s) goatherds, whom

agradezco el agasajo y buen acogimiento que hacéis a mí y a mi
thank (for) the hospitality and good welcome that you gave (to) me

scudero: que aunque por ley natural están todos los que viven
nd to my squire: for though by the law of nature all men living are

obligados a favorecer a los caballeros andantes, todavía por saber
bound to show favour to knights-errant, yet realizing

que sin saber vosotros esta obligación me acogistes y regalastes,
that without your knowing this obligation you welcomed and feasted me,

es razón que con la voluntad a mí posible os agradezca la vuestra.'
it is right that with all my possible good will I should thank you for yours.'

ALPHABETICAL LIST OF THE ESSENTIAL VOCABULARY

BASIC AND SUPPLEMENTARY WORDS AND PHRASES

A

A (prep) *to; at; on; by*
  ir a + inf = *to be going to (do sth)*
  a las tres = *at 3 o'clock*
  a pie = *on foot*
  a mano = *by hand*
ABAJO (adv) *below, under; down*
ABANDONAR *to give up; to forsake, leave*
  abandonarse a = *to give oneself up to*
ABANICO (m) *(lady's) fan*
ABIERTO (adj) *open, clear; frank*
ABONAR (a) *to subscribe (to); to buy a season ticket*
ABRAZAR *to embrace, hug*
ABRAZO (m) *embrace, hug*
ABRIGO (m) *overcoat; shelter*
abrir *to open*
ABSOLUTO (adj) *absolute*
ABSURDO (adj) *absurd*
ABUELO, -a *grandfather, -mother*
ACÁ (adv) *here; hither*
  para acá = *this way, hither*
  por acá = *hereabouts, here*
ACABADO (adj) *finished, completed*
ACABAR *to finish*
ACASO (adv) *perhaps; maybe*
  por si acaso = *just in case*
ACCESO (m) *access*
ACCIDENTE (m) *accident; chance*
  por accidente = *by chance*
7—B.E.S.

ACCIÓN (f) *action, act; share, stock*
ACEITE (m) *oil; essential oil*
  aceite de oliva = *olive oil*
  — lubricante = *lubricating oil*
aceituna (f) *olive*
aceptar *to accept*
acera (f) *pavement; side-walk*
ACERCA (adv) *about, concerning*
ACERCARSE (a) *to draw near (to)*
ACERO (m) *steel*
ACERTAR *to guess right; to hit the mark*
ACOGER *to receive; to welcome*
  ACOJO = *I receive*
ACOGIDA (f) *reception; welcome*
  buena a. = *warm welcome*
  mala a. = *unwelcome*
ACOMODAR *to accommodate, lodge; to fit, suit; to set to rights*
ACOMPAÑAR *to accompany, escort*
ACONSEJAR *to advise*
  ACONSEJARSE = *to take advice*
ACONTECIMIENTO (m) *event, incident*
ACORDAR *to agree* (pres = ACUERDO)
  ACORDARSE DE = *to remember sth, sb*
acostar *to put to bed* (pres = acuesto)

ACOSTARSE *to go to bed; to lie down*

ACOSTUMBRAR *to accustom*

ACOSTUMBRADO(A) (adj) *accustomed* (*to*)
  estar acostumbrado a = *to be accustomed to*

ACTITUD (f) *attitude*

ACTIVIDAD (f) *activity*

ACTIVO (adj) *active*

ACTO (m) *act, deed; feat*

actor, actriz (m & f) *actor, actress*

ACTUAL (adj) *of the present time* [not actual]

ACTUALIDAD (f) *present time; now*
  EN LA A. = *at present*
  ACTUALIDADES = *contemporary news, events.* **Cine de A.** = *News Cinema*

ACTUALMENTE (adv) *now; at present*

ACTUAR (1) *to act; to function* (2) *to put in motion, move*

ACUDIR *to be present at; to attend; to apply, resort to*

ACUERDO (m) *agreement; decision*
  de acuerdo (**con**) = *in agreement* (*with*)

ACUMULAR *to accumulate, pile up*

acusar *to accuse*
  acusar recibo de = *to acknowledge receipt of* [a letter, etc.]

adaptar *to adapt*
  ADAPTARSE = *to adapt oneself*

ADECUADO (adj) *adequate*

ADELANTADO (adj) *ahead; anticipated; precocious; fast* [of clock or watch]
  pagar por adelantado = *to pay in advance*

ADELANTAR *to advance, progress; to anticipate*

ADELANTE (adv) *ahead; forward*

¡Adelante! *Come in! Go ahead! Forward!*

ADEMÁS (adv) *besides; moreover*
  además de = *besides* . . .

ADENTRO (adv) *in, within, inside*

ADICIÓN (f) *addition*

ADICIONAL (adj) *additional; extra*

ADIÓS (excl) *good-bye; farewell*

ADMINISTRACIÓN (f) *management; office of m.*

ADMINISTRAR *to manage, govern*

ADMIRABLE (adj) *admirable*

ADMIRAR *to admire*

ADMISIÓN (f) *admission; permission to enter*

ADMITIR *to admit; to permit entry*

ADONDE (adv) *where to; whither*
  la ciudad adonde vamos = *the city to which we're going*
  ¿Adónde va? = *Where are you going to?*

ADORNO (m) *ornament; adornment*

ADQUIRIR *to acquire, get*

ADUANA (f) *Customs; Customs house*

ADUANERO (m) *Customs officer*

ADVERTENCIA (f) *warning*

ADVERTIR *to warn; to give notice of*

AERÓDROMO (m) *aerodrome*

AEROPLANO (m) *aeroplane*

AEROPUERTO (m) *airport*

afanar *to press, urge; to hurry sb*
  afanarse = *to hasten, hurry*

AFECCIÓN (f) *fondness, affection;* also *ailment, disease*

AFECTAR *to make a pretence of; to affect, have effect on*

AFEITAR *to shave sb*
  AFEITARSE = *to shave oneself*

AFICIÓN (f) *affection.* **La a.** [in Spain = the bull-ring public and especially the expert one]

AFICIONADO, —a in sports =
fan; *amateur*
**Mi amigo es gran aficionado de
la corrida** = *My friend is a great
lover of bullfighting, the bullfight*
AFICIONARSE *to have a liking
for*; *to take to*
AFINIDAD (f) *relationship*; *re-
semblance*
AFIRMAR *to affirm, assert*
AFORTUNADO (adj) *fortunate*;
lucky
AFUERA (adv) *out*; *outside*
DE AFUERA *from outside*
¡AFUERA! *Get out! Clear the
way!*
(noun pl) **LAS AFUERAS** = *the
suburbs*
AGASAJAR A *to treat sb kindly*;
to regale
AGASAJO (m) *kind treatment*;
hospitality; *refreshment*
AGENCIA (f) *agency*
AGENTE (m) *agent*
ÁGIL (adj) *nimble*; *quick*
agilidad (f) *agility*
AGITACIÓN (f) *excitement*; *agi-
tation*
AGITAR *to shake, stir*; *to agitate*
agotador (adj) *tiring, exhausting*
AGOTAR *to exhaust*; *to run
through* [a fortune]
AGRADABLE (adj) *pleasant*;
pleasing
AGRADAR *to please*; *be pleasing*
ESTO LE AGRADA = *this
pleases him* = *he likes it*
AGRADO (m) *pleasure*; *agreeable-
ness*
Esto no es de mi agrado = *this is
not to my liking*
AGREGAR *to add*; also *to appoint*
agricultor, -a (m & f) *farmer*
AGRICULTURA (f) *agriculture*
agrio (adj) *sour*; *rough* [of surface]

AGRUPACIÓN (f) *group*; *circle*
[of people]
agrupar *to group*
(EL) AGUA (f) *water.* (pl) **LAS
AGUAS** = *(mineral) waters*
agua dulce = *fresh water*
agua fresca = *cold water*
agua potable = *drinking water*
un salto de agua = *a waterfall*
¡Hombre al agua! = *Man over-
board!*
AGUACERO (m) *(heavy) shower*
aguador, -a *water-carrier* (m & f)
AGUANTAR *to bear, endure*; *to
resist*; *to put up with*
AGUARDAR *to wait for*; *to expect*
AGUARDIENTE (m) *alcoholic
liquor* [of inferior quality]
AGUDO (adj) *sharp*; *keen, acute*
AGUJA (f) *needle*; *bodkin*
AHOGADO (adj) *drowned*; *suffo-
cated.* **UN —** *a drowned person*
AHOGAR *to drown*; *to suffocate*
AHORA (adv) *now*
AHORA MISMO = *this very
moment*
HASTA AHORA = *up to, until
now*
POR AHORA = *for the time being*
AHORRAR *to save*; *to economise*
AHORRO (m) *thrift*
los ahorros = *savings*
Caja de Ahorros = *Savings Bank*
AIRE (m) *air, atmosphere*; *car-
riage, gait*; *aspect, look*
AL AIRE LIBRE = *in the open air*
en el aire = *in suspense*
TOMAR EL AIRE = *to take a
walk*; *to go out for a breath of air*
AJENO, -A (adj) *another's*; *foreign*
ajeno a = *foreign to, free from*
ajeno de = *free from*; *ignorant of*
AJO (m) *garlic*
Ala (f) *wing*; *brim* [of hat]
alabanza (f) *praise*

ALAMBRE (m) *wire*
alarde (m) *boasting*; *ostentation*; *military parade, review*
ALCALDE, -SA *mayor, mayoress*
ALCANCE (m) *reach*; *scope*; *extent*
 al alcance de = *within reach of*
ALCOBA (f) *bedroom*
ALCOHOL (m) *alcohol*; *liquor*
ALDEA (f) *(small) village*
ALDEANO, -A *villager*; *peasant*; *rustic* (m & f)
ALEGRAR *to rejoice, make merry*
 ALEGRARSE DE = *to be glad of*
 Me alegro = *I'm delighted*
ALEGRE (adj) *merry, gay*; *lively*
ALEGRÍA (f) *merriment*; *gaiety*; *joy*
alejar *to move to a distance*; *to withdraw*
 alejarse = *to recede, move away* (intr)
alentado (adj) *spirited*; *in good health*
alentador (adj) *encouraging*
ALENTAR (1) *to breathe* (2) *to encourage*; *to cheer up*
alfiler (m) *pin*; *scarf-pin*; *brooch*
alfombra (f) *carpet*
ALGO (indef pron) *anything*
 (adv) = *something, somewhat*
 algo más = *something more*
 algo mejor = *somewhat better*; *something better*
ALGODÓN (m) *cotton*; *cotton plant*
 algodón hidrófilo = *absorbent cotton* (= *cotton wool*)
ALGUIEN (pron) *someone, some-body*
ALGÚN = ALGUNO [before a masculine noun]
ALGUNO (adj) *some*; *any*
 alguna cosa = *something*
 algunas veces = *sometimes*
 en alguna parte = *somewhere*
 (indef pron) **ALGUNO** = *some-body, someone*

ALGUNOS (pl) = *some people*
ALHAJA (f) *jewel*
ALIADO, -A (noun & adj) *ally*; *allied*
alianza (f) *alliance*
ALIENTO (m) *breath*; *vigour*; *courage*
 SIN ALIENTO = *breathless*
 DAR ALIENTO = *to encourage, cheer up*
ALIMENTACIÓN (f) *feeding*; *meals*; *board*
alimentar *to feed*
 ALIMENTARSE CON, DE = *to feed* (*live*) *on*
aliviar *to alleviate, lighten, relieve*
ALIVIO (m) *relief*
ALMA (f) *soul*; *ghost*; *phantom*
 alma mía = *my dearest*
 con toda el alma = *with all one's heart*
ALMACÉN (m) *warehouse*; *store*; *big shop, departmental store*
almacenaje (m) *storage*
almendra (f) *almond*
ALMOHADA (f) *pillow*; *bolster*
almohadón (m) *cushion*
ALMORZAR *to lunch*
ALMUERZO (m) *mid-day meal*; *luncheon*
ALOJAMIENTO (m) *lodgings*; *quarters*
ALOJAR A *to lodge sb*
 ALOJARSE *to take lodgings*; *to live in lodgings*
ALPARGATA (f) *hemp-soled canvas shoe*
alpinismo (m) *mountaineering*
alpinista (inv n) *mountaineer*
ALQUILAR *to rent*; *to hire*
ALQUILER (m) *rent*; *hire*
ALREDEDOR (adv) *around* [of place]
 — DE + number = *about, ap-proximately*

ALREDEDORES, LOS *surroundings; outskirts, environs*
alteración (f) *alteration; emotion; agitation*
ALTERADO (adj) *disturbed; agitated*
ALTERAR *to alter; to transform*
  ALTERARSE *to be disturbed; agitated, angry*
ALTEZA (f) *height, highness*
altitud (f) *altitude; elevation*
ALTO (adj) *high; tall*
  en alto = *up high*
  alta mar = *high seas*
  un hombre alto = *a tall man*
  de lo alto = *from above*
  (adv) = *high; loud* [of voice]; *loudly*
ALTOPARLANTE (m) *loudspeaker* [of radio]
ALTURA (f) *height; tallness*
alumno, -a *pupil; student* (m & f)
ALZAR *to lift, raise* [of load, weight]
  alzarse = *to rise in revolt*
ALLÁ (adv) *there, to there, thither*
  MÁS ALLÁ = *further*
  MUY ALLÁ = *far beyond*
ALLÍ (adv) *there, in that place*
  DE ALLÍ = *from that place*
  POR ALLÍ = *that way; through there*
AMA (f) *mistress* [of the house]; *landlady; owner.* See **AMO.**
AMA DE LLAVES = *housekeeper*
AMABILIDAD (f) *kindness; amiability*
AMABLE (adj) *kind; amiable*
AMANECER *to dawn; to appear at dawn*
  AL AMANECER = *at break of day*
AMANTE (inv noun) *lover, sweetheart*
  (adj) = *loving*

AMAR *to love*
AMARGO (adj) *bitter*
AMARILLO (adj) *yellow*
ambición (f) *ambition*
ambicioso (adj) *ambitious*
AMBIENTE (m) *environment; surroundings; atmosphere*
AMBOS, -AS (adj) *both*
ambulancia (f) *ambulance*
  —de Correos = *mail van*
ambulante (adj) *roving*
  un vendedor a. = *hawker*
amenaza (f) *threat*
AMENAZAR *to threaten*
AMIGO, -A *friend* (m & f)
  ser amigo de = *to be a friend of*
  amiga = *girl friend*
AMISTAD (f) *friendship*
  romper las amistades = *to quarrel*
  hacer las amistades = *to become reconciled*
amistoso (adj) *friendly*
AMO (m) *master, owner; boss.* See **AMA**
AMOR (m) *love*
ampliación (f) *enlargement; expansion*
AMPLIAR *to enlarge, expand; to enlarge a photo*
AMPLIO (adj) *ample; roomy, extensive*
AMUEBLAR *to furnish* (*house*)
anciano, -a (adj, m & f) *aged; old; old man, old woman*
ancla (f) *anchor*
  echar anclas = *to drop anchor*
ANCHO (adj) *wide*
  sombrero de ala ancha = *broadbrimmed hat*
ANDAR *to walk; to move; to go*
andén (m) *station platform; wharf; sidewalk*
anhelar *to long for*
ANILLO (m) *ring* [for finger]; *hoop*
  — de boda *wedding ring*

animación (f) *animation, liveliness*
ANIMAL (m) *animal*
ANOCHE (adv) *last night*
ANOCHECER (1) *to grow dark*
(2) *to reach (a place) at dusk;*
(noun m) *nightfall*
ANTE (prp) *before; in front of*
ante todo = *above all*
anteayer (m noun & adv) *the day before yesterday*
antecámara (f) *entrance hall; lobby*
antemano (de antemano) (adv) *beforehand*
anteojo (m) *spyglass* (pl) = *spectacles*
anterior (adj) *former, previous*
ANTES (adv) *before, formerly* [of place or time]; *rather*
— **DE** + inf = *before (doing sth)*
antes de comer = *before eating*
antipático (adj) *displeasing; disagreeable*
ANUAL (adj) *annual; yearly*
anudar *to tie; to knot*
ANUNCIAR *to give notice; to announce*
ANUNCIO (m) *advertisement; announcement*
AÑADIR *to add; to join to*
añejo (adj) *stale, musty; old*
AÑO (m) *year*
el Año Nuevo = *New Year*
APAGAR *to put out, extinguish*
— **la luz** = *to put the light out; to switch off the light*
APARATO (m) *apparatus; (any) device;* also *pomp, show*
aparecer *to appear, show up, turn up*
apariencia (f) *appearance, aspect, look(s)*
apartar *to separate*
APARTE (adv) *apart, aside; separately*
APELLIDO (m) *surname*
APENAS (adv) *scarcely, hardly*
apetito (m) *appetite*

aplauso (m) *applause; praise*
APLAZAR *to put off, postpone*
apoyar *to support, lean on; to back, defend; to bear out, confirm*
APOYO (m) *support, prop; help, aid, backing*
aprecio (m) *appreciation; esteem*
APRENDER *to learn,* + **A** + inf = *to learn to;* **aprender a leer** = *to learn to read*
aprender de memoria = *to learn by heart*
APRESURADO (adj) *in a hurry, hurried*
APRESURARSE *to hasten, hurry*
APRETADO (adj) *firm, tight; difficult; close-fisted, stingy*
apretar *to press, tighten, make firm*
APRISA (adv) *quickly; promptly*
aprobar *to approve* (pres = **apruebo**); **aprobar en el examen** = *to pass (in) an examination*
APROVECHARSE *to take advantage of*
aproximar *to approach, move near*
APROXIMARSE *to move near* (*to* = **A**)
aptitud (f) *aptitude*
APUNTAR *to write down; to make a note of*
AQUEL, AQUELLA (adj) *that,*
AQUELLOS, -AS } *those*
AQUÉL, AQUÉLLA, AQUELLO, AQUÉLLOS, -AS (dem pron) *that one, those ones*
See p. 26, and **AQUELLO**
AQUELLO (dem pron neut) *that*
AQUÍ (adv) *here*
ÁRBOL (m) *tree*
ARCO (m) *arch; bow* [violin]
arco iris = *rainbow*
arder *to burn, blaze*
arduo (adj) *difficult, hard*
ARENA (f) *sand; arena* [sport & bullfight]

argumento (m) *argument; plot*
árido (adj) *arid, dry; barren*
ARMA (f) *weapon, arm*
armada (f) *navy, fleet*
arraigar *to take root; to settle* [in a place]
ARRASTRAR *to pull, drag*
— SE *to creep, crawl*
arrebatar *to take away; to snatch*
arrebato (m) *fit of anger; rapture*
ARREGLAR *to arrange, regulate, adjust*
ARREGLARSE *to settle, come to an agreement*
ARREGLO (m) *arrangement, agreement, compromise*
ARRIBA (adv) *up, above; upstairs*
hacia arriba = *upwards*
cuesta arriba = *uphill*
para arriba = *upwards*
ARRIESGADO (adj) *risky; daring; dangerous*
ARRIESGAR *to risk*
ARROJAR *to throw, cast, fling*
arrojarse = *to venture, risk; to throw oneself*
arroyo (m) *brook, stream*
arroz (m) *rice*
arruinar *to ruin*
ARTE (m & f) *art*
las bellas artes = *fine arts*
ARTÍCULO (m) *article*
(pl) **los artículos** = *articles, products, goods*
artículo de fondo = *leading article* [of newspaper]
artificial (adj) *artificial*
artista (inv n) *artist; craftsman*
artístico (adj) *artistic*
arzobispo (m) *archbishop*
asado (noun & adj) *roast*
ascendente (adj) *ascending, going up*
el tren ascendente = *the up train*
ASCENDER *to go up; to advance* [in rank, status]

ASCENSOR (m) *lift; elevator*
ASEGURAR *to make sure; to assure; to insure*
ASÍ (adv) *so, thus; in this manner*
ASÍ QUE⎱ *as soon as*
así como⎰
así así = *so so*
si es así = *if so*
ASIENTO (m) *seat*
asimismo (adv) *likewise; equally; also*
asistir *to be present; to look after* (*an invalid*)
ASOCIACIÓN (f) *association, union; partnership.*
asociado (m) *partner; associate*
asociar *to associate; to form a partnership*
asomar *to begin to appear; to loom up*
asomarse a *to lean out*
asombrarse *to be astonished*
asombro (m) *astonishment*
astuto (adj) *shrewd*
ASUNTO (m) *matter, subject; business, affair*
ASUSTADO (adj) *frightened*
ASUSTAR *to frighten*
atacar *to attack*
atajo (m) *short-cut*
ataque (m) *attack*
atar *to tie, fasten*
ATENCIÓN (f) *attention, civility, kindness*
en atención a = *in view of, considering* . . .
llamar la a. = *to call a.*
prestar atención a = *to pay attention to* . . .
atender *to attend, to pay attention*
atento (adj) *attentive*
atentado (m) *crime, offence* [in law]
atentar *to attempt to commit a crime* (**atiento**)
ATERRIZAJE (m) *landing* [from aeroplane]

ATERRIZAR *to land* [aviation]
atleta (m) *athlete*
atlético (adj) *athletic*
atómico (adj) *atomic*
átomo (m) *atom*
atraer *to attract*
ATRÁS (adv) *backward, behind;
    back, past.*
  hacerse atrás = *to fall back, behind*
ATRASADO (adj) *backward; late;
    slow* [of watch or clock]
atrasar *to delay; to be slow*
atraso (m) *delay; lateness; back-
    wardness*
ATRAVESAR *to cross; to go
    through; to pierce*
  atravesarse en el camino = *to
    block the road, way.*
ATREVERSE A *to dare; to venture*
atrevido (adj) *daring*
atropellado (adj) *hasty; precipitate*
atropellar *to run down, run over*
ATROPELLARSE *to act hastily,
    recklessly*
atropello (m) *outrage, abuse; attack*
atroz (adj) *atrocious*
audaz (adj) *audacious*
audiencia (f) *interview; audience*
auditorio (m) *audience* [of listeners]
AUMENTAR *to increase*
aumento (m) *increase; rise (wages)*
AÚN (adv) *still, yet, as yet*
  aún no = *not yet*
  más aún = *still more*
aun (conj) *even;* **aun peor** = *even
    worse*
AUNQUE (conj) *though, even if*
ausencia (f) *absence*
AUSENTARSE (DE) *to go away
    (from); to leave, to stay away
    from*
AUSENTE (adj) *absent*
autenticar *to authenticate; to witness*
auténtico (adj) *authentic*
AUTO (m) *automobile, motor-car*

autocamión (m) *lorry*
automático (adj) *automatic*
AUTOMÓVIL (m) *motor-car*
automovilismo (m) *motoring*
automovilista (inv n) *motorist*
autor, -a (m & f) *author; authoress*
autoridad (f) *authority*
autorización (f) *authorization*
AUTORIZAR *to authorize*
auxilio (m) *help, aid*
avanzado (adj) *advanced*
avanzar *to advance*
avaro (adj & noun) *miser(ly)*
avena (f) *oats*
AVENIDA (f) *avenue*
AVENTURAR *to take a chance,
    chances*
AVERGONZADO (adj) *ashamed*
AVERIADO (adj) *damaged; out of
    order*
averiguar *to investigate; to ascer-
    tain*
AVIACIÓN (f) *aviation*
  el camp de a. = *airfield*
AVIÓN (m) *aeroplane*
  POR AVIÓN = *by air (mail)*
AVISAR *to notify*
AVISO (m) *notification; notice;
    advertisement*
¡AY! ¡AY DE MÍ! *Alas! Woe is
    me!*
AYER (adv) *yesterday*
AYUDA (f) *help, aid*
  ayuda social = *social assistance*
ayudante, -ta *assistant* (m & f)
AYUDAR *to help*
ayunar *to fast*
ayuno (m) *fast*
AYUNTAMIENTO (m) *town hall;
    municipal office(s)*
azotea (f) *flat roof*
AZÚCAR (m) *sugar*
azucarero (m) *sugar basin*
AZUL (adj) *blue*
  azul oscuro = *dark (navy) blue*

B

bacalao (m) *salted dried codfish*
bahía (f) *bay, harbour*
BAILAR *to dance*
bailarín, -a *dancer* (m & f)
BAILE (m) *dance; ballet; ball*
  baile serio = *formal dance*
baja (f) *lowering, fall*
  una baja de precios = *fall in prices*
BAJAR *to go* or *come down; to lower*
  bajar por la escalera = *to go, come down the stairs*
  bajar los ojos = *to lower one's eyes*
  bajarse del tranvía, del auto = *to alight from tram, car, etc.*
BAJO (adj) *low; shallow; short* [of a person]; *bass* [voice]
  el piso bajo = *ground floor*
BAJO (prp & adv) *below, underneath*
  bajo cero = *below zero*
bala (f) *bullet; shot; ball*
balón (m) *ball* [for games]
balde (m) *bucket*
  de balde = *gratis; no charge*
  en balde = *in vain; with no result*
BANCO (m) (1) *bench* [seat] (2) *bank*
  banco de ahorros = *savings bank*
  un billete de banco = *banknote*
banda (f) (1) *band* [of people] (2) *strip* [of cloth]; *sash; ribbon*
  banda de música = *band* [of instrumentalists]
  la Banda Oriental = *Uruguay*
bandera (f) *banner, flag*
bandido (m) *bandit; footpad*
banquete (m) *banquet; sumptuous meal*
bañar *to bath sb; to bathe sth*
  BAÑARSE *to take a bath; to bathe*
BAÑO (m) *bath*
  cuarto de baño = *bathroom*

BAR (m) *bar* [in hotel, tavern or café]
BARATO (adj) *cheap*
BARBA (f) *beard; chin; whiskers*
  barba cerrada = *thick beard*
  barba a barba = *face to face*
barbería (f) *barber's shop*
barbero (m) *barber*
BARCO (m) *boat, ship*
barrera (f) *barrier; fence.* Also *front seat(s) at bullfight*
BARRIO (m) *district, quarter* [of town or city]
base (f) *base, basis*
básico (adj) *basic*
bastante (adv) *enough, sufficient*
  bastante bien = *quite well*
  bastante rico = *fairly rich*
bastar *to suffice, be enough*
  ¡BASTA! *That's enough! Stop it!*
bastón (m) *walking-stick*
bata (f) *dressing gown*
BATALLA (f) *battle*
batido (adj) *beaten; defeated*
BATIR *to beat; to defeat*
  batirse = *to engage in a fight, duel; to decline in health*
BAÚL (m) *travelling trunk*
  baulito = *small trunk*
bautizar *to baptise, to christen, name.* Also *to mix wine with water*
BEBER *to drink, swallow*
  beber como una cuba = *to drink like a fish*
BEBIDA (f) *drink, beverage; potion*
  tomar una bebida = *to have a drink*
becerro (m) *bullock*
BELLEZA (f) *beauty*
BELLO (adj) *beautiful; fair*
  las bellas = *the fair ones*
  las bellas artes = *the fine arts*
BENEFICIAR *to benefit, profit*
  beneficiarse = *to gain, profit*

BENÉVOLO (adj) *kind; genial, benevolent*

BERMEJO (adj) *vermilion, bright red*

BESAR *to kiss*

besar la mano⎫ *expressions of res-*
— los pies ⎭ *pect.* See p. 71

BESO (m) *kiss*

BIBLIOTECA (f) *library*

bibliotecario, -a *librarian* (m & f)

bicicleta (f) *bicycle*

bien (m) *dear one.* (pl) **BIENES** = *possessions*

BIEN (adv) *well, right(ly)*

bien que = *although*

ahora bien = *now then*

más bien = *rather, somewhat*

estar bien = *to be well*

bien . . . bien *either . . . or . . .*

¡**BIEN**! ¡**MUY BIEN**! *Good! Fine!*

si bien = *although*

bienestar (m) *well being; comfort*

BIENVENIDA (f) *welcome; safe arrival*

bienvenido (adj) *welcome*

biftec (m) *steak*

bigote (m) *moustache*

BILLETE (m) *ticket*

— de banco = *banknote*

— de abonado = *season ticket*

— de ida = *single ticket*

— de ida y vuelta = *return ticket*

— de andén = *platform ticket*

— kilométrico = *mileage ticket*

BLANCO (noun m & adj) *white*

BLANDO (adj) *soft, tender; mild, delicate*

blanquear *to whiten, whitewash; to become white*

blusa (f) *blouse*

bobo (adj) *stupid; doltish*

un bobo = *a simpleton, ninny*

BOCA (f) *mouth; entrance, opening*

boca abajo = *face downward*

boca arriba = *face upwards*

boca de agua = *hydrant*

a boca = *by word of mouth*

bocacalle (f) *turning*

bocado (m) *morsel, bite, mouthful*

BODA (f) *wedding*

BODEGA (f) *wine-cellar; hold of ship.* Also *warehouse, storeroom*

bofetada (f) *slap in the face*

BOINA (f) *beret*

bola (f) *ball; marble*

BOLSA (f) *purse; handbag*

la Bolsa = *Stock Exchange*

BOLSILLO (m) *pocket* [in clothing]

BOMBA (f) *pump; bomb*

bombero (m) *fireman; pumper*

bombilla (f) *tube for drinking maté tea*

bonísimo (adj) *very good*

BONITO (adj) *pretty*

BORDE (m) *edge, border, verge*

BORDO (m) *board (ship)*

A BORDO = *on board*

al bordo = *alongside (the ship)*

borrachera (f) *drunkenness; orgy of drunkenness*

BORRACHO (adj) *drunk*

un (una) borracho, -a = *a drunk, drunkard*

borrador (m) *rough copy, eraser*

BORRAR *to erase, rub out; to smudge*

la goma de borrar = *rubber*

BOSQUE (m) *wood, small forest*

bota (f) *boot.* Also *small leather wine bag*

botar *to cast, pitch, throw; to bounce* [of ball]

bote (m) *rowing boat*

bote salvavidas = *lifeboat*

BOTELLA (f) *bottle*

BOTICA (f) *chemist's shop; pharmacy*

BOTICARIO (m) *chemist; druggist*

botijo (m) *jar (earthenware) with handle and spout*

BOTÓN (m) *button; bud, sprout; doorknob*
  el botones = *page-boy; 'buttons'*

boxeador (m) *boxer*

boxeo (m) *boxing*

bravo (adj) *brave, manly, rough*

¡BRAVO! *Bravo!*

BRAZO (m) *arm* [of body, chair]

BREVE (adj) *brief, short, concise.*
  en breve = *shortly, soon*

BREVEMENTE (adv) *briefly; in short*

brillante (adj) *bright, shining, sparkling*

BRILLAR *to shine*

brillo (m) *brilliancy; magnificence*

BRINDAR (POR) *to drink sb's health*
  brindarse = *to offer one's help*

brindis (m) *toast; drinking sb's health*

BROMA (f) *joke, jest*

bronce (m) *bronze*

BRUMA (f) *mist; fog*

BUEN (See **BUENO**, and p. 15)

buenaventura (f) *good luck; fortune* [told by fortune-teller]
  decir la b. *to tell sb's fortune*

BUENO (adj) *good* (See pp. 15–17)
  ESTAR BUENO *to be well* [in good health]
  SER BUENO *to be good* [a good person]
  LO BUENO ES . . . = *the strange thing is . . .*
  ¡BUENA ES ÉSA! = *That's a nice kettle of fish!*
  BUENOS DÍAS = *good morning, good day*
  BUENAS TARDES = *good afternoon, good evening*

BUENAS NOCHES = *Good evening, good night*

A BUENAS = *willingly*
  (adv) *very well, all right*

buey (m) *ox*

BULTO (m) *bundle; bulky object; parcel, package*
  a bulto = *wholesale*

buñuelo (m) *fritter; bun*

BUQUE (m) *vessel, ship*
  — de cabotaje = *coaster*
  — de vapor = *steamer*
  — de guerra = *warship*
  — mercante = *merchant ship*

burla (f) *mockery, jest*
  burlas aparte = *joking aside*
  de burlas = *in jest*

BUSCAR *to look for, fetch*

BUZÓN (m) *letter-box; lid*
  el buzón de Correos = *postbox*
  echar una carta al b. = *to post a letter*

C

CABALLERO (m) *rider, horseman; knight* [much used for Sir, Mr when no name follows]
  Señoras y Caballeros = *Ladies and Gentlemen*

CABALLO (m) *horse*
  — de caza = *hunter*
  — de carrera = *racehorse*
  — de silla = *saddle horse*
  a caballo = *on horseback*
  montar a caballo = *to ride*

cabello (m) *hair of the head*
  LOS CABELLOS = *hair (head of)*

CABER *to go in* or *into; to have enough room*
  No cabe más = *That's the limit*
  No cabe duda = *There's no doubt*
  El auto cabe por esa puerta = *the car can get through that door*

No quepo aquí = *There's no room for me here*

CABEZA (f) *head* [of body]

cablegrama (m) *cablegram*

CABO (m) *end, tip*; *cape* [of land]
  llevar a cabo = *to complete, to carry out sth*

cabotaje (m) *coastal trade*

cacique (m) (*Indian*) *chief*; *political boss*

CADA (adj) *each*; *every*
  cada uno, -a (de) = *each one* (*of*)
  cada cual = *every one*

cadáver (m) *corpse*

CADENA (f) *chain*

CAER *to fall*
  caer enfermo = *to fall ill*
  dejar caer = *to let drop*
  CAERSE *to fall down*; *to lose heart*

café (m) *coffee*; *café*
  café puro = *black coffee*
  café con leche = *white coffee*

cafetera (f) *coffee pot*

CAÍDA (f) *fall*; *drop*

CAJA (f) *box, case, safe, cash box*; *cashier's desk, office*
  Caja de Ahorros = *Savings Bank*

CAJERO (m) *cashier*

CAJETILLA (f) *packet* [cigarettes, etc.]

calabozo (m) *jail*; *cell* [jail]

CALCETÍN (m) *sock*

CALCULAR *to calculate, reckon*

CÁLCULO (m) *estimate*

CALDO (m) *broth*; *buillon*
  caldo de carne = *beef tea*

calefacción (f) *heating*
  — **central** = *central heating*

CALENDARIO (m) *calendar*

CALENTAR *to heat*
  calentarse = *to get warm*

CALENTURA (f) *temperature* (*body*)
  calenturón = *high fever*

calenturilla = *slight fever*

CALIDAD (f) *quality*

CALIENTE (adj) *warm, hot*; *fiery*

CALMA (f) *calm*; *tranquillity*; *slowness* [in business]

CALMAR *to calm*

CALOR (m) *heat*
  hacer calor = *to be hot* [of weather]

calumnia (f) *slander, calumny*

CALVO (adj) *bald, bare*; *barren*

CALZADO (m) *footwear*

calzoncillos (m pl) *underpants* (*men*)

CALLADO (adj) *silent*; *quiet, reticent*

CALLAR *to keep silent*
  CALLARSE = *to stop talking*
  ¡CÁLLESE! *Stop talking!*
  ¡CALLA! *Shut up!* [rude]

CALLE (f) *street*

calleja (f) *lane*

callejón (m) *narrow passage*; *alley*

CAMA (f) *bed*; *sleeper*; *berth*
  cama de soltero = *single bed*
  cama de matrimonio = *double bed*
  el coche cama = *sleeping car*

CÁMARA (f) *hall*; *chamber*; *house* [of legislative body]
  Cámara de Comercio = *Chamber of Commerce*
  Cámara de los Comunes = *House of Commons*
  Cámara de los Lores = *Upper Chamber* (= *Senate, Lords*)

CAMARADA (inv n) *companion, pal*; *crony*

CAMARERO, -A (m & f) *waiter, waitress*

CAMBIAR *to change, exchange*
  —**un billete de banco** = *to change a banknote*
  — **dinero inglés** = *to change English money*

CAMBIO (m) *change; exchange*
Casa de Cambio = *Exchange Bureau*
CAMINAR *to walk, move along*
CAMINO (m) *road*
  ir camino de Sevilla = *to be going on the road* to *Seville*
CAMIÓN (m) }
CAMIONETA (f) } *truck, lorry*
CAMISA (f) *shirt*
CAMISETA (f) *undervest*
campamento (m) *camp; camping ground*
CAMPAÑA (f) *countryside; level country; campaign*
CAMPEÓN (m) *champion*
CAMPESINO, -A (m & f) *countryman (-woman); peasant*
CAMPO (m) *field; country* [opposed to town]
  campo santo = *cemetery*
  a campo traviesa = *cross-country*
  campo de futbol = *football ground*
  campo de aviación = *airfield*
canal (m) *canal; channel*
CANCIÓN (f) *song*
CANSADO (adj) *tired*
CANSAR *to tire, fatigue; to bore*
  CANSARSE (DE) = *to get tired (of)* + inf
  CANSARSE DE CORRER = *to tire oneself running*
CANTANTE (inv n) *professional singer*
CANTAR *to sing*
CANTIDAD (f) *quantity*
CANTINA (f) *bar; canteen*
caña (f) *cane, walking-stick*
  caña de pescar = *fishing rod*
cañería (f) *pipe* [for gas, water, etc.]
cañón (m) *cannon; barrel of rifle; gorge, ravine*
CAPA (f) *cape*

CAPACIDAD (f) *room, capacity; ability*
CAPITAL (m) *capital wealth*
  — (f) *capital city*
CAPITÁN (m) *captain*
CAPÍTULO (m) *chapter*
CARA (f) *face, countenance; front, façade*
  dar en cara = *to call to task*
  cara a cara = *face to face*
CARÁCTER (m) *character; temper; disposition*
característico (adj) *typical, characteristic*
¡CARAMBA! [mild excl] = *Dear me! Gracious! Heavens!*
CARBÓN (m) *coal*
  — **de leña** = *charcoal*
CARCAJADA (f) *guffaw; burst of laughter*
CÁRCEL (f) *prison; jail*
cardenal (m) *cardinal*
CARECER (DE) *to be lacking; not to have*
CARGA (f) *load, burden; cargo*
CARGADO (adj) *loaded; burdened*
CARGAR *to load* [vehicle or ship] *to charge* [a battery]
cargo (m) *job, post*
  hacerse cargo de = *to take charge of, to take on* [a responsibility]
CARIÑO (m) *affection*
CARIÑOSO (adj) *affectionate*
carnaval (m) *carnival*
CARNE (f) *flesh; meat*
  — **asada** = *baked, roast meat*
  — **fiambre** = *cold meat*
  — **de vaca** = *veal*
  — — **cerdo** = *pork*
  — — **ternera** = *veal*
  — — **membrillo** = *quince preserve*
  — — **carnero** = *mutton*
  — — **cordero** = *lamb*
CARNERO (m) *sheep*

CARNICERÍA (f) *butcher's shop*
carnicero, — a (m & f) *butcher*
CARRERA (f) *act of running;*
  career
— de caballos = *horse races*
CARRETERA (f) *highway; road*
carro (m) *cart; car* [in SpA]
CARTA (f) *letter*
  carta certificada = *registered*
  letter
cartel (m) *poster*
CARTERA (f) *briefcase; wallet*
cartero (m) *postman*
cartón (m) *cardboard*
CASA (f) *house, dwelling, home*
— de comercio = *business house*
— de huéspedes = *boarding house*
— de juego = *gambling house*
— de socorro = *emergency hospital*
  estar en casa = *to be at home*
CASADO (adj) *married*
  estar casado = *to be married*
CASAMIENTO (m) *marriage*
CASAR *to give in marriage; to*
  officiate at the ceremony
  CASARSE (CON) = *to get*
  married (to)
casero (adj) *home made*
  ser casero = *to be domesticated*
CASI (adv) *almost*
  casi nunca = *hardly ever*
CASINO (m) *casino; dance hall;*
  social club or *association*
CASO (m) *case; occurrence;*
  event
  en tal caso = *in such a case*
  en todo caso = *anyway, at all*
  events
  hacer caso (de) = *to mind, notice,*
  take into account
  no hacer al caso = *to be irrelevant*
castaña (f) *chestnut*
castañuelas (f pl) *castanets*
CASTELLANO (adj) *Castilian;*
  Spanish

EL CASTELLANO = *Castilian;*
  the Spanish language; the best
  Spanish
castigar *to punish*
CASUALIDAD (f) *chance*
CATALÁN-A (adj) *Catalan*
CATEDRAL (f) *cathedral*
catedrático (m) *university professor*
categoría (f) *category*
CATOLICISMO (m) *Catholicism*
CATÓLICO (adj) *Catholic*
caucho (m) *rubber (material)*
caudillo (m) *leader; chief; com-*
  mander
CAUSA (f) *cause; case at law*
CAUSAR *to cause*
CAZA (f) *hunt; hunting; chase*
CAZAR *to hunt*
cazuela (f) *(earthen) cooking pot;*
  also *stew*
cebada (f) *barley*
CEBOLLA (f) *onion*
CEDAR (f) *to cede, yield; to*
  abate
cédula (f) *official document*
— personal = *identity card or book*
CEJA (f) *eyebrow*
CELEBRAR(SE) *to celebrate,*
  applaud; to be glad of
  Lo celebro = *I'm (so) glad to hear*
  it
CÉLEBRE (adj) *famous*
CELO (m) *zeal. (pl)* **los CELOS**
  jealousy
  tener celos = *to be jealous*
CELOSO (adj) *eager; jealous*
CEMENTERIO (m) *cemetery*
CENA (f) *evening meal; supper*
CENAR *to have an evening meal*
  [dinner *or* supper]
cenicero (m) *ash-tray*
ceniza (f) *ash*
CENSURA (f) *censorship*
censurar *to blame; to censor*
centavo (m) *cent* [SpA currency]

CÉNTIMO (m) *one hundredth (part) of anything—esp. of the peseta*
CENTRAL (adj) *central*
CENTRAL (f) *head office*
 LA CENTRAL DE CORREOS = *General Post Office*
 una central eléctrica = *powerhouse*
CENTRO (m) *(town) centre; club*
CEPILLO (m) *brush [for clothes]*
— de dientes = *toothbrush*
— para el cabello = *hair-brush*
cera (f) *wax*
CERCA (adv) *near; nearly; about*
 cerca de la una = *nearly one o'clock*
 cerca de veinte personas = *about 20 people*
 CERCA DE (prp) *near [place]*
CERCANO (adj) *nearby*
CERCAR *to encircle; to surround*
CERDO, -A (m & f) *pig, hog; sow*
cereza (f) *cherry*
CERILLA (f) *match*
 una caja de cerillas = *a box of matches*
CERO (m) *zero; nought; nobody*
 ser un cero = *to be a nobody, of no account*
cerquita (adv) *very near*
 aquí cerquita = *very near here*
CERRADURA (f) *lock*
CERRAR *to close, shut; to stop up*
 cerrar la boca = *to shut up*
 cerrar los ojos = *to close one's eyes; also to turn a deaf ear*
CERRO (m) *hill*
CERTEZA (f) *certainty*
certidumbre (f) *certainty*
CERTIFICADO (m) *certificate*
CERTIFICADO (adj) *certified; registered*
 una carta certificada = *a registered letter*

CERTIFICAR *to certify; to register (a letter)*
CERVECERÍA (f) *brewery;* also *café, tavern, drinking place*
CERVEZA (f) *beer*
CESAR *to cease, stop, desist*
CESTO (m) *basket* (Also (f) LA CESTA)
 ser un cesto = *to be stupid and rude*
cicatriz (f) *scar*
cicatrizar *to heal a wound*
CIEGO, A- (adj) *blind; blind man, blind woman (m & f)*
CIELO (m) *sky*
 cielo raso = *clear sky*
 a cielo descubierto = *in the open air; openly*
 llovido del cielo = *something dropped from heaven; godsend*
CIEN, CIENTO (adj & m noun) *(a) hundred*
CIENCIA (f) *science*
CIENTÍFICO (adj) *scientific*
CIERTO (adj) *certain, sure; no doubt*
 cierto lugar = *a certain place*
 cierto día = *one day*
 por cierto = *certainly, yes indeed*
 (adv) *certainly*
cifra (f) *figure, number; cipher*
CIGARRILLO (m) *cigarette*
CIGARRO (m) *cigar; in some parts = cigarette*
 un cigarro puro = *cigar*
CIMA (f) *summit*
CINE (m) *cinema; the movies, talkies*
— de Actualidades = *news cinema*
— sonoro = *talking pictures*
CINEMATÓGRAFO (m) *(the) pictures*
CINEMATOGRAFÍA (f) *cinematography*
CINTA (f) *ribbon, tape; sash*

CINTURA (f) *waist*
cinturón (m) *belt* [for waist]
circo (m) *circus*
circular (adj) *circular*
CIRCUNSTANCIA (f) *circumstance*
  en las circunstancias = *in the circumstances*
ciruela (f) *plum*. **ciruela pasa** = *prune*
cirujano (m) *surgeon*
CITA (f) *appointment*; *quotation* [from book]
CITAR *to make an appointment*; *to quote*
CIUDAD (f) *city*
ciudadano, -a (m & f) *citizen, -ess*
CIVIL (adj) *civil*; *polite*
  LA GUARDIA CIVIL = *the Civil Guard* [Spanish gendarmerie]
  la población civil = *civil population*
CIVILIZACIÓN (f) *civilisation*
CIVILIZADO (adj) *civilised*
civilizar *to civilise*
CLARAMENTE (adv) *clearly*; *openly*
CLARO (adj) *clear, bright*; *cloudless, light*
CLARO (adv) = **CLARAMENTE**
  Está claro = *It's obvious*
  or **¡CLARO!** = *of course*; *obviously*
CLASE (f) *class*; *category*; *class* [in school]; *social class*
  un billete de primera, segunda clase = *1st, 2nd class ticket*
CLASIFICAR *to classify*; *to sort out*
clavel (m) *carnation*
clavo (m) *nail, spike*
CLÉRIGO (m) *cleric, clergyman*
CLIENTE (inv n) *client, customer*
CLIMA (m) *climate*
CLUB (m) *club*; *social centre*

cobarde (inv n, noun & adj) *coward*; *cowardly*
cobrador (m) *conductor* [of bus, tram]
COBRAR *to collect, to receive what's due*; *to charge* [price, fee]
  cobrar el sueldo (la paga) = *to draw one's salary, pay*
  cobrar un cheque = *to cash a cheque*
COBRE (m) *copper*
COCER *to boil*; *to cook*
COCIDO (m) *Sp. dish of boiled meat, vegetables and chick peas*
COCINA (f) (1) *kitchen* (2) *cookery, cooking* (3) *stove*
  la cocina española = *Sp. cookery*
  la cocina de gas = *gas stove*
COCINAR *to cook*
cocinero, -a *cook* (m & f)
COCHE (m) *coach, carriage*; *cab*; *car*
  coche dormitorio (or **coche cama**) = *sleeping car* [on train]
  coche comedor = *dining car*
  coche de plaza (or **de punto**) = *cab* [for hiring]
  coche abierto = *open (motor) car*; *touring car*
  coche cerrado = *saloon car*
cochero (m) *coachman, cabby*
código (m) *code* [of laws, regulations]
codo (m) *elbow*
COGER *to catch, seize, grasp*; *to collect, pick (up)*
  coger el sombrero = *to collect*, or *to pick up one's hat*
  coger en casa = *to find at home*
  coger en mentira = *to catch out in a lie*
COJO (adj) *lame*
col (f) *cabbage* [various kinds of]

cola (f) *tail* [of animal]
  hacer cola = *to queue up*
colaboración (f) *collaboration,
  working together; contribution*
  [to newspaper]
colaborar *to work together*
colcha (f) *bedspread*
colección (f) *collection*
COLEGIO (m) *college, school;
  seminary*
CÓLERA (f) *anger; rage*
colérico (adj) *irritable*
COLINA (f) *hill*
COLMO (m) *heap; completion;
  overmeasure*
  ser el colmo = *to be the limit*
COLOCAR *to put in place, order;
  to place in a job*
  colocar dinero = *to invest
  money*
colonia (f) *colony*
coloquio (m) *talk; conversation*
COLOR (m) *colour; dye*
— vivo = *bright colour*
— muerto = *faded colour*
COLORADO (adj) *red; ruddy*
comandante (m) *major (army);
  commander*
combate (m) *battle; fight*
combatir *to fight (con, contra)*
combinación (f) *combination; compound*
combinar *to combine*
COMBUSTIBLE (m) *fuel*
comedia (f) *comedy, play*
COMEDOR (m) *eater; diner;
  dining-room*
comentar *to remark; to comment
  upon*
comentario (m) *remark*
COMENZAR *to begin* (pres
  comienzo)
COMER *to eat; to have a meal*
  el comer = *eating*
COMERCIAL (adj) *commercial*
8—B.E.S.

COMERCIO (m) *trade; business;
  store, shop*
  el viajante de comercio = *commercial traveller*
  comercio exterior = *foreign trade*
— interior = *home trade*
COMESTIBLE (m) *eatable; item
  of food*
  LOS COMESTIBLES = *provisions; victuals*
CÓMICO (adj) *comic*
COMIDA (f) *meal of any kind;
  lunch, dinner; food*
COMISARÍA (f) *comisariat;
  purser's office* [Sp]; *police
  station*
COMISARIO (m) *commissioner;
  purser* [Sp]
COMISIÓN (f) *commission; large
  committee*
COMITÉ (m) *committee* (small)
COMO (adv) *how; as; like; in the
  same manner as*
  ¿CÓMO? (interr) *How?*
  ¿Cómo? = *How's that? What
  did you say? Why so?*
  ¿Cómo no? = *Why not?; Why,
  of course; certainly*
  ¿Cómo así? = *How so?*
  ¿Cómo está Vd.? = *How are
  you?*
cómoda (f) *chest of drawers*
CÓMODO (adj) *comfortable; con-
  venient*
COMPAÑERO, -A (m & f) *companion, friend, pal; partner;
  mate*
  compañero de viaje = *travelling
  companion; fellow traveller*
COMPAÑÍA (f) *company; association, society*
— DE SEGUROS = *insurance
  company*
  abbr: Cía., Compª.
COMPARACIÓN (f) *comparison*

COMPARAR *to compare*
COMPARTIR (CON) *to share (with)*
competencia (f) *aptitude; rivalry, competition*
competente (adj) *competent; apt*
COMPETIDOR (m) *competitor*
COMPETIR *to compete*
COMPLACER A *to oblige, accommodate, please sb*
  COMPLACERSE EN = *to be pleased with; to delight in*
COMPLACIENTE (adj) *obliging; pleasing*
COMPLEJO (adj) *complex*
COMPLETAMENTE (adv) *completely; absolutely; entirely*
COMPLETO (adj) *complete, finished; full up* [of vehicle, compartment, cinema etc.]
complicación (f) *complication; difficulty*
COMPLICADO (adj) *complicated; involved*
complicar *to complicate*
COMPONER *to mend, repair; to heal, restore; to compose, compound, construct*
  componérselas = *to deal with sth; to cope with a situation*
compostura (f) *repair; compromise; circumspection*
COMPRA (f) *purchase; thing bought*
  IR DE COMPRAS = *to go shopping*
comprador, -a (m & f) *buyer; shopper; caterer*
COMPRAR *to buy, purchase; to shop*
— **al contado** = *to pay cash*
— **al fiado** = *to buy on credit*
— **a plazos** = *to buy on instalments*
COMPRENDER *to understand; to comprise*

comprender el significado = *to understand the meaning*
comprensible (adj) *comprehensible*
comprensión (f) *understanding*
comprimir *to press, compress*
comprobar *to verify, confirm* (pres **compruebo**)
compuesto (de) (adj) *made of; compounded of*
  el compuesto = *the compound*
COMÚN (adj) *common; public; usual*
  en común = *in common*
COMUNICAR *to communicate, make known*
— **por teléfono** = *to communicate by telephone*
  COMUNICARSE CON alguien por teléfono = *to talk to sb on the phone*
comunidad (f) *community*
comunismo (m) *communism*
CON (prp) *with*
  con + inf = *by*: **con decir todo, se salvó** = *by telling everything, he saved himself*
  con dolor = *in pain*
  con + **me** = **conmigo** = *with me.* See p. 24
  con tal que = *provided that . . .*
conceder *to grant, concede, admit*
CONCEJO (m) *civic body of town in Spain; municipal council; town hall*
CONCIERTO (m) *agreement*
  un c. de música = *a concert*
CONCLUIDO (adj & pp) *concluded, finished*
CONCLUIR *to end, finish*
CONCLUSIÓN (f) *conclusion*
concreto (adj) *concrete; not abstract; definite*
  en concreto = *to sum up; in brief*
concurrencia (f) *assembly; gathering of people*

CONCURSO (m) *competition*
conde (m), **condesa** (f) *count, -ess*
condenar *to condemn; to sentence*
   [law]
CONDICIÓN (f) *condition,*
   quality, state
  a condición de que = *on condition*
   that . . .
  estar en condiciones de = *to be in*
   a condition to . . .
condicional (adj) *conditional*
CONDUCIR *to lead, guide; to*
   drive
  conducir un auto = *to drive a car*
  la carretera conduce a = *the road*
   leads to
  conducirse = *to behave oneself*
conducta (f) *conduct, behaviour*
CONDUCTO (m) *conduit, channel*
  por conducto de = *through* (*agent*)
CONDUCTOR, -A (m & f) *driver*
conferencia (f) *conference, lecture,*
   trunk call
confesar *to confess, admit*
confiado (adj) *unsuspicious, trusting*
CONFIANZA (f) *confidence*
  tener c. en = *to have confidence in*
  confiarse en = *to take sb into one's*
   confidence
confirmar *to confirm*
CONFORME (adv) *in agreement;*
   correct; acceptable; O.K.
  ¿Está Vd. conforme con eso? =
   Do you agree with (*to*) *that?*
confundir *to confuse*
  confundirse = *to become mixed*
   up, confused
CONGRESO (m) *congress; as-*
   sembly
  Congreso de los Diputados =
   House of [political] *Represen-*
   tatives; House of Commons
CONJUNTO (m) *whole, aggregate*
CONOCER *to be acquainted with;*
   to know sb; to meet

conocer de vista = *to know by*
   sight
CONOCERSE = *to know one*
   another
CONOCIDO (adj) *known, well*
   known; prominent
CONOCIDO, -A (m & f) *acquain-*
   tance
CONOCIMIENTO (m) *know-*
   ledge; bill of lading
CON QUE (conj) *so, so then*
conquistar *to conquer, subdue*
consecuencia (f) *consequence*
  en c. = *accordingly*
CONSEGUIR *to achieve; to gain;*
   to get, obtain
consejero (m) *adviser; counsellor*
CONSEJO (m) (1) *advice, counsel*
  (2) *council* [advisory body]
  consejo de ministros = *Cabinet*
  consejo de guerra = *court martial*
conserva (f) *jam.* (pl) **conservas** =
   preserves
CONSERVAR *to preserve, main-*
   tain; to conserve; to preserve,
   pickle; to can
considerable (adj) *considerable*
CONSIDERACIÓN (f) *considera-*
   tion; regard, respect
considerado (adj) *considerate;*
   thoughtful for
CONSIDERAR *to consider, think*
   over; to show kindness to
CONSIGUIENTE (adj) *consequent*
  por c. = *consequently; therefore*
CONSISTIR EN *to consist in* [*not*
   to consist *of*]
constarse (que) *to know for certain*
   (*that*) . . .
CONSTIPADO (m) *cold; cat-*
   arrh; cold in the head
  coger un constipado = *to catch a*
   cold
construcción (f) *building; construc-*
   tion

constructor (m) *builder*

CONSTRUIR *to construct; to build*

consuelo (*m*) *consolation*

CÓNSUL (m) *consul*

CONSULADO (m) *consulate*

consultar *to consult*

contacto (m) *contact*

contagioso (adj) *contagious*

(al) CONTADO (adj) *(for) cash*

CONTADOR (m) *accountant; purser* [SA]

CONTAR *to count, number; to tell a story*

  Cuéntaselo a tu abuela = *tell that to the marines*

CONTENER *to contain*

CONTENIDO (m) *contents*

CONTENTO (adj) *content; pleased; glad*

CONTESTACIÓN (f) *answer*

CONTESTAR A *to answer*

continental (adj) *continental*

continente (m) *continent*

continuación (f) *continuation*

CONTINUAR *to continue, carry on; to last, endure*

continuo (adj) *continuous*

CONTRA (prp) *against; in opposition to*

  en contra = *against*

contrabando (m) *contraband; smuggling*

contrabandear *to smuggle*

contradecir *to contradict*

CONTRARIO (adj) *contrary*

  (adv) **AL contrario**⎫
      POR el — ⎬ *on the contrary*
      POR LO — ⎭

contrario (m) *opponent; rival*

CONTRATO (m) *contract*

contribución (f) *tax; rates*

convencer *to convince*

CONVENIR *to suit, be right for; to be satisfactory (for)*

— **CON** = *to agree with sb*

— **EN algo** = *to agree to sth*

CONVERSACIÓN (f) *conversation*

CONVERSAR *to converse, talk*

convidado, -a *guest* (m & f)

convidar *to invite*

convite (m) *invitation; treat*

coñac (m) *cognac; brandy*

COPA (f) *wine glass*

  una copita = *a little drink*

copia (f) *copy; imitation*

CORAZÓN (m) *heart*

corbata (f) *necktie*

cordero (m) *lamb*

cordial (adj) *hearty; cordial*

coronel (m) *colonel*

correcto (adj) *correct*

corregir *to correct*

CORREO (m) *post; mail; correspondence*

  a vuelta de correo = *by return of post*

  por correo = *by post*

  echar una carta al correo = *to post a letter*

CORRER *to run*

— **a todo correr** = *to run at full speed*

— **la cortina** = *to draw the curtain*

— **riesgo** = *to run a risk*

— **mucha prisa** = *to be very urgent* [of sth]

CORRIDA (f) *bullfight.* See **TORO**

CORTAR *to cut; to cut up, off, out, down*

corte (m) *cut; cutting*

corte (f) *court.* **las Cortes** = *Spanish Parliament*

CORTÉS (adj) *polite; civil*

cortesía (f) *politeness; good manners*

cortina (f) *curtain*

CORTO (adj) *short; brief*

— **de oído** = *hard of hearing*

— de vista = *short sighted*
COSA (f) *thing*
  ALGUNA COSA = *something*
  NINGUNA COSA = *nothing*
  CUALQUIER COSA = *anything*
  cosa de ver, oir = *a thing worth seeing, hearing*
  cosas de (Juan) = *just like Juan*
cosecha (f) *harvest*
coser *to sew; to join by sewing*
COSTA (f) *coast; shore; beach*
  a costa de = *at the expense of*
costar *to cost*
COSTE (m) *cost, price*
  coste de vida = *cost of living*
COSTUMBRE (f) *custom; habit*
  ser c. = *to be customary*
  como de c. = *as usual*
cotización (f) *quotation* [of price]
CREAR *to create; to establish*
CRECER *to grow, grow up; to increase*
crecimiento (m) *growth*
CRÉDITO (m) *credit*
  a crédito = *on credit*
creencia (f) *belief*
CREER *to believe; to think*
  Así lo creo = *I think so*
  ¡Ya lo creo! = *I should just think so!*
creíble (adj) *credible*
CREMA (f) *cream* [of milk]
  crema facial = *face cream*
CRIADO, -A (m & f) *servant*
crianza (f) *nursing* [of baby]; *breeding*
  de buena crianza = *of good up-bringing*
criar *to breed; to rear; to bring up*
CRIMEN (m) *crime*
criminal (adj & inv noun) *criminal*
CRIOLLO, -A (adj & m & f) **creole** = *person born in America of European origin; negro born in America, not in Africa*

crisis (f) *crisis*
cristiano (adj) *Christian*
critical (adj) *critical*
criticar *to criticise*
crítico (m) *critic*
crónica (f) *newspaper article* [brief]
cruce (m) *crossing; crossroads*
crudo (adj) *uncooked; raw*
cruel (adj) *cruel*
cruz (f) *cross*
cruzar *to go across; to cross*
cuadrado (adj & m noun) *square*
cuadrilla (f) *team, group* [bullfight]
CUADRO (m) *picture; painting; frame*
CUAL, CUALES (rel pron) *which*
¿CUÁL? (inter) *which? which one?*
CUALQUIER, CUALQUIERA; CUALESQUIERA (indef pron) *any (one); any (thing)*
  CUALQUIER COSA = *any (thing)*
  EN CUALQUIER PARTE = *anywhere*
  DE CUALQUIER MODO = *anyhow*
CUANDO (adv) *when*
¿CUÁNDO? *when?*
  cuando más (or **mucho**) = *at most* = *at best*
  cuando menos = *at least*
  CUANDO QUIERA = *whenever you wish*
  cuandoquiera que = *whenever . . .*
  de cuando en cuando = *from time to time*
CUANTO, -A, -OS, -AS (adj) (inter **¿CUÁNTO?**) *how much; how many; how long*
  ¿CUÁNTOS AÑOS TIENE VD.? = *How old are you?*
  ¿CUÁNTO VALE ESTE SOMBRERO? = *How much is this hat worth?* (= *How much does this hat cost?*)

¿CUÁNTO DURARÁ? = *How long will (this) last?*

CUANTO (adv) *how; as*
  cuanto antes = *as soon as possible*

cuartel (m) *barracks*

CUARTO (m) (1) *room* (2) *fourth part of*
  cuarto de baño = *bathroom*
  Son las seis y cuarto = *It's a quarter past six*

CÚBICO (adj) *cubic*

cubierta (f) *cover; place for one at table; deck* [of ship]

CUBRIR *to cover*
  cubrirse = *to put on one's hat*

CUCHARA (f) *spoon*

CUCHILLO (m) *knife*

CUELLO (m) *neck, collar*

cuenca (f) *river basin*

CUENTA (f) *account; bill*
  La cuenta, por favor = *The bill, please*
  tener en cuenta = *take into account*

CUENTO (m) *story; tale*
  contar un cuento = *to tell a story*
  cuento de viejas = *old wives' tale; old superstition*
  sin cuento = *innumerable, countless*

cuerda (f) *string, cord*

CUERO (m) *hide; leather*

CUERPO (m) *body; corpse*
  un cuerpo sin alma = *a dull stick*
  el Cuerpo Diplomático = *the Diplomatic Corps*

CUESTA (f) *slope*
  — arriba = *uphill*
  — abajo = *downhill*

CUESTIÓN (f) *question; matter; dispute*

cueva (f) *cellar; cave*

CUIDADO (m) *care; attention*
  tener cuidado = *to be careful*
  ¡CUIDADO! *Be careful! Look out!*

cuidadoso (adj) *careful*

CUIDAR *to take care of*
  cuidar a un enfermo = *to look after* (= *to nurse*) *a sick person*
  cuidarse = *to look after oneself*

CULPA (f) *blame; guilt; fault*
  echar la culpa a = *to put the blame on sb*
  tener la culpa de = *to be to blame*

CULPABLE (adj) *guilty; culpable*

cultivador (m) *cultivator; farmer*

CULTO (adj) *cultured; educated*

CULTURA (f) *culture*

cumpleaños (m) *birthday*
  ¡Feliz cumpleaños! = *Happy birthday!*

CUMPLIR *to fulfil; to keep a promise*

Hoy cumplo 21 años = *Today I'm twenty-one*
  por cumplir = *as a matter of form*
  cumplir (una promesa, un deber) = *to fulfil (a promise, duty)*

CUÑADO, -A (m & f) *brother-in-law; sister-in-law*

CURA (m) *priest; parish priest*

cura (f) *healing; cure*

CURAR *to heal; to cure*
  curarse = *to get better; to recover* [from illness]

curiosidad (f) *curiosity*

curioso (adj) *curious; inquisitive, prying*

CURSO (m) *course; run; route; direction; course of study etc.*

CURVA (f) *curve; bend* [on road]

CUYO, -A   ⎫ (rel pron) *of which;*
CUYOS, -AS ⎭ *whose. See p. 26*

Ch

chaleco (m) *waistcoat*

champaña (m) *champagne*

CHAMPÚ (m) *shampoo*

chaqueta (f) *coat; jacket*

CHARLA (f) *chat; talk* [on radio]
CHARLAR *to chat*
charlatán, -a (m & f) *talker, chatterbox; humbug; quack*
(adj) *loquacious*
chelín (m) *shilling*
CHEQUE (m) *cheque; bank draft*
— **de viajero** = *traveller's cheque*
talonario de cheques = *cheque book*
CHICO, -A (adj) *small, tiny*
(noun m) *little boy*
(f) *little girl*
un buen chico = *decent chap*
chispa (f) *spark*
CHISTE (m) *joke*
CHISTOSO (adj) *humorous; witty; funny*
CHOCAR *to crash into; to collide; to shock*
chocolate (m) *chocolate*
chófer (m) *chauffeur; driver*
choque (m) *collision; impact*
CHORIZO (m) *pork sausage*
chuleta (f) *chop*
churro (m) [Sp] *fritter*

D

dama (f) *lady*
DAÑAR *to damage, spoil*
DAÑO (m) *damage*
hacer daño = *to hurt*
DAR *to give*
dar algo a una persona = *to give sth to sb*
dar un paseo (a pie) = *to go for a stroll*
— **en coche** = *to go for a drive (in car)*
— **en bicicleta** = *to go for a ride on bicycle*
dar la bienvenida = *to welcome*
dar la una = *to strike one o'clock*
dar ejemplo = *to set an example*

dar a luz = *to give birth (to a child); to publish (book)*
DE (prp) *of, from.* See p. 57
una taza DE té = *cup of tea*
— **PARA té** = *teacup*
más DE mil libras esterlinas = *more than £1000*
DEBAJO (DE) (adv) *under, underneath*
DEBER (m) *duty; obligation*
DEBER *to owe; to have to, must, ought*
mi amigo me debe dinero = *my friend owes me money*
+ **DE** = *supposition or belief*
Debe de haber salido = *he must have gone out* (= *I think he's gone out*)
DEBERÍA (cond) = *ought*
Vd. debería trabajar más = *You ought to work more*
DÉBIL (adj) *weak; feeble*
debilidad (f) *weakness*
DÉBITO (m) *debit; debt*
decidido (adj) *determined; decided*
decidir *to decide*
decidirse *to make up one's mind*
DECIR *to say; to tell*
QUERER DECIR = *to mean*
¿Qué quiere Vd. decir? = *What do you mean?*
es decir = *that is to say*
decir bien = *to say rightly (to speak truly)*
decir mal = *to say wrongly* (= *to be mistaken*)
se dice (que) = *it is said (that)* . . .
Así se dice = *so they say*
¡DIGO! *I say!* (= *Just listen to that!*)
decisión (f) *decision*
decisivo (adj) *decisive*
declaración (f) *statement; declaration*
DECLARAR *to declare; to state*

decorar *to adorn, ornament*; *to decorate*
DEDO (m) *finger*
— **del pie** = *toe*
DEFECTO (m) *defect, fault*
defectuoso (adj) *faulty, defective*
DEFENDER *to defend*
defensa (f) *defence*
DEJAR *to leave, let*; *to let go*; *to allow, permit*
  DEJAR DE = *to stop, leave off*
    dejar de hablar = *to stop talking*
    Dejar + inf = *to cause sth to . . .*
    dejar caer = *to let drop*
    dejar atrás a = *to leave sb behind one*
    dejar en paz = *to leave alone*
DELANTE (adv) *in front of*; *ahead*
DELGADO (adj) *thin*
delicado (adj) *delicate*; *gentle*; *refined*
DELICIA (f) *delight*
DELICIOSO (adj) *delicious*
DEMANDA (f) *demand*; *request*
  en gran d. = *in great demand*
DEMÁS (adj) *other(s)*; *(the) rest*
  LO DEMÁS = *the rest*
  LOS, LAS DEMÁS = *the others*
  por lo demás = *as for the rest*
DEMASIADO (adj & adv) *too*; *too much*
  trabajar demasiado = *to work too hard*
  demasiado pobre = *too poor*
  demasiada gente = *too many people*
democracia (f) *democracy*
DEMOCRÁTICO (adj) *democratic*
demostración (f) *proof* [by showing]
DEMOSTRAR *to show* [the truth of]; *to prove*
denso (adj) *thick, close*; *compact*
dentadura (f) *set of teeth* [natural or artificial]

dentífrico (m) *dentifrice*
dentista (inv n) *dentist*
DENTRO (adv) *inside, within*
  POR DENTRO = *on the inside*; *inside*
  dentro DE = *inside of*
    dentro de un año = *within a year*
  dentro de poco = *before long, shortly*
denunciar *to denounce*
departamento (m) *department*; *section*; *compartment*
DEPENDER DE *to depend on, upon*
dependiente (adj) *dependent*
  (noun m) *clerk, employee*; *shop-assistant*
DEPORTE (m) *sporting activity*; *recreation*; *amusement*
deportista (inv n) *sportsman, -woman*
depositar *to deposit*; *to put away*
DEPÓSITO (m) *deposit*; *depository*; *warehouse*
  en depósito = *in bond*
DERECHO (adj) *right (side) of*; *just, lawful*
  mano derecha = *right-hand side*
  A LA DERECHA = *to the right*
  (m noun) *right* [in law]
    Derecho Civil = *Civil Law*
    los derechos = *tax, customs duty*; *fees*
  (adv) *straight on, ahead*
    ir derecho a casa = *to go straight home*
derivado (de) (adj) *derived (from)*; *descended from*
derrota (f) *defeat*
derrotar *to defeat*
desagradable (adj) *unpleasant, disagreeable*
desagradecido (adj) *ungrateful*
desalentarse *to lose heart*

DESAPARECER *to disappear*
desaprobar *to disapprove; to object*
desarmar *to disarm*
desarme (m) *disarmament*
DESARROLLAR *to develop; to unfold*
  desarrollarse = *to develop, evolve; to unfold*
DESARROLLO (m) *development*
desastre (m) *disaster*
desatar *to untie*
DESAYUNARSE *to have breakfast*
DESAYUNO (m) *breakfast; first meal* [= Sp coffee & rolls]
descalzarse *to take off one's shoes*
descalzo (adj) *barefoot(ed)*
DESCANSAR *to rest, take a rest; to be* (or *lie*) *at rest*
DESCANSO (m) *rest, repose; quiet*
descarga (f) *unloading; discharge* [of gun, ship]
descargar *to unload* (*ship*); *to discharge* (*gun*)
descendente (adj) *descending; going* or *coming down*
  el tren descendente = *the down train*
DESCENDIENTE (inv n) = *descendant*
descenso (m) *descent; way down*
desconfianza (f) *distrust; suspicious fear*
desconocer (1) *to be unacquainted with* (2) *to disavow knowledge of*
descontar *to discount*
describir *to describe*
descripción (f) *description*
descubierto (adj) *uncovered; bareheaded*
descubrimiento (m) *discovery*
DESCUBRIR *to discover*
descubrirse = *to take one's hat off*

descuento (m) *discount*
descuidado (adj) *careless; neglectful*
descuidar *to neglect*
descuido (m) *neglect; carelessness*
DESDE (prp) *since, from, after*
  desde entonces = *since then*
  desde luego = *of course; whereupon; admittedly*
  desde que = *since, ever since*
  desde niño = *since childhood*
  desde Londres hasta Madrid = *from London to Madrid*
  desde hoy = *from today*
desdichado (adj) *unfortunate; wretched*
DESEAR *to desire, wish; to want*
desembarazarse (de) *to get rid of (of)*
desembarcadero (m) *wharf; quay*
DESEMBARCAR *to unload; put ashore*
  desembarcarse = *to go ashore, land*
DESENGAÑO (m) *disillusionment; disappointment*
  sufrir un d. = *to be disillusioned*
deseo (m) *desire, wish*
desesperado (adj) *desperate*
desfavorable (adj) *unfavourable*
DESGRACIA (f) *misfortune; mishap*
  POR DESGRACIA = *unfortunately*
  caer en D. = *to lose favour*
desgraciado (adj) *unfortunate, unlucky*
  un desgraciado, -a = *a poor wretch, unfortunate person*
DESHACER *to undo*
  deshacerse de = *to get rid of*
deshielo (m) *thaw*
desierto (adj & noun) *deserted; uninhabited.* (noun m) *desert; waste; wilderness*
DESIGUAL (adj) *unequal*
desinfectante (m) *disinfectant*

desmayarse *to faint*
desmayo (m) *faint*
DESNUDO (adj) *naked*
desobedecer *to disobey*
desorganización (f) *disorganisation*
DESPACIO (adv) *slowly*
¡Despacio! = *Go easy!*
DESPACHO (m) *office*
— de billetes = *booking office*
despedida (f) *farewell; dismissal*
DESPEDIR *to dismiss; to see off*
[of a friend]
despedirse (de) = *to take leave
(of); to say good-bye (to)*
DESPERTAR *to waken*
despertarse = *to wake up*
despreciable (adj) *despicable; con-
temptible*
desprecio (m) *scorn; contempt*
DESPUÉS (adv) *afterwards*
— de = *after, next to*
— + inf: después de llegar = *after
arriving*
— de todo = *after all*
destinatario, -a (m & f) *addressee;
consignee*
destructivo (adj) *destructive*
DESTRUIR *to destroy; demolish;
to ruin* (pres = destrujo)
desvalido (adj) *destitute; helpless*
detalle (m) *detail*
detención (f) *delay, stop, stay; de-
tention, arrest*
DETENER *to stop, detain; to
arrest*
detenerse = *to tarry, stay*
DETRÁS (adv) *behind, after; back*
por detrás = *from behind; behind
one's back*
detrás de mí = *behind me* . .
detrás de la casa = *behind the
house*
DEUDA (f) *debt*
DEVOLVER *to give back, return,
pay back*

DÍA (m) *day*
— de fiesta = *feast day; holiday*
— siguiente = *next day*
— laborable = *working day*
el día de Año Nuevo = *New Year's
Day*
hace tres días = *three days ago*
Buenos días = *Good morning;
good day*
DIABLO (m) *devil; Satan*
¡Cómo diablos! *How the devil!*
¡Qué diablo! *The devil!*
diamante (m) *diamond*
DIARIO (adj & m noun) *daily;
daily paper*
DIBUJAR *to draw; to make a
drawing; to depict*
DIBUJO (m) *drawing; sketch*
DICCIONARIO (m) *dictionary*
— de bolsillo = *pocket dictionary*
dicho (m) *saying*
dieta (f) *diet; prescribed meals*
DIFERENCIA (f) *difference*
DIFERENTE (adj) *different*
DIFÍCIL (adj) *difficult*
DIFICULTAD (f) *difficulty*
DIGNO (adj) *worthy*
dimisión (f) *resignation* [from post
or office]
dimitir *to resign*
DINERO (m) *money*
DIOS (m) *God*
Vaya Vd. con D. = *good-bye*
diplomático (adj & m noun) *diplomatic; diplomat*
diputado (m) *deputy; member of the
House of Commons*
DIRECCIÓN (f) *direction; postal
address. Also management; ad-
ministration*
DIRECTO (adj) *direct*
DIRECTOR, -A (m & f) *director,
manager; chief; editor* [news-
paper]
— espiritual = *father confessor*

— **de orquesta** = *conductor*
DIRIGIR *to direct*
— **un negocio** = *to manage a business*
— **una carta** = *to address a letter*
DIRIGIRSE A *to make one's way to*
disciplina (f) *discipline*
discípulo, -a (m & f) *pupil, student; disciple*
DISCO (m) *gramophone record; disc*
discoteca (f) *library of gramophone records*
DISCULPA (f) *excuse*
DISCULPAR (A) *to excuse (sb)*
disculparse = *to apologise*
DISCURSO (m) *speech (public); address*
discusión (f) *discussion*
DISCUTIR *to discuss; to argue; to dispute*
disminuir *to diminish, decrease*
DISTANCIA (f) *distance*
distante (adj) *distant*
a *X* **kilómetros de distancia** = *X Km. away*
¿Qué distancia hay de Madrid a Sevilla? = *How far is it from Madrid to Seville?*
distinción (f) *distinction*
distinguido (adj) *distinguished*
DISTINGUIR *to distinguish; make out*
DISTINTO (adj) *plain; clear; different*
una vida muy distinta = *a very different (way of) life*
distraer *to amuse; to entertain*
DISTRAERSE = *to amuse oneself*
distraído (adj) *absent-minded; distracted*
distribución (f) *distribution*
distribuir *to distribute*

DISTRITO (m) *district*
DIVERSO (adj) *diverse, different* (pl) *various; several*
DIVERTIDO (adj) *amusing; entertaining*
divertir *to amuse sb*
DIVERTIRSE = *to enjoy oneself; to have a good time*
DIVIDIR *to divide*
división (f) *division; section; compartment*
divorciar *to divorce*
divorciarse = *to be, to become divorced*
divorcio (m) *divorce*
DOBLAR *to double; to make double; to fold; to turn*
— **un papel** = *to fold a piece of paper*
— **la calle** = *to turn a corner* [of a street]
DOBLE (adj) *double, twofold* (noun) **el doble** = *fold; crease*
DOCENA (f) *dozen*
DOCTOR, -A (m & f) *doctor; physician*
DOCUMENTACIÓN (f) *personal identity papers; documents* [generally]
DÓLAR (m) *dollar* [U.S.A.]
DOLER *to pain; to grieve*
Me duele la cabeza = *I have a headache*
DOLOR (DE) (m) *pain (in)*
dolor de cabeza = *pain in the head* [headache]
dolorcito (m) *slight pain*
dolorido (adj) *painful, aching; doleful, afflicted, grieved*
DOMÉSTICO (adj) *domestic* (noun m & f) = *domestic servant*
dominar *to dominate; to master* [a subject]
dominar el castellano = *to master Spanish*

DON (m) title for a gentleman, used only before Christian names = *Sir, Mr* or *Esquire*. A politely familiar form of address: *Don Pablo*, written *D. Pablo. Señor* can be used before it: *Señor Don Pablo Giménez: Sr. D. Pablo* etc. (f) = **DOÑA**

doncella (f) *lady's maid; servant; girl*

DONDE (adv) *where*
¿**Dónde está el tren?** = *Where's the train?*
¿**De dónde viene el tren?** = *Where does the train come from?*
¿**Hacia dónde vamos?** = *Where are we going* (= *in which direction*)?

dondequiera (adv) *wherever*

DOÑA (see **DON**). Used only before Christian names: *Doña María de Sayas.* Equivalent to *Miss* or *Mrs.*

DORADO (adj) *golden; gilt*

DORMIDO (adj) *asleep*
estar dormido = *to be asleep*

DORMIR *to sleep*
dormirse = *to fall asleep*

dote (f) *dowery*
las dotes = *talents, gifts* [*from nature*]

drama (m) *drama; serious play*

dramático (adj) *dramatic*

DUCHA (f) *shower bath*

DUDA (f) *doubt*
poner en duda = *to query, question*
SIN DUDA = *doubtless; undoubtedly*

DUDAR *to doubt*
— **DE** = *to be doubtful of; to distrust*

DUDOSO (adj) *doubtful; dubious; risky*

DUEÑO, -A (m) = *owner, proprietor, landowner; master*

ser dueño de = *to own; to be master of*
(f) = *owner, proprietress, landlady; married lady; chaperon*

DULCE (adj) *sweet* [like honey]; *pleasant, agreeable*
(noun m) *sweetmeat; candy; bonbon; sweet* [after dinner]

DULZURA (f) *sweetness; meekness; gentleness*

duque, duquesa (m & f) *duke; duchess*

DURACIÓN (f) *duration*

duradero (adj) *lasting*

DURANTE (prp) *during*
durante uno año = *for the whole course of a year*

DURAR *to last; to endure*

dureza (f) *hardness; solidity; obstinacy; hardness of heart*

DURO (adj) *hard; solid; firm; stubborn; stingy; harsh*

DURO (m) *dollar; 5 peseta piece* [Sp]
un duro sevillano = *a bad (counterfeit) coin*

E

E = Y (conj) *and* (E is used before words beginning I or HI but not hie)
padre e hijo = *father and son*

ECHAR *to throw, pitch, hurl, fling*
echar carnes = *to put on weight*
echar flores = *to compliment*
echar suertes = *to draw lots*
echar a + inf = *to start*
echar a correr = *to start running*
See also **BUZÓN, CORREO**
echarse = *to lie down*

EDAD (f) *age*
menor de edad = *under age*

mayor de edad = *of age*
de edad madura = *of mature age*
¿Qué edad tiene él? = *What age is he?*
edición (f) *edition*; *publication*; *issue*
EDITAR *to publish*; *to issue in print*
editor (m) *publisher*
EDUCACIÓN (f) *education*; (*good*) *breeding*
mala educación = *bad upbringing*; *ill breeding*
EDUCAR *to bring up*; *to educate*
mal educado = *ill-bred*; *rude*
efectivo (adj) *effective, real*; *actual*
EFECTO (m) *effect*
en efecto = *in fact*
(pl) **efectos** = *assets*; *chattels*
eficaz (adj) *competent, capable* [of persons]
efficacious [of things]
eficiencia (f) *efficiency*
egoísmo (m) *selfishness*; *egoism*
ejecutar *to do, make*; *to execute*
EJEMPLAR (m) *copy*; *pattern*; *specimen*
sin ejemplar = *without precedent*
EJEMPLO (m) *example, instance*
por ejemplo = *for example*
dar ejemplo = *to set an example*
ejercer *to exercise, practise*
ejercicio (m) *exercise*; *practice*
EJÉRCITO (m) *army*
EL *the.* (pl) **LOS**
el domingo = *on Sunday*
los domingos = *on Sundays*
ÉL (pl) **ELLOS** (pers pron) *he, him, it*; *they, them* (m)
elástico (m noun & adj) *elastic*
ELECCIÓN (f) *election*; *choice*
electricidad (f) *electricity*
eléctrico (adj) *electric*
elegante (adj) *elegant*; *fashionable*
elegir *to elect*; *to choose*

ELLA (pl) **ELLAS** (pers pron) *she, her, it*; *they, them* (f)
ELLO (neuter pers pron) *it*
Ello es que . . . = *The fact is that . . .*
EMBAJADA (f) *embassy*
embajador (m) *ambassador*
EMBARCADERO (m) *landing-stage*; *quay*; *docks*
EMBARCAR *to ship*; *to put on board*
EMBARCARSE = *to go on board*; *to embark*
embarco (m) *embarcation*
embargo (m) *hindrance*; *embargo*
SIN EMBARGO = *nevertheless, however*
emborracharse *to get drunk*
e. con vino = *to get drunk on wine*
embrollo (m) *muddle, tangle, confusion*
embustero, -a (m & f) *liar, cheat, trickster*
eminente (adj) *eminent, prominent*
EMOCIÓN (f) *emotion*; *feeling*
emocionante (adj) *moving, thrilling*; *exciting*
EMPEZAR *to begin.* (pres **empiezo**)
empleado, -a (m & f) *employee*; *clerk*
EMPLEAR *to employ*
EMPLEO (m) *employment*
emprender *to engage in*; *to undertake*
EMPRESA (f) *enterprise*; *undertaking*
empujar *to push*
empujón (m) *push, violent shove*
a empujones = *jostling, pushing*
EN (prp) *in, on, at.* See p. 57
entrar en la casa = *to go into the house*
estar en casa = *to be at home*
en la mesa = *on the table*

EN SEGUIDA = *at once*
enamorado (adj) *in love; lovesick*
  estar enamorado (de) = *to be in love (with)*
enamorar *to woo; to make love to*
  enamorarse (de) = *to fall in love (with)*
encaje (m) *lace*
encantado (adj) *delighted*
encantador, -a (adj) *charming; delightful*
encantar *to charm, to delight*
encarcelar *to imprison*
ENCARGAR *to entrust; put in (under) the care of; to order (goods)*
  encargarse de = *to take charge (care) of*
encendedor (m) *lighter*
  —de bolsillo = *cigarette lighter*
encender *to light; kindle; to light up*
  encender la luz = *to put on (switch on) the light*
  — un fuego = *to light a fire*
ENCIMA (DE) (adv) *above, overhead; on top of; on, upon*
encoger *to shrink, contract*
ENCONTRAR *to meet; to find*
  encontrarse con = *to run across sb*
encuentro (m) *encounter, meeting*
enderezar *to straighten*
ENEMIGO, -A (adj & noun) *enemy*
energía (f) *energy*
enérgico (adj) *energetic*
enfadar *to annoy; to anger*
  enfadarse = *to lose one's temper*
ENFERMAR *to fall ill*
ENFERMEDAD (f) *illness; malady*
enfermero, -a (m & f) *nurse* [for the sick]
ENFERMO, -A (adj & noun) *sick, ill; sick person*
ENFRENTE (adv) *in front; opposite*

— DE *in front of; opposite to*
engañar *to deceive, cheat*
  ENGAÑARSE = *to make a mistake; to deceive oneself*
ENGAÑO (m) *deceit; trick; trickery*
ENGAÑOSO (adj) *deceitful; deceptive*
engordar *to grow, become fat*
engrasar *to oil* [a car, etc.]
enhorabuena (f) *congratulation*
enhoramala (adv) *in an evil hour; in a bad time*
ENORME (adj) *enormous; huge; vast*
enriquecerse (con) *to grow rich (by, on)*
ENSALADA (f) *salad*
ensayo (m) *trial, test; essay; experiment; rehearsal*
enseñar *to teach*
ensuciar *to dirty, soil*
ENTENDER *to understand*
— DE = *to be familiar with; to know about*
  entender mal = *to misunderstand*
entendimiento (m) *intellect, mind; understanding*
ENTERO (adj) *entire, whole*
enterrar *to bury*
entierro (m) *burial*
ENTRADA (f) *entrance; entry; ticket of admission*
ENTRAR (A, EN, POR) *to go (in, into, by); to come in*
  entrar en la casa por la puerta = *to enter the house by the door*
ENTRE (prp) *between, among, amid*
  entre tanto = *meanwhile*
  entre manos = *in hand*
entrega (f) *handing over, delivery*
entregar *to deliver, hand over*
entremeses (m pl) *side-dishes; hors d'œuvres*

Alphabetical List of the Essential Vocabulary   117

ENTRETANTO (adv) *meanwhile*
ENTREVISTA (f) *interview*
entristecerse *to become sad*
entusiasmo (m) *enthusiasm*
entusiasta (inv noun) *enthusiast*
(adj) *enthusiastic*
ENVEJECER *to grow old*
envenenar *to poison*
ENVIAR *to send; to despatch*
envidia (f) *envy*
envidiable (adj) *enviable*
envidiar *to envy*
envidioso (adj) *envious*
ENVÍO (m) *shipment; despatch of parcel or remittance*
envolver *to wrap up, make into a parcel*
envolverse = *to become or be implicated*
equilibrio (m) *equilibrium; balance*
EQUIPAJE (*m*) *baggage; luggage*
equipar *to equip*
equipo (m) *equipment, fittings; team* [in sport]
EQUIVALENTE (adj) *equivalent*
EQUIVOCACIÓN (f) *mistake, error*
EQUIVOCARSE *to make a mistake*
errar *to wander, roam*
errante (adj) *wandering; roaming*
ERRÓNEO (adj) *wrong*
ERROR (m) *mistake, error*
escala (f) *ladder; scale (of an instrument, or in) music; stopping-place*
hacer escala (en) = *to stop (at a port)*
ESCALERA (f) *staircase; stairs*
escalfado (adj & pp) *poached*
huevos escalfados = *poached eggs*
escalón (m) *step of stairs; stepping stone*
ESCAPARSE *to escape; to run away from*

escape (m) *escape, flight, evasion*
a todo escape = *at full speed*
un escape de gas = *an escape of gas*
escasez (f) *scarcity; shortage*
escaso (adj) *scarce; lacking*
escoger *to choose, select*
escogido (adj) *chosen, selected*
esconder *to hide sth*
esconderse = *to hide oneself*
ESCRIBIR *to write*
papel de escribir = *writing paper*
escribir a máquina = *to type*
máquina de escribir = *typewriter*
escritor, -a (m & f) *writer; author*
escritorio (m) *writing-desk*
ESCUCHAR *to listen (to); to heed*
ESCUELA (f) *school*
— **primaria** = *primary school*
— **secundaria** = *secondary school*
— **superior** = *institute of higher education*
escultor, -a (m & f) *sculptor*
escultura (f) *sculpture*
ESE, ESA,   } *that;*
ESOS, ESAS (dem adj) } *those*
ÉSE, ÉSA, -S, ESO, -S (dem pron) *that one, those (ones)*
esencia (f) *essence; perfume*
ESENCIAL (adj) *essential*
ESFORZARSE *to try hard; to exert oneself* (**EN** *in*; **POR** *in order to*)
ESFUERZO (m) *effort; strong endeavour*
esmero (m) *diligence*
ESO (neut pron) *it*
eso es = *that's it*
eso mismo = *that very thing*
no es eso = *it's not that*
ESPACIO (m) *space*
ESPALDA (f) *shoulder; back (of body)*
a espaldas vueltas = *behind one's back; treacherously*

dar de espaldas = *to fall on one's back*
ESPAÑOL, -A (adj) *Spanish*
— (noun m & f) *Spaniard*
EL ESPAÑOL = *the Spanish language*
ESPANTADO (adj) *frightened*
ESPANTAR *to frighten*
ESPANTARSE = *to be astonished, to marvel*
ESPANTO (m) *fright; terror*
ESPANTOSO (adj) *frightful, terrible; wonderful*
ESPECIAL (adj) *special*
especialidad (f) *speciality*
especializarse en *to specialise in*
ESPECIE (f) *species, sort, kind*
en especie = *in kind*
espectáculo (m) *spectacle, sight; show* [theatre, bullfight, etc.]
espectador, -a *spectator* (m & f)
ESPEJO (m) *looking-glass; mirror*
espera (f) *wait, waiting; pause*
en espera (de) = *waiting (for)*
ESPERAR *to hope; to expect*
— **A UNA PERSONA** = *to wait for sb*
— + inf = *to expect to*
espero ir a Inglaterra = *I expect to go to England*
ESPESO (adj) *thick; dense*
espinaca (f) *spinach*
ESPÍRITU (m) *spirit; soul*
(pl) (*evil*) *spirits, demons*
espléndido (adj) *splendid*
esponja (f) *sponge*
espontáneo (adj) *spontaneous*
ESPOSO, -A (m & f) *married partner; husband, wife*
espuma (f) *foam, froth; lather*
esquí (m) *ski*
esquiador, -a (m & f) *skier*
esquiar *to ski*
estable (adj) *stable*

ESTABLECER *to found, establish*
establecerse = *to settle oneself*
establecimiento (m) *establishment; institution*
ESTACIÓN (f) *railway station; season*
estadística (f) *statistics*
ESTADO (m) *state; condition*
estado de guerra = *martial law*
los Estados Unidos = *the United States*
en mal estado = *in bad condition*
estampilla (f) *rubber stamp with facsimile signature* [Sp]; *postage stamp* [SpA]
ESTANCIA (f) *stay; sojourn; living-room.* SpA = *farm*
estaño (m) *tin*
ESTAR *to be.* See p. 39
estar en casa = *to be at home*
ESTAR PARA + inf = *to be about to*
estar a punto de = *to be on the point of*
¿A cuántos estamos? = *What's the date?*
estatua (f) *statue*
ESTE (m) *east; orient*
ESTE, ESTA, ⎱ (dem adj) *this;*
ESTOS, ESTAS ⎰ *these*
See p. 26
ÉSTE, ÉSTA; ESTO ⎫ (dem prons)
ÉSTOS, ÉSTAS ⎭ *this (one); these (ones)*
See p. 26, and **ESTO**
estilo (m) *style*
estimación (f) *esteem*
estimar *to esteem*; also *to estimate*
estimular *to stimulate*
estímulo (m) *stimulation; encouragement*
estirar *to stretch*
— **las piernas** = *to stretch one's legs (go for a walk)*
ESTO (pron neut) *this; this one*

estómago (m) *stomach*
  tener mucho estómago = *to be thick skinned*
ESTORBAR *to hinder*
ESTORBO (m) *hindrance*
estornudar *to sneeze*
estrechar *to tighten; to contract; to press*
— la mano = *to shake hands*
estrecho (M noun & adj) *narrow; tight*
  un zapato estrecho = *a tight shoe*
  (El) Estrecho de Magallanes = *Magellan Straits*
ESTRELLA (f) *star*
ESTRICTO (adj) *strict*
estropeado (pp & adj) *lame, crippled; damaged*
estropear *to spoil*
ESTUDIANTE (m & f) *student*
ESTUDIAR *to study*
estudioso *(adj) studious*
estufa (f) *stove*
ESTÚPIDO (adj) *stupid*
etcétera (f) *et cetera*
eterno (adj) *eternal; everlasting*
etiqueta (f) *label; etiquette*
  estar de etiqueta = *to be distant, cool*
  de etiqueta = *formal; ceremonious*
evidencia (f) *evidence; obviousness*
EVIDENTE (adj) *evident*
evitable (adj) *avoidable*
EVITAR *to avoid; to shun*
EXACTO (adj) *exact, accurate, precise; punctual*
exagerar *to exaggerate*
examen (m) *examination; inquiry; investigation*
EXAMINAR *to examine; to question; to inspect; to search*
exceder *to exceed*
excelencia (f) *excellence*
  Su Excelencia = *His (or Your) Excellency*
9—B.E.S.

EXCELENTE (adj) *excellent*
excepción (f) *exception*
excepcional (adj) *exceptional*
EXCEPTO (adv) *except*
exceptuar *to except*
EXCESIVO (adj) *excessive*
exceso (m) *excess*
excitación (f) *excitement*
excitante (adj) *exciting; stimulating*
EXCITAR *to excite; to stimulate*
exclamación (f) *exclamation*
EXCLAMAR *to exclaim*
excursión (f) *excursion; trip*
excursionista (inv n) *excursionist; tripper*
excusado (adj & m noun) *excused, exempted*
  el excusado = *W.C.; toilet*
excusar *to excuse sb*
  EXCUSARSE = *to apologise*
exhibición (f) *exhibition; exposition*
exhibir *to exhibit*
existencia (f) *existence*
existente (adj) *extant; existent*
EXISTIR *to exist*
ÉXITO (m) *success*
  tener éxito = *to be successful*
expansión (f) *expansion*
expansivo (adj) *expansive; sociable; communicative*
experiencia (f) *experience*
experimentado (adj) *experienced*
experimental (adj) *experimental*
experimentar *to experiment*
experimento (m) *experiment*
experto (m noun & adj) *expert*
EXPLICACIÓN (f) *explanation*
  dar una E. = *to explain (one's conduct)*
EXPLICAR *to explain; to expound*
  EXPLICARSE = *to explain oneself*
exploración (f) *exploration*
explorador (m) *explorer; (boy) scout*

explorar *to explore; to scout, reconnoitre*

explosión (f) *explosion*

explosivo (m noun & adj) *explosive*

EXPORTACIÓN (f) *export (trade); exporting, exportation*

exportador (m) *exporter*

EXPORTAR *to export*

EXPRESAR(SE) *to express (oneself)*

expresión (f) *expression*

expresivo (adj) *expressive*

EXPRESO (m noun & adj) *express, clear*
  un tren expreso = *express train*
  un expreso = *express train*

extender *to extend; to draw up a document*
  extender un cheque = *to draw a cheque*

extensión (f) *extension; extent*

extenso (adj) *extensive*

EXTERIOR (adj) *exterior; external; foreign*
  comercio exterior = *foreign trade*

EXTRANJERO (adj) *foreign*

EXTRANJERO, -A (noun m & f) *foreigner; abroad*
  ir(se) al extranjero = *to go abroad*
  estar en el extranjero = *to be abroad*

EXTRAÑO (adj) *odd, strange; extraneous*

EXTRAORDINARIO (adj) *extraordinary*

extravagante (adj) *eccentric, odd; freakish*

extremidad (f) *extremity*

EXTREMO (m) *extreme; utmost point; highest degree*
  con (por) extremo = *extremely; in the highest degree*
  (adj) *extreme; final; furthest; utmost*

F

FÁBRICA (f) *factory*

fabricación (f) *manufacture; make*

FABRICANTE (inv n & adj) *manufacturer; maker*

FABRICAR *to manufacture; to make*

FÁCIL (adj) *easy*
  fácil + inf = *easy (to) + inf*: **Es fácil hacer eso** = *It's easy to do that*

FACILIDAD (f) *facility; easiness*

FACILITAR *to make easy; to expedite*

FACTURA (f) *bill; invoice*

falda (f) *skirt; lap*

FALSO (adj) *false; untrue; sham*

FALTA (f) *mistake; error; lack of*
  sin falta = *without fail*
  falta de medios = *lack of means*
  falta de dinero = *shortage of money*
  hacer falta = *to be necessary; to be missing*
  Vd. me hace mucha falta = *I need you very much*

FALTAR *to be wanting; to fall short; to fail*
  Me faltan diez pesetas (pesos) = *I'm short of 10 pesetas (pesos)*
  faltar para = *to lack (in time)*
  Faltan diez minutos para los dos = *It's 10 minutes to two o'clock*
  ¡No faltaba más! *That's out of the question!*

FAMILIA (f) *family; household*

familiar (adj) *familiar; domestic* (noun) **un familiar** = *bosom friend; household figure; member of one's family; servant*
  un estilo familiar = *a colloquial style*

FAMOSO (adj) *famous; great*

fantasía (f) *imagination*; *whim*; *conceit*

fantástico (adj) *fantastic*; *fanciful*

farmacéutico (m) *chemist, pharmacist*

FARMACIA (f) *chemist's shop*; *drug-store*

faro (m) *lighthouse*; *headlight*

FAVOR (m) *favour*
  hacer el favor de = *to do the favour of* (= *to oblige*)
  a favor de = *on behalf of*
  ¿Quiere Vd. hacerme el favor de ... ? = *Would you please ... ?*
  por favor = *please*

favorable (adj) *favourable*

FECHA (f) *date*

fechar *to date* (*put the date on*)

felicitación (f) *congratulation*

felicitar *to congratulate*; *to compliment*

FELIZ (adj) *happy*; *fortunate*

felizmente (adv) *fortunately, happily*

fe (f) *faith*
  tener fe a = *to have faith in*

FEO (adj) *ugly, plain*

FERIA (f) *fair*; *market*; *holiday*

FERROCARRIL (m) *railway*

festejos (m pl) *festivities*

fiado (adj) *on trust*; *on credit*
  comprar (vender) al fiado = *to buy (sell) on credit*

FIAR *to trust*; *to guarantee*; *to bail*
  fiarse de = *to rely upon*; *to give credit to*

fidedigno (adj) *trustworthy*

FIEBRE (f) *fever*; *temperature*

FIEL (adj) *faithful*; *loyal*; *exact, accurate* (*copy*)

fiero (adj) *fierce*; *proud*; *haughty*

FIESTA (f) *feast day, festival*; *feast*; *entertainment*; *party*
  día de fiesta = *holiday*; *rest day*

tener una fiesta (en casa) = *to have a party (at home)*

figura (f) *figure*; *bodily form*; *shape*

FIJAR *to fix, fasten*; *to make fast*

FIJO (adj) *fixed*; *firm*
  precio fijo = *fixed price*

fila (f) *row, line*
  en fila = *in a line*

filete (m) *fillet of steak*

FIN (m) *end, ending*; *conclusion*
  a fin de = *in order to*
  EN FIN = *finally*
  por fin = *at last*
  sin fin = *endless*
  al fin = *in the end*; *at last*

FINAL (adj) *final*
  finalmente = *finally*

finalizar *to end*

fingir *to pretend*

FIRMA (f) *signature*; *firm's name*; *firm*

FIRMAR *to sign*

firme (adj) *firm, stable*
  estar en lo firme = *to be positive*

firmeza (f) *firmness*

fisión (f) *fission* [in physics]

FLACO (adj) *thin, lean*; *feeble, frail*
  flaco de memoria = *bad memory*

FLAMENCO (adj) *Flemish*; = *of Andalusia*; *gypsy-like*; (noun) *Andalusian gypsy*; also *gypsy music and dancing*

FLOJO (adj) *slack, loose*; *lax, lazy*. SpA parts of = *timid*; *cowardly*
  vino flojo = *weak wine*

FLOR (f) *flower*

flota (f) *fleet*

flotante (adj) *floating*

FLÚIDO (m) *fluid*

fluir *to flow*

fonda (f) *inn*; *eating house*

FONDO (m) *bottom*; *background, rear part*
  (pl) **fondos** = *funds*

FORASTERO (adj) *exotic*
(noun m & f) = *stranger* [from inside the country]

FORMA (f) *form, shape*
de ninguna forma = *in no sense*
de forma que = *so that*

formal (*adj*) *formal; sedate; respectable*

formalidad (f) *formality; exactness*

FORMAR *to form; to fashion*
formarse = *to take form; to develop*

fortaleza (f) *fortress; fortitude*

fortificar *to fortify*

FORTUNA (f) *fortune*
por fortuna = *fortunately*

fósforo (m) *phosphorous; match* [for lighting]

FOTOGRAFÍA (f) *photograph; photography; photographer's*

fotografiar *to photograph*

fotógrafo (m) *photographer*

FRACASAR *to come to naught; to fail*

FRACASO (m) *failure; downfall; calamity*

fraile (m) *friar; monk; priest*

FRASE (m) *sentence; phrase; idiom*

frecuentar *to frequent; to haunt*

FRECUENTE (adj) *frequently*

frecuentemente (adv) *often*

fregar *to rub; to wash up; to scour*

freir *to fry*

FRENO (m) *brake*

FRENTE (f) *forehead; countenance*
(adv) = *opposite; across the way*

frente (m) *military front*

fresa (f) *strawberry*

FRESCO (adj) *fresh; cool; recent; new-laid* [of eggs]

fresco (m) *coolness; cool air*

FRÍO (adj) *cold*
hacer frío = *to be cold* [of weather]

tener frío = *to be cold* (of person]
(m noun) **el FRÍO**
(pl) **los fríos** SpA = *malaria*

FRITO (pp & adj) *fried*
pescado frito = *fried fish*

FRONTERA (f) *frontier; boundary*

FRUTA (f) *fruit*

frutería (f) *fruit shop*

FUEGO (m) *fire*
encender el fuego = *to light the fire*
apagar el fuego = *to put out the fire*

FUENTE (f) *spring, well; fountain; source* [of river]

FUERA (DE) (adv) *out, outside (of); away*
estar fuera de casa = *to be out* (= *not at home*)

¡FUERA! ¡AFUERA! *Out! Get out! Out of it!*

FUERTE (adj) *strong*

FUERZA (f) *strength*
por fuerza = *forcibly*

fulano, -a (m & f) *So-and-so*

fumador, -a (m & f) *smoker; smoking carriage*

fumante (adj) *smoking; fuming*

FUMAR *to smoke* [cigarette etc.]

FUNCIÓN (f) *function; entertainment; social party*

FUNCIONAR *to function; to work* [of a machine]
Esta máquina no funciona = *this machine (engine) doesn't work*

funcionamiento (m) *working* [of a machine]

FUNCIONARIO (m) *public official; civil servant*

fundación (f) *founding, foundation; establishment* [of an institution]

FUNDAMENTAL (adj) *fundamental*

fundamento (m) *groundwork, basis*

FUNDAR *to found; to establish*

FURIOSO (adj) *furious*; *very angry*
fusil (m) *rifle*; (*shot*) *gun*
FUTBOL (m) *football* (*soccer*)
FUTURO (EL or LO) *future*
  en LO futuro = *in future*

G

GABINETE (m) *cabinet* [of government]; *private* (*sitting*) *room*; *consulting room* [of a doctor]
GACETA (f) *gazette*; *newspaper*
gala (f) *gala*; *full dress*
  galas de novia = *bridal trousseau*
galante (adj) *courteous*; *attentive to ladies*
GALLETA (f) *biscuit*
gallina (f) *hen*
gallo (m) *cock*
  Misa del gallo = *midnight mass*
GANA (f) *desire*; *appetite*
  de buena gana = *willingly*
  de mala gana = *reluctantly*
  TENER GANA(S) DE = *to wish to, have a mind to*
  No tengo gana de comer = *I don't want to eat* (*dine*)
ganado (m) *cattle*
GANANCIA (f) *gain, profit*
GANAR *to gain, win, earn*
  ganarse la vida = *to earn one's living*
GANCHO (m) *hook*; *peg*
GANSO, -A *gander*; *goose*
GARAJE(= GARAGE) (m) *garage*
garantía (f) *guarantee*
garantizar *to guarantee*
garbanzo (m) *chickpea*
GAS (m) *gas*
GASOLINA (f) *gasolene*; *petrol* [for car, etc.]
GASTADO (adj) *worn out*; *useless*

GASTAR *to spend, expend*; *to waste, wear out*
  gastar palabras = *to waste one's breath*
GASTO (m) *expenditure*; *expense*
  (pl) los gastos = *expenses*
GATO, -A *cat* (m & f)
gaucho, -a *Argentine cowboy*; *Gaucho woman* (m & f)
GENERAL (adj) *general, common, usual*
  en (or por lo) general = *as a rule*; *generally*
general (m) (*army*) *general*
GÉNERO (m) *kind, sort*
  (pl) = *goods*
generoso (adj) *generous*; *excellent* [of wine]
GENIO (m) *genius*; *temperament, character*; *temper*
  tener mal genio = *to be bad-tempered*
GENTE (f) *people*; *folk*; *crowd*
  gente de bien = *honest people*
  gente de color = *coloured people*
  gente de traza = *well behaved people*
  mucha gente = *many people*
  poca gente = *few people*
GESTO (m) *look*; *gesture*; *face*
  estar de buen gesto = *to be in good humour*
GIRAR *to revolve*; *to turn round*
GIRO (m) *turn, trend*
  — postal = *money order*
gitano, -a (noun m & f & adj) *gypsy*
globo (m) *globe*; *sphere*
gloria (f) *glory*; *bliss*
gobernador (m) *governor*
gobernante (adj) *governing*
gobernar *to govern, rule*
GOBIERNO (m) *government*
goce (m) *enjoyment*
golf (m) *golf*

golfo (m) *gulf* [sea]; *abyss*
  el Golfo de Vizcaya = *Bay of Biscay*
GOLPE (m) *blow*; *stroke*; *knock*
  un buen golpe de fortuna = *a good stroke of luck*
golpear *to beat, strike, hit*
  (past def) = **golpeé**, etc.
goma (f) *gum* [for sticking]; *rubber*
— **de borrar** = [rubber] *eraser*
GORDO (adj) *fat*; *stout*
gordura (f) *fatness*
gorra (f) *man's cap*; *woman's bonnet*
gota (f) *drop*
  gota de agua = *drop of water*
GOZAR (DE) *to enjoy* (*sth*)
GOZO (m) *enjoyment*; *joy*; *mirth*
GRACIA (f) *grace*; *witty saying*
  (pl) **GRACIAS** = *thanks*
  dar gracias a = *to give thanks to*
gracioso (adj) *graceful*; *witty*; *funny*
GRADO (m) *step* [of staircase]; *grade, rank, degree*
  de grado = *willingly*
  de mal grado = *unwillingly*
gradual (adj) *gradual*
gradualmente (adv) *gradually*
gramática (f) *grammar*
gramófono (m) *gramophone*
GRAN short form of **GRANDE**, used only in the singular: *large, big, great*
GRANDE (adj) *big*; *large*; *great*; *grand*
  (m noun) = **grandee** [Sp] *great man*
grandeza (f) *greatness*
granizar *to hail, to be hailing*
granizo (m) *hail*; *hailstorm*
GRANO (m) *grain*; *cereal*; *single seed*
  ir al grano = *to come to the point*

grasa (f) *grease*
gratis (adv) *gratis*; *free of charge, cost*
gratitud (f) *gratitude*
grato (adj) *pleasing*; *pleasant*
  su grata carta = *your* (*kind*) *letter*
grave (adj) *grave, serious*; *critical*
grifo (m) *water tap*
GRINGO (adj & noun) A familiar and disrespectful term applied to foreigners, especially English and Americans. **hablar en gringo** = *to talk gibberish*. [The word is more common in SpA than in Sp]
gris (adj) *grey*
GRITAR *to cry out*; *to shout*
GRITO (m) *shout*; *scream*
grosería (f) *rudeness*
grosero (adj) *rude, discourteous*
GRUESO (adj) *thick*; *bulky*; *stout*; (coll) *pregnant*
grupo (m) *group*; *set*
GUANTE (m) *glove*
GUARDAR *to guard, keep*; *protect*
guardarropa (m) *cloakroom*
GUARDIA (m) *policeman*
— **civil** = *Civil Guard* (Sp *gendarme*)
  (f) *guard* [body of armed men]
  estar de guardia = *to be on guard duty*
GUERRA (f) *war*; *warfare*
  buque de guerra = *warship*
GUÍA (inv n) *guide*; *leader*
  (f) *guide book*; *guide sign*
  la Guía de Ferrocarriles = *Railway Guide*
  la Guía de Teléfonos = *Telephone Directory*
GUIAR *to guide, direct*; *to lead*; *to drive*
guisado (m) *stew*
guitarra (f) *guitar*

GUSTAR (1) *to taste, to try* (2) *to be pleasing to*: **Esto me gusta** = *that pleases me* (render *I like that*)
  Como Vd. guste = *as you like*
  gustar de = *to have a taste for, to like* [wine, etc.]
GUSTO (m) *taste; pleasure; liking*
  dar gusto = *to please*
  darse gusto = *to have a nice time*
  de mi gusto = *to my taste*
  tener gusto en = *to take pleasure in*

H

HABER (aux) *to have* (vtr) *to have*. See p. 33
  haber de = *to have to; must*
    Hemos de salir = *We must go out*
  HA = *ago*: **cinco años ha** = *5 years ago*
  Impersonal use:
  HAY = *there is; there are*
  HABÍA⎫
  HUBO⎬ *there was; there were*
  HABRÁ = *there will be*
  HABRÍA = *there would be*
  No hay de qué = *Don't mention it; you're welcome*
  no hay más que = *it is enough that . . . ; there's only . . .*
  hay que comer algo = *one must eat something*
HABITACIÓN (f) *lodging, abode; room; suite of rooms*
habitante (m) *inhabitant*
habitar *to inhabit*
HABITUAL (adj) *usual; customary*
habituar *to accustom; to habituate*
HABITUARSE *to become accustomed; to get used (to)*
habla (f) *speech*

estar sin habla = *to be speechless*
hablador, -a (adj) *talkative* (noun m & f) (-A) = *gossip, chatterbox*
HABLAR *to speak, talk*
  hablar claro = *to speak clearly*
  hablar de memoria = *to talk at random; to speak from memory*
  hablar alto = *to speak up, talk loudly*
  hablar mal de = *to speak ill of* [a person]
HACER *to do; to make*. See p. 45

Of the weather:
  hacer frío, calor = *to be cold, hot*
  hace buen, mal tiempo = *the weather's good, bad*
  hace viento = *it's windy*

Of time ago:
  hace un mes, un año = *a month, a year ago*
  hace mucho tiempo = *a long time ago*
  hace poco = *a short time ago*
  hacerse tarde = *to grow late*

  hacer la maleta = *to pack one's suitcase*
  hacer saber = *to let know*
  hacer noche en = *to spend the night in, at . . .*
  hacer lo posible = *to do one's best*
  hacer(se) la barba = *to shave*
  hacer daño = *to hurt; to harm*
HACIA (prp) *towards*
— **arriba** = *upwards*
— **abajo** = *downwards*
— **atrás** = *backwards*
— **las seis de la tarde** = *about 6 o'clock p.m.*
HACIENDA (f) *estate; property; farm; ranch* [Sp America]
  hacienda pública = *public finances*
  Ministro de Hacienda = *Minister of Finance; Chancellor of the Exchequer*

hacha (f) *hatchet; axe*
halagar *to flatter*
HALLAR *to find; to come across; to find out*
  hallar el camino = *to find one's way*
  hallarse = *to be in a place, to fare, feel* [of health]
HAMBRE (f) *hunger*
  tener hambre = *to be hungry*
harina (f) *flour; meal*
HASTA (prp) *up to; till, until*
  hasta ahora = *until now*
  hasta la estación = *as far as the station*
  Hasta luego = *good-bye* [for a while]; *so long*
  Hasta la vista = *au revoir; until we meet again*
hazaña (f) *exploit; feat; act*
HECHO (m) *fact; deed; event*
  de hecho = *in fact, actually*
  (adj) *made; done; ready made;*
  bien h. = *well made; well done*
  mal hecho = *badly made; badly done*
helada (f) *frost*
HELADO (adj) *frigid, frozen; cold, indifferent*
  (noun) **helado** = *ice-cream*
HELAR *to freeze*
hiela *it's freezing*
hembra (f) *female*
heredar *to inherit*
heredero, -a (m & f) *heir, -ess*
HERIDO (adj & noun m & f) *wounded*
  mal h. = *dangerously wounded*
  una herida = *a wound*
HERIR *to wound; to hurt, harm; to offend*
HERMANO, -A (m & f) *brother; sister*
HERMOSO (adj) *beautiful*
  ¡Qué día tan hermoso! = *What a fine day!*

heroico (adj) *heroic*
herramienta (f) *tool; implement*
hidalgo, -a (m & f) *nobleman (-woman)*
  (pl m) = **hijosdalgo**
HIELO (m) *ice*
HIERBA (f) *grass*
HIERRO (m) *iron*
higo (m) *fig*
HIJO, -A (m & f) *son; daughter*
HILO (m) *thread*
  ropa de hilo = *linen* (*cloth*)
hinchar *to swell*
hinchazón (m) *swelling*
hispánico (adj) *Hispanic*
hispanista (m) *Spanish scholar*
hispano (adj) *Spanish*
hispanoamericano (adj & noun m & f) *Spanish-American*
HISTORIA (f) *history; story*
histórico (adj) *historic(al)*
HOGAR (m) *home; hearth*
HOJA (f) *leaf* [of tree *or* book]
¡HOLA! [friendly] *greeting* = *Hello! Cheerio! Ahoy!* [at sea]
holgazán, -a (adj) *lazy*
HOMBRE (m) *man*
  — **de negocios** = *businessman*
  — **de Estado** = *statesman*
  — **de letras** = *scholar*
  — **de ciencia** = *scientist*
  — **de dinero** = *moneyed man*
  ser muy hombre = *to be very much a man*
  ¡Hombre! [Exclamation of surprise] = *Well I never!*
hombro (m) *shoulder*
  a hombros = *on the shoulders*
HONDO (adj) *deep*
hondura (f) *depth*
HONOR (m) *honour, fame, celebrity*
  (pl) = *honours; privileges; title*
honorable (adj) *honourable*

HONRA (f) *respect*; *reputation*; *chastity* [in women]
HONRADO (adj) *upright, honest*
HORA (f) *hour*; *time* [of day]
 ¿Qué hora es? = *What's the time?*
 Es la una = *It's one o'clock*
 Son las dos = *It's two o'clock*
 dar la hora = *to strike the hour*
 Es hora de + inf = *it's time to ...*
 media hora = *half an hour*
 a última hora = *at the last moment*
HORARIO (m) *time table*
horizontal (adj) *horizontal*
horizonte (m) *horizon*
horno (m) *oven*; *furnace*
 alto horno = *blast furnace*
horrible (adj) *horrible*
hortaliza(s) (f) *vegetable(s)*
hospedarse *to stay, put up* [at a hotel or boarding house]
HOSPITAL (m) *hospital*
HOTEL (m) *hotel*; *house, villa*
 tener un hotel en el campo = *to have a country house*
HOY (adv) *today*; *nowadays*
 hoy día = *at the present time*; *nowadays*
 por hoy = *for the present*
 de hoy en adelante = *from now onwards*
hoyo (m) *hole*; *dimple*
hueco (adj & noun m) *hollow*
HUELGA (f) *strike* [of workers]
HUERTA (f) *kitchen garden*; *orchard*; *irrigated land*
HUESO (m) *bone*; *stone* [of fruit]
HUÉSPED, -A (m & f) *guest*
 casa de huéspedes = *guest-house*; *boarding house*
HUEVO (m) *egg*
— **fresco** = *new laid egg*
— **duro** = *hard boiled egg*
 huevos escalfados = *poached eggs*
— **estrellados** = *fried eggs*

— **pasados por agua** = *soft boiled eggs*
huir *to run away*; *to flee*
humanidad (f) *humanity*; *mankind*
humano (adj) *human*
 un ser humano = *human being*
humedad (f) *humidity*; *dampness*
húmedo (adj) *damp*; *humid*
humilde (adj) *humble*
humillación (f) *humiliation*
humillar *to humiliate*
HUMO (m) *smoke*; *fumes*
humor (m) *humour*; *disposition*; *temper*
 estar de buen (mal) humor = *to be in a good (bad) temper*
humorista (adj & inv noun) *humorist*; *humorous*
hundirse *to sink* [of ship]; *to crumble, collapse*
¡HURRA! *Hurrah!*
hurtar *to steal*
hurto (m) *theft*

I

ibérico (adj) *Iberian* [pertaining to ancient Sp & Portugal] (*Iberia*)
íbero (adj) *Iberian*
íberoamericano (adj) *Ibero-American*
IDA (f) *going away*; *departure*
 ida y vuelta = *out and back, round trip*
 billete de ida y vuelta = *return ticket*
 idas y vueltas = *comings and goings*
IDEA (f) *idea*
ideal (adj) *ideal*
idear *to conceive the idea of*; *to devise, contrive, plan, design*
idem (pron) *the same*; *ditto*
idéntico (adj) *identical*

identidad (f) *identity*
  carta de identidad = *identity card*
identificar *to identify*
  identificarse (con) *to identify oneself (with)*
IDIOMA (m) *language*
idiomático (adj) *idiomatic*
IGLESIA (f) *church; clergy*
IGUAL (adj) *equal; level, even; uniform*
  (noun m) *equal*
  Me es igual = *It's all the same to me*
  no tener igual = *to have no equal; to be unique*
  por igual = *equally*
  sin igual = *unequalled*
igualar *to equal*
igualdad (f) *equality*
ilegal (adj) *illegal, unlawful*
ilegalidad (f) *illegality; unlawfulness*
ileso (adj) *unhurt; unscathed; safe*
ilimitado (adj) *unlimited; unbounded*
ILUMINAR *to light up; to illuminate*
ilustración (f) *illustration; picture* [in book]
ilustrar *to illustrate*
imaginación (f) *imagination*
imaginar *to imagine*
  imaginarse = *to think to oneself; to suspect*
  Imagínese Vd. (que) = *Just think (that)*
imitación (f) *imitation*
imitador, -a (adj) *imitative*
imitar *to imitate*
impacientarse *to grow impatient; to lose patience*
impaciente (adj) *impatient*
imparcial (adj) *impartial*
IMPEDIR *to prevent; to hinder*
imperdible (m) *safety-pin*

imperfección (f) *imperfection*
IMPERFECTO (adj) *imperfect; defective; incomplete*
IMPERIO (m) *empire*
impermeable (adj) *waterproof*
  (noun m) *raincoat*
impersonal (adj) *impersonal*
importación (f) *import trade; imports*
importador, -a (m & f) *importer*
IMPORTANCIA (f) *importance*
IMPORTANTE (adj) *important*
IMPORTAR (1) *to be of importance; to matter* (2) *to import* (*goods*) (3) *to amount* [of a sum, account]
  No importa = *It doesn't matter* (= *Never mind*)
  No me importa = *I don't care* (= *it doesn't matter to me*)
  la cuenta importa 1,000 pesetas (pesos) = *the bill comes to 1,000 pesetas (pesos)*
  Ellos importan mercancías = *They import goods*
IMPORTE (m) *amount* [of bill, account]; (*total*) *cost*
imposibilidad (f) *impossibility*
IMPOSIBLE (adj) *impossible*
IMPRENTA (f) *printing; printing office, firm*
impresión (f) *impression; printing*
impresionar *to cause an impression; to impress*
imprevisto (adj) *unforeseen*
  de imprevisto = *unaware*
  (noun pl) **los imprevistos** = *incidental* or *unforeseen expenses*
improbable (adj) *improbable*
improductivo (adj) *unproductive; unfruitful; unprofitable*
impropio (adj) *inappropriate; unfit; unsuitable*
IMPRUDENTE (adj) *unwise; imprudent*

IMPUESTO (m) *tax; duty*
(*Customs*)
impulso (m) *impulse*
impuro (adj) *impure; adulterated*
inactividad (f) *inactivity*
inactivo (adj) *inactive*
inagotable (adj) *inexhaustible*
inalterable (adj) *unchangeable*
inapreciable (adj) *invaluable*
inauguración (f) *inauguration;
opening (ceremony)*
inaugurar *to inaugurate; to open
to the public*
incapaz (adj) *incapable; unable*
incendiar *to set fire to*
incendiarse = *to catch fire*
incendio (m) *fire; conflagration*
incertidumbre (f) *uncertainty*
incidente (m) *incident; occurrence*
INCIERTO (adj) *uncertain; doubtful*
inclinación (f) *inclination; tendency;
bent*
inclinar *to tilt; to influence*
INCLINARSE = *to lean towards;
to stoop; to bend down*
INCLUIR *to include*
INCLUSO (adj) *included; en-
closed* [in a letter, etc.]
incomodidad (f) *inconvenience; discomfort*
INCÓMODO (adj) *uncomfortable*
INCOMPLETO (adj) *incomplete;
unfinished*
incondicional (adj) *unconditional*
incorporar *to incorporate; to unite;
to join*
incorporarse = *to sit up in bed;
to stand on one's feet; to form
a company* [business]
increíble (adj) *incredible*
incurable (adj) *incurable*
indecisión (f) *indecision; hesitancy*
INDECISO (adj) *undecided; vague;
doubtful*

independencia (f) *independence*
independiente (adj) *independent*
INDICAR *to point out; to indicate;
to suggest*
indiferente (adj) *indifferent*
Me es i. = *It's all the same to
me*
indignación (f) *indignation; anger*
indigno (adj) *unworthy; ignoble*
INDIRECTO (adj) *indirect*
indispensable (adj) *indispensable;
very necessary*
indistinto (adj) *indistinct; vague*
individual (adj) *individual*
(adv) **-mente** = *singly; individually*
indudable (adj) *undoubted*
indulgente (adj) *tolerant; forbearing*
INDUSTRIA (f) (1) *diligence; un-
remitting application* (2) **de i.** =
*on purpose; manufacture; in-
dustry*
industrial (adj) *industrial*
(noun m) *industrialist*
inepto (adj) *inept; incompetent*
inesperado (adj) *unexpected*
inestimable (adj) *invaluable; price-
less*
inexacto (adj) *inaccurate; wrong*
inexperto (adj & noun) *inexperienced*
(noun) *inexperienced person*
infancia (f) *childhood*
infección (f) *infection*
infeccioso (adj) *infectious*
infectar *to infect*
infectarse = *to become infected*
INFERIOR (adj) *lower; inferior*
inferioridad (f) *inferiority*
infiel (adj) *unfaithful; false*
infierno (m) *hell*
infinito (adj) *endless; infinite*
inflamar *to inflame, stir*
inflar *to inflate* [tyre]
influir *to influence*
información (f) *information; report*

INFORMAR *to inform; to let know*

INFORME (m) *report; written report*

INGENIERO (m) *engineer*

— **civil** = *civil engineer*

— **agrónomo** = *agricultural engineer*

— **electricista** = *electrical engineer*

— **industrial** = *industrial engineer*

— **químico** = *chemical engineer*

— **de minas** = *mining engineer*

ingenio (m) *wit; skill; talent*

ingenioso (adj) *ingenious, talented*

ingratitud (f) *ingratitude*

ingrato (adj) *ungrateful; thankless*

ingresar (en) *to enter; to come in for money, profits, etc.*

ingreso (m) *entry, entrance; money received*

  los ingresos = *earnings, revenue, income*

inhumano (adj) *inhuman*

inicial (adj & f noun) *initial*

INICIAR *to initiate, start*

iniciativa (f) *initiative; enterprise*

injusticia (f) *injustice*

injusto (adj) *unfair, unjust*

INMEDIATAMENTE (adv) *immediately*

INMEDIATO (adj) *immediate*

INMENSO (adj) *immense, huge*

inmoral (adj) *immoral*

inmortal (adj) *immortal*

INMÓVIL (adj) *motionless; fixed*

innecesario (adj) *unnecessary*

innumerable (adj) *countless; innumerable*

inocencia (f) *innocence*

inocente (adj) *innocent*

inofensivo (adj) *inoffensive*

inoportuno (adj) *inconvenient; inopportune*

INQUIETO (adj) *uneasy; restless*

inscripción (f) *registration; record; entry* [in a record]

INSECTO (m) *insect*

inseguridad (f) *insecurity*

inseguro (adj) *insecure; unsteady; unsafe*

insensato (adj) *senseless; foolish*

inservible (adj) *unserviceable; useless*

insignificante (adj) *insignificant*

insípido (adj) *tasteless; insipid*

insistente (adj) *insistent; persistent*

INSISTIR *to insist*

insociable (adj) *unsociable*

insolente (adj & noun m & f) *insolent*

insoportable (adj) *unbearable*

inspección (f) *inspection; survey; inspector's office*

INSPECCIONAR *to inspect, survey, examine; to supervise*

inspector, -a (m & f) *inspector, examiner, supervisor*

inspiración (f) *inspiration*

inspirar *to inspire; to inhale*

INSTANTE (m) *instant, moment*

  al instante = *at once*

  (adj) = *pressing, urgent*

instinto (m) *instinct*

  por i. = *instinctively*

INSTRUCCIÓN (f) *instruction, teaching; education.* (pl) *instructions*

—**primaria** = *primary education*

— **secundaria** = *secondary education*

— **pública** = *public education*

— **superior** = *higher education*

instructor, -a (m & f) *teacher; teacher*

instruido (adj) *educated*

INSTRUIR *to teach; to educate*

instrumento (m) *instrument; implement; appliance*; in law = *indenture; deed*

insultar *to insult*

insulto (m) *insult*

íntegro (adj) *entire, whole; upright, honest*

intelectual (adj & inv noun) *intellectual*

inteligente (adj) *intelligent*

INTENCIÓN (f) *intention; purpose; aim*
  tener la intención de + inf = *to intend to* ...

INTENTAR *to try, attempt; to mean to; to start a lawsuit*

INTENTO (m) *intent, purpose, aim*
  de intento = *purposely, on purpose*

INTERÉS (m) *interest (%); concern*
  (often pl) **se pagarán los intereses** = *the interest will be paid*
  los intereses = *business interests*
  tipo de interés = *rate of interest*

interesado, -a *person interested* (m & f)

INTERESANTE (adj) *interesting*

interesarse *to be interested; to be concerned*

INTERIOR (m) *interior, inside*
  (adj) = *internal, inner; home (national) affairs*

interminable (adj) *endless; interminable*

INTERNACIONAL (adj) *international*

interno, -a (m & f) *boarding student*

interpretar *to interpret*

INTÉRPRETE (m) *interpreter*

interrogar *to question; to cross-examine*

interrumpir *to interrupt*
  — **un viaje** = *to break a journey*

interrupción (f) *interruption*

ÍNTIMO (adj) *intimate; close*
  un amigo íntimo = *an intimate friend*

intolerante (adj) *intolerant*

intranquilo (adj) *uneasy; restless*

intransigente (adj) *uncompromising*

introducción (f) *introduction*

introducir *to usher in; to put in; to insert*
  introducirse en = *to get in, gain access to; to interfere in*

INÚTIL (adj) *useless; needless; fruitless*
  -mente (adv) = *to no purpose*

invariable (adj) *invariable, unchanging; constant*

invención (f) *invention*

inventar *to invent; to make up* [a story]

inventario (m) *inventory; stock-taking*

investigación (f) *enquiry; research; investigation*

investigar *to enquire into*

INVIERNO (m) *winter; rainy season* [in some tropical countries]

invitación (f) *invitation*

invitar *to invite; to treat* [to a drink, meal]

inyección (f) *injection; liquid injected*

IR *to go.* See pages 48–49
  IRSE *to go away*
  ir + inf *to be going to do sth*:
    voy a comer = *I'm going to eat*
  Esta carretera va a Sevilla = *This road goes to Seville*
  ir en auto = *to go by car*
  ir de compras = *to go shopping*
  ir por agua = *to go to fetch water*
  ir a caballo = *to go (ride) on horseback*
  ir a medias = *to go halves*
  ir delante = *to go ahead*
  ¿Cómo le va? = *How are you?*
    [Much used in parts of SpA]
  Vamos claros = *Let's get this clear*

¡Vámonos! *Let's get out of here*
¡Vaya Vd. con Dios! = *farewell*
¡Vaya! = *Come, come! That's
enough!* or *Of course!* or *You
don't say so!*
See also **ANDAR** p. 44 in Part 1
and p. 91 of Vocabulary
irregular (adj) *irregular*
irregularidad (f) *irregularity*
irresponsable (adj) *irresponsible*
ISLA (f) *island; city block*
IZQUIERDO (adj) *left, left-
handed*
  A LA IZQUIERDA (= **a la
  mano izquierda**) *to the left-
  hand side; on the left*

J

JABÓN (m) *soap*
  pastilla de J. = *tablet of soap*
jactancioso (adj) *boastful*
JACTARSE (DE) *to boast (of)*
jalea (f) (*fruit) jelly*
JAMÁS (adv) *never; ever*
  nunca jamás⎫
  por jamás⎭*never more*
JAMÓN (m) *ham*
jarabe (m) *syrup*
JARDÍN (m) *garden*
jarro (m) *jug; pitcher*
JEFE (m)⎫ *chief; head; leader;*
jefa (f)⎭   *superior*
  jefe político = *governor* [of pro-
  vince]
jerez (m) *sherry.* [Made in Jerez
  de la Frontera]
jerga (f) *slang*
JORNADA (f) *one day's march,* or
  *one day's work; stage, stop-
  ping place*
  jornada de 8 horas = *8-hour day*
jornal (m) *day's work; day's pay*
jornalero (m) *person who works by
  the day; journeyman*

jota (f) *dance, and tune* [Aragón
  and Valencia]
jota = name of letter **J**
  no saber una jota = *to be a complete ignoramus*
  sin faltar una jota = *not a jot
  missing*
JOVEN (adj & inv. n) *young; a
  youth*
  un joven = *a youth*
  jovencillo, -a = *youngster* (m & f)
joya (f) *jewel*
joyería (f) *jeweller's shop*
jubilar *to pension off; to set aside
  as useless*
  jubilarse = *to be superannuated*
júbilo (m) *glee; joy; jubilation*
judía (f) *runner bean; Jewess*
judío, -a (adj) m & f *Jewish*
  (noun) = *Jew, Jewess*
JUEGO (m) *game; play; amusement*
  juego limpio = *fair play*
  juego de niños = *child's play*
JUEZ (m) *judge*
  — municipal = *local magistrate*
jugador, -a (m & f) *player; gambler*
JUGAR *to play a game; to gamble*
  jugar al futbol = *to play football*
  jugar a las cartas = *to play cards*
jugo (m) *juice, sap, marrow*
jugoso (adj) *juicy, succulent*
juguete (m) *toy; plaything*
juguetón (adj) *playful*
JUNTA (f) *board; council; union*
  celebrar una junta = *to hold a
  meeting*
  junta directiva = *executive board*
JUNTAR *to join, connect, unite*
  juntarse = *to be closely united; to
  draw near*
JUNTO (adj) *united; close at hand*
  (adv) = *close to, nearby*
juramento (m) *oath*
jurar *to swear*

JUSTICIA (f) *justice*; *court of justice*; *punishment*
  la justicia = *the police*; *officers of the law*
  de justicia = *justly*, *deservedly*
justificación (f) *justification*
justificar *to justify*
JUSTO (adj) *just*, *strict*; *exact*, *correct*
  al justo = *fitly*; *duly*
juvenil (adj) *juvenile*; *youthful*
juventud (f) *youth*
JUZGAR *to judge*; *to try* [in court of law]; *to pass judgment*

K

KILO (m) abbr. Kg⎱
KILOGRAMO (m) ⎰ *kilogramme*
kilométrico (adj) *kilometric*
  billete kilométrico = *kilometric ticket* [= one for so many kilometres on Sp railways]
KILÓMETRO abbr **Km.** (m) *kilometre*
kiosco (m) *small pavilion*; *kiosk*

L

LABIO (m) *lip*
LABOR (f) *work*; *task*; *labour*
LABORAR *to work*; *to till*
laborioso (adj) *laborious*; *industrious*
labrador (m) (*land*)*worker*
LADO (m) *side*
  lado a lado = *side by side*
  al lado (de) = *beside*
  a un lado = *to one side, aside*
  dejar a un lado = *to set aside*
  lado superior = *top side*
  al otro lado de = *on the other side of*
ladrón, -a (m & f) *thief, robber*
lago (m) *lake*

LÁGRIMA (f) *tear*
lamentar *to regret*; *to mourn*
  lamentarse por la desgracia = *to regret* (*deeply*) *a misfortune*
lámina (f) *plate, sheet* [of metal]; *print, picture*
lámpara (f) *lamp*
LANA (f) *wool*; *woollen fabric*
  calcetines de lana = *woollen socks*
lance (m) *incident, occurrence*
  de lance = *secondhand*; *at cut price*
langosta (f) *lobster*
LÁPIZ (m) *pencil*; crayon
LARGO (adj) *long*; *extended*
  largos años = *long life*; *many years*
  a lo largo = *at a distance*; *lengthwise*
  (noun m) = *length*
  de largo a largo = *from end to end*; *lengthwise*
  (adv) = *largely*; *profusely*
LÁSTIMA (f) *pity*
  es lástima = *it's a pity*
  ¡Qué lástima! = *What a pity!*
LATA (f) *tin plate*; *tin* (*can*)
  EN LATA = *tinned* (*canned*)
  una lata de sardinas = *a tin of sardines*
  sardinas en lata = *tinned sardines*
  es una lata = *it's a nuisance, an annoyance*
lateral (adj) *lateral*
  (adv) **-mente** = *sideways*
latir *to beat, throb*
latitud (f) *breadth, width*; *latitude*
latón (m) *brass*
laudable (adj) *praiseworthy*
lavado (adj) *washed*
lavamanos (m) *washstand*
lavandera (f) *laundress*; *washerwoman*
lavandería (f) *laundry*
LAVAR *to wash*; *to launder*
  lavarse = *to wash oneself*

lavarse las manos = *to wash one's hands*

lazo (m) *bow; tie; knot*

leal (adj) *loyal; faithful*

LECCIÓN (f) *lesson*

lectura (f) *reading; reading matter*

LECHE (f) *milk*

lechería (f) *dairy*

lechero, -a (m & f) *milkman, milk-maid*
  (adj) = *milky*

lechugo (f) *lettuce*

LEER *to read*

legal (adj) *legal*

legión (f) *legion*

legítimo (adj) *legitimate*

LEGUMBRE (f) *vegetable*

LEJANO (adj) *distant*

LEJOS (adv) *far away; remote*
  a lo lejos = *in the distance*

LENGUA (f) *tongue; language*
  lengua madre = *mother tongue*
  tener en la lengua = *to be about to say*

lenguaje (m) *vernacular*
  — **bajo** = *bad (loose) language*

lente (m) *lens.* (pl) = *glasses*

LENTO (adj) *slow; sluggish*

leña (f) *firewood; kindling wood*

león, -a (m & f) *lion; lioness*

letra (f) *letter* [of alphabet]; *hand-writing*
  letras = *learning*
  letra de cambio = *bill of exchange*

letrado (adj) *learned, erudite*

letrero (m) *sign; placard; poster*

LEVANTAR *to lift, raise; to pick up*
  — **la mesa** = *to clear the table*
  LEVANTARSE = *to get up; to get out of bed*

levante (m) *east coast; east wind*

LEY (f) *law; (set of) rules*
  las leyes del juego = *the rules of the game*

fuera de ley = *lawless*

liberación (f) *release; liberation*

LIBERAR *to set free, release* [from obligation, etc.]

LIBERTAD (f) *freedom; liberty*
  — **de comercio** = *free trade*
  — **de cultos** = *freedom of religion*
  — **de palabra** = *freedom of speech*

LIBRA (f) *pound (lb & £)*
  — **esterlina** = *pound sterling*

LIBRE (adj) *free*

LIBRERÍA (f) *bookseller's*

LIBRO (m) *book*
  — **de caja** = *cash book*
  — **de cuentas** = *account book*

LICENCIA (f) *leave; permission; licence*

licor (m) *any liquid; liquor; liqueur*

ligar *to tie*

ligereza (f) *lightness; swiftness*

LIGERO (adj) *light; slight; nimble*

limitación (f) *limitation*

limitado (adj) *limited*

limitar *to limit*

límite (m) *boundary; limit; border*

limón (m) *lemon*

limonada (f) *lemonade*

limosna (f) *alms*

limpiar *to clean*

LIMPIO (adj) *clean; cleanly; neat*

LINDO (adj) *pretty; attractive*

LÍNEA (f) *line; lineage; equator*
  en línea = *in line*

LÍQUIDO (noun m & adj) *liquid*

liso (adj) *smooth, even, flat*

LISTA (f) *list; catalogue*
  — **de platos** = *bill of fare, menu*
  — **de vinos** = *wine list*

LISTO (adj) *ready; quick; clever*
  estar listo para = *to be ready to . . .*
  ser listo = *to be clever*

literal (adj) *literal*

literatura (f) *literature*

LO (neuter article) *the* (& pers
pron) *it, him*
LOCAL (m) *place; site; premises*
(adj) = *local*
LOCALIDAD (f) *locality; loca-
tion*
LOCO (adj & noun m & f) *mad,
insane, crazy; crazy person*
volverse loco = *to go mad*
locomotora (f) *locomotive*
locura (f) *insanity; madness;
folly*
lógico (adj) *logical; reasonable*
es lógico = *it stands to reason*
LOGRAR *to obtain, gain, pro-
cure; to succeed in*
lograrse = *to be successful*
longaniza (f) *pork sausage* [for
slices]
LONGITUD (f) *length; longitude*
LOS (m pl def article). See EL
(pers pron) = *them*
LOS, LAS QUE = *those who,
which*
lote (m) *lot; share; part*
lotería (f) *lottery*
LUCHA (f) *struggle; fight;
wrestling; argument*
LUCHAR *to fight; struggle; to
wrestle*
lucir *to shine, glitter; to light*
LUEGO (adv) *soon after; then*
(= *immediately*)
hasta luego = *au revoir, so long*
desde luego = *naturally, of course*
(tan) luego que = *as soon as*
(conj) *therefore*
LUGAR (m) *place, spot; site*
en primer L. = *first, in the first
place*
en segundo L. = *secondly, in the
second place*
en lugar de = *instead of*
dar lugar a = *to give rise to*
hacer lugar = *to make room*
10—B.E.S.

lugar de nacimiento = *birthplace*
LUJO (m) *luxury*
de lujo = *luxurious; exquisite*
lujoso (adj) *luxurious; sumptuous;
lavish*
lumbre (f) *grate fire; light*
LUNA (f) *moon; glass plate (mirror)*
luna de miel = *honeymoon*
luto (m) *mourning*
de luto = *in mourning*
LUZ (f) *light; daylight*
a primera luz = *at daybreak*
salir a luz = *to come (leak) out;
to be divulged; to be published*

LL

llamada (f) *call, shout, summons*
LLAMADO (adj) *named, called*
llamador (m) *door knocker*
(m & f) *caller* [at the door]
LLAMAR *to call, summon; to
name*
LLAMARSE = *to be called,
named*
¿Cómo se llama Vd? = *What's
your name?*
Yo me llamo Juan = *My name is
John*
llamar a la puerta = *to knock* or
ring at the door
llamar la atención = *to call attention; to draw attention*
llano (m) *plain; flat country*
llano (adj) *plain, even, flat*
llanto (m) *flood of tears; fit of
weeping*
LLAVE (f) *key* [of door]; *switch*
ama de llaves = *housekeeper*
LLEGADA (f) *arriving* [act];
arrival
LLEGAR(A) *to arrive (at, in); to
reach; to attain*
llegar a casa = *to get home*

llegar a la frontera = *to reach the frontier*

llegar a tiempo = *to arrive in time*

llegar a ser médico = *to succeed in becoming a doctor*

llegar a las manos = *to come to blows*

LLENAR *to fill, pack, stuff*

llenarse (1) *to stuff oneself* [with food] (2) *to fill up* [of a place, compartment, train, ship, etc.]

LLENO (DE) (adj) *full (of); filled (with)*

— **alegría** = *filled with rejoicing*

— **polvo** = *covered with dust*

— **de bote en bote** = *full to the brim; packed* [house, cinema, etc.]

(noun m) = *abundance; glut*

LLEVAR *to carry; to wear; to bear (tolerate)*

llevar algo a un amigo = *to take sth to a friend*

la carretera lleva a Valencia = *the road leads to Valencia*

llevar un traje = *to wear a dress*

Aquí llevamos un mes = *We've been a month here* [in this place]

llevar una vida tranquila = *to lead a quiet life*

llevar a cabo = *to carry out, to finish sth*

llevarse bien = *to get along nicely* (**mal** = *badly*)

volver a llevar = *to carry (take) back*

llevar al crédito = *to place to the credit of*

LLORAR *to weep, cry; to lament; to drip* [of a tap, etc.]

estar llorando = *to be weeping, crying*

llorar con un ojo = *to weep crocodile tears*

LLOVER *to rain*

llueve = *it is raining*

estar lloviendo = *to be raining*

llueva o no = *rain or shine*

lluvia (f) *rain*

M

macho (m) *male*

MADERA (f) *wood, timber*

de madera = *made of wood; wooden*

MADRE (f) *mother; matron*

— **política** = *mother-in-law*

MADRUGADA (f) *dawn; small hours*

de madrugada = *at dawn*

MADRUGAR *to get up at dawn; to get up early*

MADURO (adj) *ripe*

maestro (adj) *masterly*

obra maestra = *masterpiece*

MAESTRO, -A (m & f) *teacher; expert*

— **de escuela** = *schoolmaster; schoolmistress*

maestro de obras = *builder*

mágico (adj) *magical; wonderful; marvellous*

MAGNÍFICO (adj) *magnificent; splendid*

MAL (adj) [contraction of **MALO**, used only before *m* nouns] *bad*

MAL (m) *evil, misfortune, harm; illness, pain*

el bien y el mal = *the good and the evil*

MAL (adv) *badly*

Hemos comido mal = *We ate badly* [had a bad meal]

maleta (f) *suitcase*

malgastar *to waste*

— **el dinero** = *to throw money away*

MALO (see **MAL**) (adj) *bad; evil*

ser malo = *to be bad (a bad man)*

estar malo = *to be ill*
mala educación = *ill breeding*
mala suerte = *bad luck*
mala voluntad = *spite; ill will*
¡Mal haya! *Confound him, her, it!*
mal hecho = *badly made, done*
de mal en peor = *from bad to worse*
malsano (adj) *unhealthy; sickly*
maltratar *to maltreat, abuse, spoil*
mancha (f) *stain, spot*
MANDAR *to command; to order*
  mandar por vino = *to send for wine*
mandarina (f) *tangerine orange*
mandato (m) *command; order*
mando (m) *power, authority; position of command*
MANEJAR *to handle, manage, operate*
MANEJO (m) *handling, management*
  manejo doméstico = *housekeeping; running a home*
MANERA (f) *manner; way* [of doing]
  de manera que = *so that*
  de esta manera = *in this way*
  sobre manera = *exceedingly*
  de ninguna manera = *not at all*
manga (f) *sleeve*
manifestación (f) *statement; public demonstration*
MANIFESTAR *to show; to demonstrate*
MANO (f) *hand*
  a mano = *by hand*
  de propia mano = *with one's own hand*
  a mano derecha (izquierda) = *to the right (left) hand side*
  entre manos = *on hand, in process*
  por su mano = *by oneself*
manta (f) *blanket*

— de viaje = *travelling rug*
MANTECA (f) *pork fat; lard; butter*
MANTENER *to maintain; to support*
  mantener correspondencia = *to keep up correspondence*
  mantenerse = *to support oneself*
MANTEQUILLA (f) *butter*
MANZANA (f) *apple*
manzanilla (f) *white sherry* [like the wine made in Sanlúcar de Barrameda and elsewhere in Andalucía]; *also camomile*
MAÑANA (f) *morrow; morning; forenoon*
  por la mañana = *in the morning*
  las ocho de la m. = *8 a.m.*
  mañana = *tomorrow*
  mañana por la mañana = *tomorrow morning*
  pasado mañana = *the day after tomorrow*
muy de M. = *very early*
MAPA (m) *map; chart*
MÁQUINA (f) *machine; engine; apparatus*
— de afeitar = *safety razor*
— coser = *sewing machine*
— escribir = *typewriter*
— combustión interna = *internal combustion engine*
— pneumática = *air pump*
— escribir a máquina = *to type*
MAR (m & f) *sea; flood*
— alta = *rough sea*
— de bonanza = *calm sea*
— llena = *high water*
  la mar de cosas = *very many things*
MARAVILLA (f) *marvel, wonder*
  por maravilla = *very seldom*
maravillar *to admire; to regard with wonder*
  maravillarse (de) = *to marvel (at)*

MARAVILLOSO (adj) *marvellous*; *wonderful*

MARCA (f) *mark*; *make*; *stamp*
de marca = *excellent* [of its kind]
marca de fábrica = *trade mark*

MARCAR *to mark*; *to note, observe*
marcar la ropa = *to mark (the) linen*

MARCHA (f) *march*; *progress*

MARCHAR *to walk*; *to go (move, march, function)*
Ese reloj no marcha = *That clock has stopped*
MARCHARSE = *to go away*

mareado (adj) *seasick*

MAREARSE *to become (sea)sick*

mareo (m) *seasickness*

MARIDO (m) *husband*

marina (f) *shipping*; *seamanship*
marina mercante = *merchant navy*

marino (adj) *marine, nautical*

marítimo (adj) *maritime, marine*; *of the sea*

mármol (m) *marble*

martillo (m) *hammer*

MAS (conj) *but*

MÁS (adv) *more.* **LO MÁS** *most*
más tarde = *later*
MÁS tarde **QUE** = *later than . . .*
LO MÁS tarde = *the latest*; *at the latest*
en más = *above, over*
a lo más = *at most*; *at the outside*
más bien que = *rather than*
trabajar más = *to work harder*
más o menos = *more or less*; *about*
más **DE** 10 pesetas = *more than 10 pesetas*
ni más ni menos = *exactly*
Necesito más información = *I need more information*
estar de más = to be unwanted

masa (f) *mass*; *aggregation*; *heap*; *lump*

matador (m) *killer*
— de toros = *matador*

MATAR *to kill*; *to extinguish* [a fire, a light]
matarse = *to kill oneself*

matemáticas (f pl) *mathematics*

MATERIA (f) *matter, material, stuff*; *subject matter*
materias primas = *raw materials*

material (adj) *material*; *rough*

materno (adj) *maternal*

MÁXIMO (adj & noun) *maximum*

MAYOR (adj) *greater, bigger*; *older*
el, la mayor = *biggest*; *eldest*
(pl) los, las mayores
ser mayor (menor) de edad = *to be of (under) age*
por mayor = *wholesale*

mayoría (f) *majority*

mecánico (adj) *mechanical*
(noun) *mechanic, engineer*

MEDIA (f) *stocking*
medias de seda = *silk stockings*

mediado (adj) *half full* or *half empty*
a mediados de = *about the middle of*

MEDIANOCHE (f) *midnight*

MEDICINA (f) *medicine*

MÉDICO (m) *physician*; *doctor*
(adj) = *medical*

MEDIDA (f) *measure*; *measurement*
hecho a la medida = *made to measure*
tomar medidas = *to take steps*

MEDIO (adj) *half*
media hora = *half an hour*
las dos y media = *half past two*
por término medio = *on an average*
(adv) = *half*

medio vestido = *half dressed*
dormido a medias = *half asleep*
(noun m) = *middle, centre*
en medio de = *in the midst of*;
between
los medios = *means*; *resources*
MEDIODÍA (m) *mid-day*; *noon*
MEDIR *to measure, weigh, judge*
medir las palabras = *to weigh one's words*
MEJOR (adj) *better.* **EL, LO MEJOR** = *the best*
cuanto más ... tanto mejor ... = *the more ... the better ...*
mejora (f) *improvement*
mejorar *to improve, get better*
mejorarse = *to recover from an illness*; *to improve in health*
melocotón (m) *peach*
melón (m) *melon*
membrillo (m) *quince* [preserve]
MEMORIA (f) *memory*; *recollection*; *souvenir*
flaco de memoria = *inclined to forget*; *forgetful*
de memoria = *from memory*; *by heart*
mención (f) *mention*
hacer mención de = *to mention sth, sb*
mencionar *to mention*
mendigo, -a *beggar* (m & f)
mengano, -a *Mr (Mrs) So-and-so*
See **fulano**
MENOR (adj) *less, smaller*; *younger*; *junior* [in age]
menor de edad = *minor, under age*
por menor = *retail*
MENOS (adv) *less*
las dos menos cinco = *five minutes to two*
las dos menos cuarto = *a quarter to two*
menos DE diez pesetas = *less than 10 pesetas*

lo menos posible = *the least possible*
al (or **a lo**) **menos** = *at least*
estar de menos = *to be wanting, lacking, missing*
todo menos eso = *anything but that*
menos mal = *not so bad*
menos mal que ... = *it's a good thing that ...*
mensaje (m) *message*
mensajero, -a *messenger* (m & f)
mensual (adj) *monthly*
(adv)-**mente** = *monthly*
mente (f) *mind*; *understanding*
MENTIR *to tell a lie (lies); to be misleading*
¡Miento! = *Sorry, I made a mistake (when I said that)*
mentira (f) *lie, untruth*
mentiroso (adj) *untruthful*
(noun m & f) = *liar*
MENÚ (m) *menu; bill of fare*
menudo (adj) *minute, small*
a menudo = *often*
MERCADO (m) *market; market place*
MERCANCÍA (f) *merchandise*
(pl) = *goods*
mercante (adj) *mercantile; trading*
MERECER *to deserve, be worthy of; to be worth*
meridional (adj) *southern*
merienda (f) *light meal*
— **campestre** = *picnic*
MÉRITO (m) *merit; worth; excellence*
un libro de mérito = *an excellent book*
mermelada (f) *jam; preserve; marmalade*
MES (m) *month; monthly wage*
MESA (f) *table; table-land*
mesa de noche = *bedside table*
poner la mesa = *to set the table*

alzar la mesa = *to clear the table*
mesa franca = *open table*
metal (m) *metal*
metálico (adj) *metalic*
METER *to put* (*in*); *to insert*
  meter ruido = *to make a noise*
  meter la pata = *to put one's foot in it*
  meterse = *to intrude, meddle, interfere*
  meterse con = *to pick a quarrel with*
metódico (adj) *methodical*
método (m) *method*
métrico (adj) *metric*
  el sistema métrico = *the metric system*
METRO (m) *meter; unit of length*
metro (m) ⎱ *underground*
metropolitano (m) ⎰ *railway*
MEZCLAR *to mix, mingle*
  mezclarse (con) = *to mix* (*with*); *to take part; to intermarry*
mezquino (adj) *mean, stingy*
MIEDO (m) *fear*
  tener miedo = *to be afraid*
miel (f) *honey*
  luna de miel = *honeymoon*
MIEMBRO (m) *member* [of community, society]; *limb* [of the body]
MIENTRAS (adv) *while; when*
  mientras (que) yo escribo = *while I'm writing*
  mientras tanto = *meanwhile, in the meantime*
MIL (adj & m noun) (*a*) *thousand*
milagro (m) *miracle, wonder*
militar (m) *military man; soldier*
  (adj) = *military*
MILLA (f) *mile*
millar (m) (*a*) *thousand*
MILLÓN (f) *million*
MINERAL (adj & m noun) *mineral*

MÍNIMO (m noun & adj) *minimum*
ministerio (m) *ministry; cabinet*
  — **de Hacienda** = *Ministry of Finance* (= *Treasury*)
  — **de Instrucción Pública** = *Ministry of Education*
  — **de Relaciones Exteriores** = *Foreign Office*
MINISTRO (m) (*cabinet*) *minister*
minoría (f) *minority*
MINUTO (m) *minute* (*of time*)
  (adj) = *minute, tiny*
miope (adj) *short-sighted*
MIRADA (f) *look, glance*
  mirada fija = *stare*
MIRAR *to look* (*at*), *gaze*
  — **a una persona** = *to look at a person*
  — **por** = *to look after*
  la ventana mira al jardín = *the window looks out on the garden*
  mirar fijamente a = *to stare at a person*
misa (f) *mass*
  — **mayor** = *high mass*
  oir misa = *to hear mass*
miserable (adj) *miserable, unhappy; close-fisted*
  (noun m & f) = *wretch; despicable person*
miseria (f) *poverty, want; stinginess*
misericordia (f) *mercy*
MISMO (adj) *same; self*
  ahora mismo ⎱ *at once, now,*
  ya mismo ⎰ *immediately*
  yo mismo, -a = *myself.* See page 25
  Me da lo mismo = *It's all the same to me*
  lo mismo que = *the same as . . .*
  por lo mismo = *for the same* (= *that very*) *reason*
  así mismo = *likewise*

misterio (m) *mystery*
misterioso (adj) *mysterious*
MITAD (f) *half*
mixto (adj) *mixed; mingled*
MODA (f) *fashion; style*
  a la moda = *fashionable*
  estar de moda = *to be in fashion*
  pasado de moda = *outmoded, out of fashion*
modelo (m) *model*
moderación (f) *moderation*
moderado (adj) *moderate; temperate*
moderar *to moderate*
MODERNO (adj) *modern*
modesto (adj) *unpretentious; modest*
modificar *to modify*
modismo (m) *idiom*
modista (f) *dressmaker*
MODO (m) *way; method; manner*
  de ningún modo = *by no means; on no account*
  de todos modos = *anyhow; at any rate*
  de modo que = *so that*
  al modo de = *in the style of*
  no hay modo de + inf = *it's impossible to . . .*
mojar *to wet, moisten*
moler *to grind; to pulverise*
MOLESTAR *to disturb, trouble, annoy; to vex*
  ¿Le molesta si fumo? = *Do you mind if I smoke?*
  No se moleste Vd. = *Don't bother*
MOLESTIA (f) *discomfort; inconvenience; nuisance*
molesto (adj) *annoying; uncomfortable*
molino (m) *mill; millhouse*
  molinillo (m) = *little mill* [for grinding coffee, etc.]
momentáneo (adj) *momentary*
MOMENTO (m) *moment*
  al momento = *immediately*

monarquía (f) *monarchy*
monasterio (m) *monastery*
mondar *to clean; to trim, peel*
MONEDA (f) *coin; money; currency*
  moneda corriente = *currency*
  moneda de plata = *silver money*
  La Moneda (= **Casa de la Moneda**) = *the Mint*
monje, -a (m & f) *monk; nun*
mono, -a *monkey* (m & f)
monopolio (m) *monopoly*
monótono (adj) *monotonous*
MONTAÑA (f) *mountain;*
  las montañas = *highlands*
montañoso (adj) *mountainous; hilly*
montar *to mount, get on top; to amount*
  montar a caballo = *to ride on horseback*
  montar en cólera = *to fly into a rage*
MONTE (m) *mountain, mount; woodland*
  monte alto = *forest*
  monte bajo = *scrub, thicket*
  Monte de Piedad = (*municipal*) *pawnshop*
montera (f) *bullfighter's hat*
montón (m) *heap, pile*
  un montón de cosas = *a lot of things*
  un montón de gente = *a crowd of people*
monumento (m) *monument; memorial*
morada (f) *dwelling*
moral (adj) *moral*
MORDER *to bite*
MORENO (adj) *brown, dark; swarthy*
  una morena = *a brunette*
MORIR *to die*
  (pp & adj) **MUERTO**

morir de hambre, de frío = *to die of hunger, cold*
morirse por = *to be extremely fond of; to be dying to do stg*
morirse de risa = *to die of laughing*
¡Muera! = *Down with (it)!*
moro (adj & noun) *Moorish; Moor*
mortal (adj) *mortal*
mortalidad (f) *death-rate*
mosca (f) *fly (insect)*
mostaza (f) *mustard*
MOSTRADOR (m) *counter [shop]; bar*
MOSTRAR *to show; to display; to point out*
MOTIVAR *to cause; to give rise to*
MOTIVO (m) *motive*
con motivo de = *owing to, by reason of, on the occasion of*
motocicleta (f) *motor bicycle*
MOTOR, -A (adj & noun m) *motor; engine*
— de combustión interna = *internal combustion engine*
— Diesel = *Diesel engine*
MOVER *to move, shift; to prompt; to persuade*
mover a piedad = *to rouse to pity*
moverse = *to stir, move*
movible (adj) *movable; mobile*
MOVIMIENTO (m) *movement*
poner en M. = *to set in motion*
MOZO, -A (n) *youth, young person (m & f)*
un mozo = *youth; bachelor; waiter; porter*
un buen mozo = *a fine looking youth, boy*
la moza = *maid; waitress*
una buena moza = *a fine girl*
MUCHACHO, -A (m & f) *boy; girl*
MUCHÍSIMO (adj) *very much*
MUCHO (adj) *much; many*
mucho tiempo = *a long time*

MUCHO (adv) *much; very*
MUCHO MÁS = *much more*
mucho más rápido = *much more quickly; far quicker*
hace mucho tiempo = *a long time ago; long ago*
hablar mucho = *to talk a lot*
MUDANZA (f) *change; alteration*
MUDAR *to change*
— aires = *to go for a change*
— casa = *to move house*
MUDO (adj & noun m & f) *dumb, mute (person)*
muela (f) *molar tooth*
dolor de muelas = *toothache*
muelle, -a (adj) *soft; tender; luxurious*
muelle (m) *quay; docks; spring*
muerte (f) *death*
MUERTO (adj) *dead*
muerto (m) *dead body; corpse*
los muertos = *the dead*
MUESTRA (f) *specimen, sample; shop sign; model, pattern*
MUJER (f) *woman; wife*
— casera = *good housewife*
tomar mujer = *to take a wife; to marry a wife*
mulato, -a (m & f) *mulatto; cross of black and white [races]*
multitud (f) *crowd; mass of people; the mass*
multiplicación (f) *multiplication*
multiplicar *to multiply*
MUNDIAL (adj) *of all the world; world*
guerra mundial = *world war*
MUNDO (m) *world*
todo el mundo = *everyone, everybody*
en todo el mundo = *throughout the world*
mucho mundo = *many people*
munición (f) *ammunition. (pl) = munitions*

murmurar *to whisper*; *to grumble*
MURO (m) *wall*
muscular (adj) *muscular*
músculo (m) *muscle*
MÚSICA (f) *music*
musical (adj) *musical*
músico (m) *musician*
MUY (adv) *very*
  muy bueno = *very good*
  estar muy cansado = *to be very tired*
  Muy Señor mío = *Dear Sir* [opening of a letter]

N

nabo (m) *turnip*
NACER *to be born*
NACIDO (pp & adj) *born*
  bien (mal) nacido = *well (ill) bred*
nacimiento (m) *birth*
  de n. = *from birth*
NACIÓN (f) *nation*
nacional (adj) *national*
nacionalidad (f) *nationality*
NADA (f) *nothing*; *nothingness*; *nonentity*
  (indef pron) *not anything, nothing*
  nada de eso = *none of that*; *not so*
  de nada = *you're welcome* [in reply to 'thank you']
  por nada = *for nothing*; *in no circumstances*
  (adv) = *not at all, by no means*
nadar *to swim*
NADIE (indef pron) *nobody*; *no one*; *none*
naranja (f) *orange*
NARIZ (f) *nose*; *sense of smell*
  las narices = *nostrils* [also used for *nose*]
nata (f) *cream*; *choice part*
  (pl) = *whipped cream with sugar*

natación (f) *swimming*
natalidad (f) *birth rate*
nativo (adj) *native*; *indigenous*
NATURAL (adj & inv n) *native*; *natural*
  ser natural de = *to be a native of* . . .
  Soy natural de aquí = *I was born here*
NATURALEZA (f) *nature*
naturalizarse *to become naturalised*
NATURALMENTE (adv) *naturally* [= *of course* in conversation]
naufragar *to be shipwrecked*
navaja (f) *jack-knife*
navegar *to navigate*; *to sail*
NAVIDAD (f) *Christmas Day*
  las navidades = *Christmas time*; *round about Christmas*
naviero (m) *ship owner*
navío (m) *ship*
neblina (f) *mist*; *fog*
NECESARIO (adj) *necessary*
NECESIDAD (f) *necessity*; *want*
  por necesidad = *from necessity, necessarily*
  tener N. de = *to be in need of*
NECESITAR *to need, want*
necesitarse = *to be in need*
necio (adj) *stupid*; *idiotic*
  (noun m & f) *fool*; *stupid person*
negación (f) *denial*; *negation*
negar *to deny*
  negarse a = *to refuse to*
  él se negó a hablar = *he refused to speak*
negativo (adj) *negative*
NEGOCIANTE (m) *trader*; *dealer*; *merchant*
NEGOCIO (m) *business*; *deal*; *transaction*
  los negocios = *business affairs*
  negocio redondo = *a good stroke of business*

un hombre de negocios = *a businessman*
NEGRO (adj & noun) *black*
  un negro, una negra = *a negro, negress*
nervioso (adj) *nervous*; *energetic*
neumático (m) (*pneumatic*) *tyre*
neutral (adj) *neutral*
neutralidad (f) *neutrality*
nevado (adj) *snowy*; *snow-white*
nevar *to snow*
  nieva = *it is snowing*
nevera (f) *ice-box*; *refrigerator*
NI (conj) *neither*; *nor*
  NI Vd. NI yo = *neither you nor I*
  ni siquiera = *not even*
NIEBLA (f) *fog*
NIETO, -A (noun m & f) *grandson*; *granddaughter*
NIEVE (f) *snow*
NINGÚN [used only before m nouns] = **NINGUNO**
NINGUNO (adj) *none, no one*
  ningún hombre = *no man*
  ninguna cosa = *nothing*
  (indef pron) = *none*; *no one*
  no ha venido ninguno = *not a person has come*
  ninguno de ellos = *none of them*
NIÑA (f) of **NIÑO** *girl*; *child*
niñez (f) *childhood*
NIÑO, -A (m & f) *boy*; *child*
  los niños, las niñas = *the children* (m & f)
NIVEL (m) *level*; *levelness*
  a nivel = *true level*
  nivel del mar = *sea level*
NO (adv) *no*; *not*
  no es necesario = *it's not necessary*
  no hay nada = *there's nothing*
  no ha venido nadie = *nobody has come*
  no bien = *no sooner*; *as soon as*
  no tener razón = *to be wrong*

no común = *unusual*
no obstante = *in spite of*; *nevertheless*
noble (adj) *noble*. (inv noun) = *nobleman*
nobleza (f) *nobility*
noción (f) *notion, idea*; *element* [in a statement]
nocturno (adj) *nightly*; *nocturnal*
NOCHE (f) *night*
  ANOCHE = *last night*
  esta noche = *this night, tonight*
  MEDIANOCHE = *midnight*
  POR LA NOCHE ⎫ = *at night,*
  DE NOCHE   ⎭ *night*
  hacer noche en = *to spend the night at . . .*
  hacerse de noche = *to grow dark*
  todas las noches ⎫ *every night*
  cada noche   ⎭
Nochebuena (f) *Christmas Eve*
nombramiento (m) *appointment, nomination*
NOMBRAR *to name*; *to appoint* [of a post, job]
NOMBRE (m) *name*; *surname*; *noun*
  nombre de pila = *Christian name*
  por nombre = *by name*; *by the name of*
  nombre y apellido = *full name*
nordeste (m) *north-east*
normal (adj) *normal*
normalidad (f) *normality*
noroeste (m) *north-west*
NORTE (m) *north*
nostalgia (f) *homesickness*; *nostalgia*
NOTA (f) *note*; *mark*; *sign*
  tomar nota (de) = *to make a note of*
notable (adj) *noticeable*; *notable*; *remarkable*
NOTAR *to note*; *to notice, observe*

NOTICIA (f) *item of news*
  las noticias = *the news*
  atrasado de noticias = *behind the times*
notificar *to notify*
NOVEDAD (f) *news, change; novelty*
  llegar sin novedad = *to arrive without incident* [= *safely*]
novillada (f) *bullfight with young bulls*
novillero (m) *young bullfighter*
novillo (m) *young bull*
novia (f) *fiancée; sweetheart; bride*
novio (m) *fiancé; suitor; bridegroom*
nuclear (adj) *nuclear*
nudo (m) *knot*
nuera (f) *daughter-in-law*
NUEVO (adj) *new*
  de nuevo = *again; anew*
  ¿Qué hay de nuevo? = *What's the news?*
  nada de nuevo = *no news*
  nuevo flamante = *brand new*
nuez (f) *nut; walnut*
nulo (adj) *nul, void; of no account*
numeral (adj) *numeral*
NÚMERO (m) *number*
  número uno = *number one*
  sin número = *innumerable*
NUNCA (adv) *never*
  nunca jamás = *never again; never more*
nuncias (f pl) *wedding; marriage*

O

O (conj) *or; either*
  O bueno O malo = *either good or bad*
obedecer *to obey*
obediente (adj) *obedient*
obispo (m) *bishop*

objeción (f) *objection*
  hacer objeción = *to object*
OBJETO (m) *object; thing*
  — de arte = *work of art*
  con objeto de = *in order to*
obligación (f) *obligation, duty*
  tener la o. de = *to be one's duty to*
obligar *to force, compel*
obligatorio (adj) *compulsory*
OBRA (f) *work; creation;* (pl) *building*
  obra literaria = *book*
  hay obra = *work is going on*
  hay obras = *building is going on*
obrar *to act, take action*
obrero, -a (adj & noun m & f) *workman; workwoman*
  los obreros = *the workers*
obscuridad (f) *darkness*
obscuro (adj) *dark*
  azul obscuro = *dark blue*
  a obscuras = *in the dark(ness)*
obsequiar *to treat, entertain; to make presents to*
obsequio (m) *gift; present; treat*
  en obsequio de = *out of respect for*
observación (f) *observation*
OBSERVAR *to observe, notice; to remark*
obstáculo (m) *obstacle, hindrance*
obstante (adv) *in* **NO obstante** = *nevertheless; in spite of*
obstrucción (f) *obstruction*
  — del tráfico = *traffic-jam*
obstruir *to obstruct, block, choke*
  — el camino = *to block the road*
obtener *to obtain*
OCASIÓN (f) *occasion; opportunity*
  de ocasión = *secondhand*
ocasionar *to cause, occasion; to move, excite*
occidental (adj) *western*
OCCIDENTE (m) *west; western world*

océano (m) *ocean*
ocio (m) *idleness; leisure*
  ratos de ocio=*leisure moments*
ocioso (adj) *idle; fruitless*
  palabras ociosas=*idle words*
oculista (inv n) *oculist*
OCULTAR *to hide; to conceal*
  ocultarse=*to hide oneself*
OCULTO (adj) *hidden, concealed*
OCUPADO (pp & adj) *occupied,
  busy, engaged*
OCUPAR *to occupy, take possession of; to fill (a job); to live in*
  ocuparse (de, en)=*to be engaged
  in; to care about, pay attention
  to*
ocurrencia (f) *event; happening*
ocurrir *to happen; to take place; to
  occur to, come to mind*
  ¿Qué le ocurre?=*What's happening to him? What's the
  matter with him?*
odiar *to hate*
ODIO (m) *hatred; odium*
odioso (adj) *hateful*
OESTE (m) *west*
ofender *to offend*
ofensa (f) *offence; insult*
oferta (f) *offer; supply*
OFICIAL (adj) *official*
  (noun m)=*officer*
OFICINA (f) *office; workshop;
  laboratory*
OFICIO (m) *work, occupation,
  function; trade, business*
OFRECER *to offer*
  ofrecerse=*to volunteer*
OÍDO (*m*) (*sense of*) *hearing; ear*
  de oído=*by ear*
  ser duro de oído=*to be hard of
  hearing; to have no ear for
  music*
  dar oídos=*to listen to*
OIR *to hear*
— misa=*to attend mass*

¡OJALÁ! *Would that ... Oh
  that ... God grant that ...
  May ...*
  ¡Ojalá que no viniera!=*May he
  never come!*
ojeada (f) *glimpse*
OJO (m) *eye*
  a ojo=*by eye*
  a los ojos de=*in the presence of*
  ¡Ojo!=*Look out!*
¡Ole! (excl) *Well done! Bravo!*
oler *to smell*
  No huele bien=*It doesn't smell
  nice* (=*something fishy about
  it*)
olor (m) *smell*
oloroso (adj) *fragrant*
OLVIDADO (pp & adj) *forgotten*
OLVIDAR *to forget*
  olvidarse de=*to forget about*
OLVIDO (m) *forgetfulness*
  echar en olvido=*to forget*
OLLA (f) *pot; stewpot.* Also Sp
  stew
omisión (f) *omission; neglect*
omitir *to omit; to leave out*
ÓMNIBUS (m) *omnibus; motor
  coach*
onda (f) *wave*
ondear *to form waves; to wave hair*
ondulación (f) *undulation; wavy
  form*
  ondulación permanente=*permanent wave* (hair)
ondulado (adj & pp) *waved, wavy*
operación (f) *operation*
OPINIÓN (f) *opinion*
OPONER *to oppose; to object*
  oponerse=*to be opposed; to be
  opposite*
OPORTUNIDAD (f) *opportunity;
  chance*
oportuno (adj) *timely, opportune*
oposición (f) *opposition; competition* [for a job]

óptico (m) *optician*
  (adj) = *optical*
optimismo (m) *optimism*
opuesto (adj & pp) *opposite*; *contrary*
opulento (adj) *rich*
oración (f) *prayer*; *oration*
orar *to pray*
ORDEN (m) *order*
  en orden = *in order*
  a sus órdenes = *at your service*
orden (f) *command*; *order of knighthood*
  a la orden = *to order*
ORDINARIO (adj) *ordinary*; *common*; *coarse*
OREJA (f) (*outer*) *ear*
organización (f) *organisation*; *arrangement*
organizar *to organise*
orgullo (m) *pride*
ORGULLOSO (adj) *proud*; *haughty*
oriental (adj) *eastern*; *oriental*
  Banda Oriental = *Uruguay*
ORIENTE (m) (*the*) *East*; (*the*) *Orient*
  el Próximo Oriente = *Near East*
  Centro Oriente = *Middle East*
  Extremo Oriente = *Far East*
origen (m) *origin*; *source*
original (adj) *original*
ORILLA (f) *bank* [of river]; *edge*
ORO (m) *gold*
  de oro = *of gold*; *golden*
orquesta (f) *orchestra*
OTOÑO (m) *autumn*
otorgar *to consent*; *to agree to*
OTRO (adj) *other*
  al otro lado = *on the other side*; *across*
  otra vez = *again*
  el uno o el otro = *either* (*one*)
  ni el uno ni el otro = *neither* (*one*)

por otra parte = *in addition*, or *on the other hand*
en (alguna) otra parte = *somewhere else*
otra cosa = *something else*

P

paciencia (f) *patience*
paciente (inv noun & adj) *patient*
pacífico (adj) *peaceful*; *peace-loving*
PADRE (m) *father*; *priest* (RC)
  los padres = *parents*
paella (f) Sp *dish* [rice with meat, fish, chicken, etc.]
paga (f) *payment*; *wages, pay, salary*; *earnings*
PAGAR *to pay* (*for*); *to repay*
  pagar una visita = *to return a visit*
  El me pagó el almuerzo = *He stood me lunch*
PÁGINA (f) *page*; *sheet*
PAGO (m) *payment*
PAÍS (m) *country* (*nation*); *region*
paisaje (m) *landscape*; *scenery*
paisano (m & f) *countryman*; *countrywoman*
  (adj) = *from the same country or region*
paja (f) *straw*
pájaro (m) *bird*; also *sly* (*shrewd*) *fellow*
  pájaro bobo = *booby*; *lout*
PALABRA (f) *word*; *speech*
  palabra por palabra = *word by word*
  por palabra = *by word* [of mouth]
  gastar palabras = *to waste one's breath*
  llevar la palabra = *to be the spokesman*
palacio (m) *palace*
palco (m) *box* [in theatre

pálido (adj) *pale*
palillo (m) *toothpick*
  los palillos = *castanets*
palmo (m) *span* (= 8–9 ins)
  palmo a palmo = *inch by inch*
PALO (m) *stick, cudgel; pole;*
  mast
paloma (f) *pigeon; dove*
pampa (f) *pampa, extensive plain*
  [SpA]
pampero, -a (m & f) *pampa-man,*
  woman; (m) = *violent wind*
  [SpA]
PAN (m) *bread; loaf of bread*
  pan bazo = *brown bread*
  pan duro = *stale bread*
  pan tierno = *fresh bread*
panadería (f) *baker's shop*
pandereta (f) *tambourine*
  panderete (m) = *small tambourine*
panecillo (m) *roll of bread*
pantalla (f) *screen* [cinema]; *also*
  lamp-shade
PAÑO (m) *cloth, woollen stuff; any*
  woven stuff, drapery
  paños menores = *undergarments*
PAÑUELO (m) *handkerchief;*
  small shawl
Papa (m) *Pope*
  papá = *daddy*
papa (f) *potato* [SpA]
PAPEL (m) (1) *paper* (2) *rôle, part*
  papel blanco = *blank paper*
  papel moneda = *paper money*
  mil pesetas (pesos) en papel =
    1,000 pesetas (pesos) in paper
    money
  papel secante = *blotting paper*
  papel de fumar = *cigarette paper*
  un trozo de papel = *a piece (scrap)*
    of paper
  hacer el papel de = *to play the*
    part of
  hacer un buen papel = *to do a*
    good job

papelería (f) *stationer's shop*
PAQUETE (m) *packet, package,*
  parcel
PAR (adj) *on a par, equal; even*
  (number)
  a la par = *at par* [of exchange]
par (m) *pair; couple*
  un par de huevos fritos = *a couple*
    of fried eggs
PARA (prp) *for; in order to.* See
  p. 58
  ¿Para qué . . . ? = *Why?*
  para que = *so that . . .*
  para siempre = *for ever, for good*
  ¿Para qué habla Vd? = *Why*
    (= *with what object*) *do you*
    speak?
  ¿Para qué sirve eso? = *What is*
    that for?
parada (f)   ⎫ *stop; halt;*
paradero (m) ⎭ *stopping place*
parado (adj) *stopped* [of clock]; *not*
  busy; unoccupied, unemployed
  los parados = *the unemployed*
paraguas (m) *umbrella*
paralelo (adj & noun m) *parallel*
PARAR (1) *to stop, check, parry* (2)
  to stay, put up (at)
  pararse = *to come to a stop; to*
    stop (intr)
  parar un golpe = *to parry a blow*
  parar en una pensión = *to put*
    up (stay) in a boarding house
  parar en seco = *to stop dead* [of a
    car, etc.]
  el ómnibus para aquí = *the bus*
    stops here
  el tren no para aquí = *the train*
    doesn't stop here
  el reloj se ha parado = *the clock*
    has stopped
parcial (adj) *in part, partial; unfair*
  -mente = *in part*
PARECER *to seem to be; to*
  appear

al parecer = *apparently*
parece mentira = *it seems to be a lie (nonsense)*
Me parece que = *it seems to me that . . .*
¿Qué le parece? = *How does it strike you?*
Juan tiene que parecer ante el juez = *John has to appear before the judge*
parecerse = *to look like one another*
PARECIDO (adj) *resembling; similar*
bien parecido = *good looking*
mal parecido = *bad looking; not nice looking*
PARED (f) *wall* [of a house]
PAREJA (f) *pair; couple; dancing-partner*
pariente, -a *relative, relation* (m & f)
parlamento (m) *parliament; parley*
paro (m) *stoppage of work; lock-out*
PARQUE (m) *park*
— zoológico = *zoo*
parroquia (f) *parish; parish church*
PARTE (f) *part, portion, share; place*
estar de la parte de = *to be on the side of*
la parte superior = *the top part*
de parte de = *on behalf of, by order of*
dar parte = *to notify*
en parte = *in part, partly*
hacer de su parte = *to do his best*
por mi parte = *for my part*
por todas partes = *on all sides; everywhere*
ser parte en = *to be a party to*
en alguna parte = *somewhere*
en otra parte = *elsewhere*
por otra parte = *on the other hand*

en ninguna parte = *nowhere*
particular (adj) *peculiar; special; private*
PARTIDA (f) *departure; group*
— de bautismo = *baptismal certificate*
PARTIDO (m) *party* [political]; *game, match*
un partido de futbol, tenis = *game of football, tennis*; also *match*
partir *to split, divide; to set out on a journey*
partir la diferencia = *to split the difference*
PASADO (adj) *past, previous; last*
pasado mañana = *the day after tomorrow*
el año pasado = *last year*
pasaje (m) *passage; passage money; number of passengers*
PASAJERO, -A *passenger* (m & f)
un tren de pasajeros = *passenger train*
PASAPORTE (m) *passport*
PASAR *to pass, pass by; to go across or through; to happen*
¿Qué pasa? = *What's happening?* (= *What's the matter?*)
pasar el río = *to cross the river*
pasar el tiempo = *to spend time*
pasar una semana en = *to spend a week in . . .*
pasar de largo = *to pass by; to ignore*
pasar en silencio = *to take no notice of*
pasarlo bien = *to have a good time*
PASARSE SIN = *to do without*
pasarse sin fumar = *to go without smoking*
PASCUA (f) *Easter*
PASE (m) *pass, permit; authorisation*

PASEAR(SE) *to take a walk; to walk about*
  pasear en auto = *to go for a drive* [in a car]
PASEO (m) *walk, stroll; drive* [in car]
  dar un paseo = *to take a walk*
  enviar a paseo a uno = *to send sb packing*
PASO (m) *step; pace; act of passing; passage*
  el paso de los Andes = *the crossing of the Andes*
  un paso a nivel = *level crossing*
  el paso doble = *military two-step* [dance]
  a buen paso = *quickly*
  a cada paso = *at every step; very often*
  a paso de tortuga [tortoise] = *at a snail's pace*
  abrir paso = *to clear the way*
  de paso = *incidentally*
  paso a paso *step by step*
pastel (m) *pastry; confectionery*
pastelería (f) *pastry shop*
pastilla (f) *pastille; piece of, slab*
  pastilla de jabón = *cake of soap*
  — — **chocolate** = *piece (slab) of chocolate*
PATA (f) *leg, foot, paw* [of animal]; also *duck* (**pato** = *drake*)
PATATA (f) *potato* [Sp]
  patatas fritas = *fried potatoes*
patente (f) *patent*
  (adj) = *patent, manifest*
patio (m) *court-yard; pit* [theatre]
  — **de trabajo** = *work yard*
PATRIA (f) *native country*
  patria chica = *home town*
patriótico (adj) *patriotic*
PATRÓN, -A (m & f) *patron saint; protector; boss, skipper; owner* [of an establishment]

la patrona de la casa de huéspedes = *landlady of guest house*
el patrón del café = *the landlord of the café*
pausa (f) *pause*
pavo (m & f) *turkeycock, -hen*
  pavo real = *peacock*
PAZ (f) *peace; peace of mind*
  ¡**Paz**! *Hush! Silence!*
  dejar en paz = *to leave sb alone* [not to disturb sb]
pecado (m) *sin*
pecar *to sin*
pecho (m) *chest; breast, bosom*
PEDAZO (m) *piece, fragment, bit*
  en pedazos = *in pieces, bits*
PEDIR *to request, to ask for*
  — **prestado** = *to ask for a loan*
  — **limosna** = *to ask for alms*
pegajoso (adj) *sticky, adhesive*: also *contagious, catching*
PEGAR (1) *to stick* [with glue, etc.] (2) *to strike*
  pegar fuego (A) = *to set fire to*
peinar *to comb*
  peinarse = *to comb one's hair*
peine (m) *comb*
peineta (f) *large Spanish comb*
pelar *to cut or pluck* (hair, feathers); *to peel or shell*
  duro de pelar = *extremely difficult to do*
  pelar una naranja = *to peel an orange*
  pelarse = *to be losing (casting) hair*
PELÍCULA (f) *film* [for camera]
  una película sonora = *a sound film; talkie*
PELIGRO (m) *danger; peril*
  correr peligro = *to run a risk*
peligroso (adj) *dangerous; risky*
PELO (m) *hair; down* [birds]; *pile* [of cloth]

(con) pelos y señales = (*with*) *full details*

estar a medios pelos = *to be half-seas over, tipsy*

estar hasta los pelos = *to be fed up to the teeth*

tomar el pelo = *to pull sb's leg*

hacerse el pelo = *to have a haircut*

tener pelos = *to be tough*

no tener pelos en la lengua = *to be outspoken*

pelota (f) *ball; ball game* [Basque]

pelotari (inv m noun) *pelota player*

PELUQUERÍA (f) *hairdresser's shop; barber's shop*

peluquero, -a *hairdresser* (m & f)

PENA (f) *penalty, punishment; grief, sorrow, trouble*

estar con mucha pena = (1) *to be very sorry* (2) *to be greatly vexed*

a duras penas = *with great difficulty*

valer la pena = *to be worth while*

tener la pena de + inf = *to be very sorry* (to) . . .

pendiente (adj) *overhanging; dangling; pending* (= *outstanding*)

pendientes (m pl) *ear-rings*

penique (m) *penny*

pensamiento (m) *thought; pansy* [flower]

pensado (adj) *thought out; deliberate*

PENSAR *to think; to contemplate*

pensar en alguna cosa = *to think of sth, over*

sin pensar = *thoughtlessly*

PENSIÓN (f) (1) *pension; scholarship* (2) *price of board and lodging* (3) *boarding-house*

Pensionista (inv n) *boarder*

Pentecostés (m) *Whitsuntide*

Domingo de Pentecostés = *Whit Sunday*

PENÚLTIMO (adj) *last but one*

PEOR (adj & adv) *worse*

el, la, lo peor; los (las) peores = *the worst*

peor que peor = *worse and worse*

tanto peor = *so much the worse*

PEQUEÑO (adj) *small, little; very young; humble* (*person*)

una niña pequeña = *a very small girl; little girl*

pera (f) *pear*

percha (f) *coat hanger; hat-rack*

PERDER *to lose*

perder de vista = *to lose sight of*

perder el juicio = *to go out of one's mind*

perderse = *to lose one's way; to get lost*

Ése no se perderá = *That chap has no flies on him*

pérdida (f) *loss*

perdido (pp & adj) *lost; mislaid; misguided*

PERDÓN (m) *pardon; forgiveness*

con perdón = *by your leave, excuse me*

PERDONAR *to pardon; to forgive*

Perdone Vd. = *Excuse me*

perecer *to perish; come to an end*

perecerse por alguna cosa = *to crave, pine for sth*

pereza (f) *laziness, sloth*

perezoso (adj) *lazy, indolent*

perfección (f) *perfection*

a la p. = *perfectly*

PERFECTO (adj) *perfect*

PERFECTAMENTE = [in speaking] *quite so*

perfume (m) *scent; perfume*

pericia (f) *expertness; skill*

PERIÓDICO (m) *newspaper* (adj) = *periodical, periodic*

periodista (m & f) *journalist*
PERÍODO (m) *term; period; age,*
era
perito (adj & noun m) *expert*
PERJUDICAR *to hurt, injure*
perjudicial (adj) *harmful, injurious*
perjuicio (m) *injury; damage*
PERMANECER *to remain; to stay*
permanencia (f) *act of remaining,*
staying at a place
permanente (adj) *permanent*
permiso (m) *permission; permit;*
leave
  con permiso = *by your leave;*
  with your permission
PERMITIR *to permit, allow*
  Permítame hablar = *Allow me to*
  speak
PERO (conj) *but; yet*
PERRO, -A (m & f) *dog; bitch*
  un perro chico, una perra gorda =
  SP *copper coins* (= *5 céntimos,*
  10 céntimos)
  un perro viejo = *an old hand;*
  experienced person
perseguir *to follow; to follow up*
PERSONA (f) *person*
  (pl) *people*
PERSONAL (adj) *personal*
personalidad (f) *personality; indi-*
viduality
perspectiva (f) *outlook, view*
  (pl) **perspectivas** = *prospects*
persuadir *to persuade, convince*
persuasivo (adj) *persuasive*
PERTENECER *to belong to; to*
pertain to
perturbación (f) *disturbance*
perturbar *to disturb*
PESADO (adj) *heavy*
  sueño pesado = *sound sleep*
PESAR *to weigh; to weigh upon;*
to regret
  Me pesa mucho = *I am very sorry*
PESAR (m) *sorrow, grief, regret*

  a pesar de = *in spite of*
  a mi pesar = *against my wish(es)*
pesca (f) *fishing*
pescado (m) *fish* [for table]
pescador (m) *fisherman*
pescar *to fish; to fish for*
peseta (f) Sp *monetary unit*
PESO (m) *weight; heaviness; also*
monetary unit [SpA]
  peso bruto = *gross weight*
  peso neto = *net weight*
  peso corrido = *overweight*
pestaña (f) *eyelash*
petróleo (m) *petroleum; mineral oil*
pez (m) *live fish*
piano (m) *piano*
picador (m) *picador* [in bullfight]
picadura (f) *sting, pricking; cut*
tobacco
PICAR *to prick; to sting; to goad*
[in bullfighting]
  la pimiento pica = *pepper stings*
  (*the tongue*)
  el sol pica = *the sun burns* (*one's*
  skin)
  el picador pica el toro = *the*
  picador pricks (*goads*) *the bull*
pícaro, -a (m & f) *rascal, knave*
PICO (m) *point, peak; beak*
  y pico [after a number] = *and a*
  little more
  500 pesetas y pico = *500-odd pts*
PIE (m) *foot*
  a pie = *on foot*
  de pie = *standing*
  ponerse de pie = *to stand up*
  de pies a cabeza = *from head to*
  foot
piedad (f) *piety; mercy*
  Monte de Piedad = *municipal*
  pawnshop
  ¡Por piedad! *For mercy's sake!*
PIEDRA (f) *stone*
PIEL (f) *skin; fur; leather*
  abrigo de pieles = *fur coat*

PIERNA (f) *leg*

PIEZA (f) *piece, bit*; *room* [in a house]

el hotel tiene 100 piezas = *the hotel has 100 rooms*

pijama (m) *pyjamas*

PILA (f) *pile, heap*; *electric battery*

piloto (m) *pilot* [of ship, aeroplane]; *navigating officer*

pimienta (f) *pepper*

PINTAR *to paint*; *to depict*

pintoresco (adj) *picturesque*

pintura (f) *painting*; *paint, pigment*

pipa (f) *tobacco pipe*; *hogshead* [wine]

piropo (m) *compliment*; *flattery* [used of/to a lady]

pisar *to tread*; *to tread on*

piscina (f) *fishpond*; *swimming-pool*

PISO (m) *floor, storey*; *flat (apartment)*; *pavement, paving*

piso bajo = *ground floor*

pista (f) *track*; *trail*

pitillera (f) *cigarette case*

pitillo (m) *cigarette* [Sp]

pito (m) *whistle* [instrument and sound]; *catcall*

no valer un pito = *not to be worth a straw*

PLACER *to please*

(noun m) = *pleasure*

a placer = *at one's convenience*

PLAN (m) *plan*

plancha (f) *plate, sheet* [of metal]; *smoothing-iron*

planchar *to iron*; *to press, smooth*

PLANO (adj) *smooth, level, even*

PLANTA (f) *plant*; *plantation*; *sole* [of foot]

plantar *to plant*; *to erect, set up*

plantarse = *to stand firm*

plástico (noun m & adj) *plastic*

PLATA (f) *silver*; *silver coin*; *money* [SpA]

hablar en plata = *to talk in plain language*

plátano (m) *banana*; *plantain*

PLATO (m) *plate, dish*; *course* [on menu]

platos del día = *(special) dishes of the day* [on menu]

comida de 4 platos = *four-course dinner*

PLAYA (f) *beach*; *seaside*

PLAZA (f) *public square*; *market place*; *vacancy, post*

plaza de toros = *bullring*; *arena*

plaza mayor = *principal square* [in town or city]

un auto de 5 plazas = *a five-seater car*

sacar a plaza = *to publish, to make public*

plazo (m) *instalment* [hire-purchase]; *fixed date or term*

vender (comprar) a plazos = *to sell (by) on instalments*

el plazo vence el 1° del mes = *the instalment falls due on the 1st of the month*

plomo (m) *lead* [metal]

PLUMA (f) *pen*; *plume*; *feather*

pluma estilográfica = *fountain pen*

POBLACIÓN (f) *population*; *city, town, village*

POBLADO (noun m & adj) *town*; (adj) = *populated*

POBLAR *to populate*; *to inhabit*

POBRE (adj) *poor*; *unfortunate* (noun m & f) *poor person*

los pobres = *the poor*

pobreza (f) *poverty*

POCO (adj) *little*; *small*; *not much*

(adv) *briefly*; *in a short time*

tan poco como = *as little as*

dentro de poco = *before long*

hace poco = *a short time ago*

a poco = *soon*

poco a poco = *little by little*
poco común = *unusual*
tener en poco = *to think little of*
(noun m) un poco (de) = *a little
(of)*
PODER *to be able; can; may. See
p. 46*
Puede que llueva = *It may rain*
no poder más = *not to be able to
do more*
no poder ver a uno = *to detest sb*
(noun m) *power; authority; influence*
en poder de = *in the hands of*
PODEROSO (adj) *powerful; in-
fluential*
poesía (f) *poetry*
poeta (m) *poet*
poético (adj) *poetic*
POLICÍA (f) *police*
agente de policía = *plain-clothes
detective*
Comisaría de Policía = *Police
Station*
(noun) m *policeman*
político (m) *politician*
(adj) = *political*
POLVO (m) *dust; powder*
(pl) polvos = *toilet powder*
— para la cara = *face powder*
quitar el polvo = *to dust*
pollo (m) *chicken*: also (*artful*)
young man
pompa (f) *pomp; ostentation;
splendour*
PONER *to put; to place*
poner fin a = *to put a stop to*
poner en duda = *to call in question; to challenge*
poner en claro = *to make clear*
poner en libertad = *to set free,
release*
poner en ridículo = *to make a
fool of*
poner el corriente = *to inform*

poner mal = *to run down, dis-
credit*
poner por escrito = *to write down*
PONERSE:
— de pie = *to stand up*
— de acuerdo = *to reach agreement;
to agree*
— en ridículo = *to make an ass of
oneself*
— el sombrero = *to put on one's hat*
— a + inf = *to begin to:*
ponerse a escribir = *to begin to
write*
— el sol = *to set* [of the sun]
poniente (m) *west; west wind*
popa (f) *stern, poop* [of ship]
popular (adj) *popular*
popularidad (f) *popularity*
POR (prp) *for; by; through. See
pp. 58–59*
por Madrid = *through, by, via
Madrid*
por la mañana = *in the morning*
— la tarde = *in the afternoon*
— la noche = *in the night*
comprar (vender) por 50 pesetas
= *to buy (sell) for 50 pesetas*
por adelantado = *beforehand; in
advance*
— escrito = *in writing*
— supuesto = *of course*
— lo tanto = *therefore*
— si acaso = *if by chance; just in
case*
— lo pronto = *for the time being*
una carta por contestar = *a letter
to be answered*
por una semana = *for a week*
trabajar por dinero = *to work for
money*
¿POR QUÉ . . . ? = *Why?*
pormenor (m) *detail*
PORQUE (conj) *because*
porrón (m) *glass bottle with
pointed spout for wine* [Sp]

portador (m) *porter; carrier*
portal (m) *porch; entrance*
portamonedas (m) *purse; small handbag*
PORTAR *to carry, bear*
portarse = *to behave, comport oneself*
portátil (adj) *portable*
PORTE (n) *cost of carriage, postage; porterage*
  porte franco = *carriage, postage prepaid*
portero, -a *porter; janitor* (m & f)
PORVENIR (m) *future*
posada (f) *inn; small hotel, lodging house*
posar *to place, lay down; to put up at an inn* (**posada**)
POSEER *to possess; to own*
posesión (f) *possession*
  las posesiones = *possessions, property*
positivo (adj) *positive*
POSTAL (adj) *postal*
  tarjeta postal = *post card*
  franqueo postal = *postage*
posterior (adj) *back; later, subsequent*
potable (adj) *drinking*
  agua potable = *drinking water*
pozo (m) *well of water; pool* [in river]
PRÁCTICA (f) *practice; custom*
  poner en P. = *to put into practice*
practicable (adj) *practicable; practical*
PRACTICAR *to practise; to do habitually*
práctico (adj) *practical; experienced*
prado (m) *meadow*
PRECIO (m) *price; cost*
  precio corriente = *current price*
  no tener precio = *to be invaluable*
  tener en precio = *to esteem*
precioso (adj) *valuable; beautiful*

PRECISO (adj) *precise, exact; necessary*
  SER PRECISO = *to be necessary*
  Es preciso que Vd . . . = *You must . . .*
  Es preciso ir a . . . = *One must go to . . .*
  la hora precisa = *the exact hour* (*time*)
predecir *to predict, forecast*
predicción (f) *forecast*
preferencia (f) *preference*
preferible (adj) *preferable*
PREFERIR *to prefer*
  (pres) **prefiero**
pregón (m) *public announcement*
pregonar *to announce publicly*
PREGUNTA (f) *question; enquiry*
  hacer una pregunta = *to ask a question, make an enquiry*
PREGUNTAR *to ask a question*
  preguntarse = *to wonder*
  Me pregunto quién es = *I wonder who he is*
premiar *to reward; to award a prize*
PREMIO (m) *reward; prize*
  premio gordo de la lotería = *1st prize in the lottery*
  a premio = *at a premium*
prenda (f) *pledge; security; guarantee*
  en prenda = *as security*
  prendas de vestir = *articles of clothing*
PRENSA (f) *printing press; press*
  prensa periódica = *the* (*daily*) *press, newspapers*
preocupación (f) *concern; worry; anxiety*
preocupar(se) *to worry*
preparación (f) *preparation*
PREPARADO (adj) *prepared; ready*
preparar *to prepare*
  estar preparado = *to be ready*

prepararse para la lucha = *to get
ready for the struggle*
presencia (f) *presence; being
present*
presenciar *to be present at; to
witness*
presentación (f) *introduction*
PRESENTAR *to introduce* [one
person to another]; *to display;
to make a present*
presentarse = *to present oneself*
presente (adj) *present*
tener presente = *to bear in mind;
to take into account*
presidencia (f) *presidency; chair-
manship*
presidente (m) *president; chairman*
**Presidente del Consejo de
Ministros** = *Prime Minister*
presidir *to take the chair; to pre-
side*
preso, -a *prisoner* (m & f)
PRESTADO (adj & pp) *lent,
loaned*
pedir prestado = *to ask for a
loan*
tomar prestado = *to borrow*
PRESTAR *to lend*
presumir *to presume, surmise; to
boast; to be conceited*
prevenido (adj) *forewarned; prepared for*
prevenir *to foresee, forestall*
prevenirse = *to be ready; to be on
guard*
previsión (f) *expectation; foresight*
PRIMAVERA (f) *spring*
PRIMER contraction of
PRIMERO. See p. 19
PRIMERO (numeral adj) *first;
former*
primer piso = *first floor*
a primera vista = *at first sight*
(adv) = *in the first place*
PRIMO, -A *cousin* (m & f)

PRINCIPAL (adj) *principal; main;
chief; leading*
(noun m) = *head of a firm,
business*
príncipe ⎱
princesa ⎰ *prince, princess*
PRISA (f) *hurry, haste*
a prisa (or **aprisa**) = *quickly*
correr mucha prisa = *to be very
urgent*
tengo que darme prisa = *I must
get a move on*
estar de prisa = *to be in a hurry*
PRIVADO (adj) *private*
PRIVAR *to deprive; to prohibit; to
debar*
privilegio (m) *privilege*
probabilidad (f) *probability*
probable (adj) *probable*
-mente = *probably*
PROBAR *to prove; to test; to
taste*
probar a + inf = *to try to*
probar el vino = *to try* (= *taste*)
the wine
probarse = *to try on* [of a garment]
Quiero probarme el traje = *I want
to try on the suit* (*costume*)
problema (m) *problem*
procedente (de) *coming from*
proceder (1) *to proceed, go on* (2)
to take action
proceso (m) *lawsuit; trial*
— **de quiebro** = *bankruptcy suit*
procesión (f) *procession*
PROCURAR *to try, endeavour; to
obtain*
procurar camino = *to find a way*
PRODUCIR *to produce, manufacture; to yield, bear* [agri-
culture]
productivo (adj) *productive*
PRODUCTO (m) *product*
profesión (f) *profession; occupation*
profesional (adj) *professional*

profesor, -a (m & f) *teacher; professor*

profundidad (f) *depth; profundity*

PROFUNDO (adj) *deep, profound; low*
   un sueño profundo = *a deep sleep*
   una casa profunda = *a house that goes back a long way*

programa (m) *programme; schedule; syllabus*

progresar *to progress; to improve*

prohibición (f) *prohibition*

PROHIBIDO (adj & pp) *prohibited; forbidden*
   estar prohibido = *to be forbidden*

PROHIBIR *to forbid, prohibit*

prójimo (m) *neighbour; fellow man*

proletario (adj) *working class; poor*

promedio (m) *average; mean; middle*

promesa (f) *promise*

PROMETER *to promise*
   prometerse en matrimonio = *to become engaged*

PRONTO (adj) *prompt; quick, fast* (adv) *soon; promptly*
   tan pronto como = *as soon as*
   al pronto = *at first*
   de pronto = *suddenly*
   por lo pronto = *for the time being*
   estar pronto (para) = *to be ready (for)*

pronunciación (f) *pronunciation*

pronunciamiento (m) *rebellion*

pronunciar *to pronounce; to make a speech*
   pronunciarse = *to rise in rebellion*

propietario, -a *owner* (m & f); *landlord, landlady*

propina (f) *tip; gratuity*

PROPIO (adj) *one's own; proper; fit*
   el propio patrón = *the boss himself*
   propio para el caso = *fit (suitable) for the occasion*

PROPONER *to propose; to propound*
   proponer ideas = *to submit ideas*
   proponerse = *to plan, mean; to determine (to)*

PROPÓSITO (m) *proposal; purpose; intention*
   a propósito de = *apropos*
   de propósito = *on purpose*

PROSEGUIR *to pursue; to prosecute; to go on, continue*

prosperar *to prosper*

prosperidad (f) *prosperity*

próspero (*adj*) *prosperous*

protección (f) *protection*

proteger *to protect*

protegido (adj, pp & noun) *protected; favourite*

protestar *to protest*

PROVECHO (m) *profit, benefit*
   ¡Buen provecho! = *May it benefit you!* [said to diner(s) as one passes or sits down]

proveer *to provide, supply* [with provisions or stock]

provenir (de) *to arise from, to be due to*

proverbio (m) *proverb*

PROVINCIA (f) *province*

provisión (f) *provision*
   (pl) **provisiones** = *provisions, groceries etc.*

provisional (adj) *provisional; temporary*

PRÓXIMO (adj) *next, nearest; proximate*
   la semana próxima = *next week*

proyecto (m) *project; plan, design*

prudente (adj) *prudent; wise*

PRUEBA (f) *proof; trial, test; fitting* [of a garment]
   a prueba = *on trial*
   a prueba de = *-proof* as in **a prueba de agua** = *waterproof*

publicación (f) *publication*

publicar *to publish*
PÚBLICO (adj & noun m) *public*
  en público = *in public*
puchero (m) (1) *cooking pot* (2)
  stew [Sp] *of meat and vege-*
  tables
PUEBLO (m) *village; working*
  people; population; nation
  el pueblo español = *the Spanish*
  people
  pueblo natal = *native village*
PUENTE (m or f) *bridge*
puerta (f) *gate; entrance*
PUERTO (m) *port, harbour; haven,*
  shelter
PUES (conj) *for, as; because, since;*
  well, then
  ¿Y pues? = *And what of it?*
  ¿Pues y qué? = *Well, what*
  then?
  Pues sí = *Yes indeed*
  ¡Pues! = *Of course! Exactly!*
PUESTO (m) *place, position;*
  stall, booth; job
pulga (f) *flea*
pulgada (f) *inch*
pulgar (m) *thumb*
pulmón (m) *lung*
pulmonía (f) *pneumonia*
pulso (m) *pulse*
  tomar el pulso = *to take* (*feel*) *the*
  pulse
PUNTA (f) *point, end, tip*
PUNTO (m) *point, dot; full stop;*
  stitch
  punto de taxis = *taxi-rank*
  punto de partida = *starting point*
  punto de vista = *point of view*
  en punto = *exactly, sharp* [of the
  time of day]
  estar a punto de = *to be on the*
  point of
puntual (adj) *punctual*
  ser puntual = *to be on time*
puño (m) *fist*

de propio puño = *in one's own*
  handwriting
PURO (adj) *pure; clear; clean*
  a puro = *by dint of*
  de puro = *extremely*
  (noun m) **un puro** = *a cigar*
puramente (adv) *simply; merely*

Q

QUE (rel pron) *who, whom, which,*
  that. See pp. 25–26
  el que, la que = *he who, she who,*
  the one which (m & f)
  los que, las que = *those who,*
  which (m & f)
QUE = *than* [in comparisons]:
  Juan es más grande que María
  = *John is taller than Mary*
QUE (conj) = *that*:
  El me dijo que vendría = *He*
  told me that he would come
QUÉ is used in exclamations:
  ¡ Qué muchacha! = *What a*
  girl!
and in questions:
  ¿Qué pluma quiere Vd.? =
  What pen do you want?
QUEDAR *to remain, stay*
  Me quedan diez pesetas = *I*
  have 10 pesetas left
  La carta quedó por contestar =
  The letter was left to be
  answered
  ¿En qué quedamos? = *Where*
  do we stand (*what do we do*
  now)?
  Quedamos conformes = *We are*
  in agreement
QUEDARSE:
  quedarse atrás = *to remain be-*
  hind
  quedarse con = *to keep, retain*
  quedarse fresco = *to remain in-*
  different

Me quedo en casa = *I'm staying at home*

queja (f) *complaint; grievance*

quejarse (a uno de otro) *to complain* [to one person about another]

quemadura (f) *burn, scald*

QUEMAR *to burn; to scald*

QUERER *to wish (for); to want; to like, love*

　QUERER DECIR = *to mean*

　El quiere a María = *He loves Mary*

　Yo quisiera (que) = *I should like (that)*

　sin querer = *without intention*

QUERIDO (adj & pp) *wished, desired; beloved*

　querido mío⎫ *my darling*
　querida mía⎭

queso (m) *cheese*

QUIEN, QUIENES (rel pron) *who.* See pp. 25–26

　Aquellos amigos de quienes Vd. ha hablado = *Those friends of whom you have spoken*

QUIÉN, QUIÉNES (inter pron) *Who?*

　¿De quién es esta pluma? = *Whose is this pen?*

quienquiera　⎫ (indef pron) = *who-*
quienesquiera⎭ *ever, whosoever*

QUIETO (adj) *quiet; still; calm*

quietud (f) *quietness*

químico (adj & noun m) *chemical; chemist*

QUITAR *to remove, take away; to take off; to deprive of*

　quitarse el sombrero = *to take off one's hat*

QUIZÁ or **QUIZÁS** (adv) *perhaps; maybe*

R

racimo (m) *bunch; cluster*

radio (m) *radius, circuit; radium*

RADIO (f) *radio* [receiving] *set; broadcasting*

radiotelegrama (m) *radiotelegram; wireless telegram*

RAMA (f) *branch*

RÁPIDO (adj) *quick, rapid* (noun m) = *express train*

rápidamente (adv) *quickly*

RARO (adj) *uncommon, unusual; odd, strange*

rasgo (m) *stroke, flourish; deed, feat; feature* (pl) *facial features*

　a rasgos grandes = *broadly; in outline*

RATO (m) *short time; little while*

　a ratos = *from time to time*

　a ratos perdidos = *in leisure moments*

　pasar el rato = *to spend the time*

ratón (m) *mouse*

RAZA (f) *race; lineage; breed*

RAZÓN (m) *reason; motive; rightness*

　tener razón = *to be right*

　no tener razón = *to be wrong*

razonable (adj) *reasonable*

　ser razonable = *to be reasonable* (= *sensible*)

　a razón de = *at the rate of*

　perder la razón = *to go mad*

razonar *to reason*

REAL (adj) *real, actual; royal*

　camino real = *highway*

realidad (f) *reality; truth*

　en realidad = *in fact; actually*

realmente (adv) *actually; in fact*

recado (m) *message; errand*

recatado (adj) *prudent; shy, coy*

receta (f) *cookery recipe; prescription*

RECIBIR *to receive; to get*

RECIBO (m) *receipt*

reciente (adj) *recent; fresh*

recíproco (adj) *reciprocal*; *mutual*
RECLAMAR *to claim, demand*
RECLAMO (m) *claim, complaint*;
   advertisement [in newspaper,
   etc.]
RECOGER *to gather, collect*; *to
   pick up*; *to take back.*
   recogerse = *to withdraw*
RECOMPENSA (f) *reward*
recompensar *to reward*
RECONOCER *to recognise*; *to
   admit*; *to search luggage* [in
   the Customs]
reconocimiento (m) *recognition*
RECORDAR *to remember, recall*;
   to remind
   recordarse = *to remember*
   No me recuerdo = *I don't remember*
recto (adj) *straight* [line]; *upright,
   honest*
RECUERDO (m) *memory*; *re-
   membrance, recollection*; *souvenir*
   (pl) **recuerdos** = *regards*
rechazar *to refuse*; *to reject*
red (f) *net*; *network*
redacción (f) *editing*; *editorial
   office*; *editorial staff*
redactar *to draft, write*; *to edit*
REDONDO (adj) *round*; *circular*
reducción (f) *reduction*; *decrease*
reducir *to reduce*
reemplazar *to replace*
referencia (f) *reference*; *mention*;
   narration
REFERIR *to refer*; *to narrate*
   referirse a = *to refer to*
reflexionar *to think* (*deeply*)
reforma (f) *reform*; *reformation*
REFRESCAR *to refresh*; *to cool*;
   to renew
   refrescarse = *to take a refreshment*; *to take the air*; *to cool
   off*

REFRESCO (m) *refreshment*(*s*);
   cool drink
refugiarse *to take refuge, shelter*
refugio (m) *shelter*; *refuge*
REGALAR *to make a present*; *to
   give*
REGALO (m) *present*; *gift*
régimen (m) *regime, system*; *conduct*
   r. alimenticio = *diet*
   de régimen = *ordinary*; *normal*
REGIÓN (f) *region*
regional (adj) *regional*
regir *to rule, govern*
registrar *to inspect, examine*; *to
   register, record*
registro (m) *search, inspection,
   examination*; *registry*; *registration*
REGLA (f) *ruler* [for ruling lines];
   rule, regulation
   en regla = *in due form*
   por regla general = *generally, as a
   rule*
regocijo (m) *rejoicing*; *joy*
REGRESAR *to come* or *go back*;
   to return
REGRESO (m) *return* [going or
   coming back]
regulación (f) *act of regulating*
REGULAR (adj) *regular*; *moderate*; *fairly good*
   por lo regular = *as a rule*
   ¿Cómo está Vd.? = *How are you?*
   Answer: **regular** = *fairly well*
regularidad (f) *regularity*; *orderli-
   ness*; *common use*
reina (f) *queen*
REINO (m) *kingdom*
   El Reino Unido = *the United
   Kingdom*
REIR *to laugh*
   reirse de una persona = *to laugh
   at sb*
   echarse a reir = *to burst out
   laughing*

reja (f) *iron window-grating*
relación (f) *relation (connection);
report, narrative, memoir*
  relaciones exteriores = *foreign
affairs*
  relaciones comerciales = *commercial relations*
relacionar *to relate; to narrate*
  relacionarse = *to get acquainted;
to form contacts, connections*
RELATO (m) *statement, report*
RELIGIÓN (f) *religion*
RELIGIOSO (adj & noun) *religious*
  un religioso = *monk*
  una religiosa = *nun*
RELOJ (m) *clock; watch*
  reloj de bolsillo = *pocket watch*
  reloj de pulsera = *wrist watch*
  reloj de pared = *clock* [wall]
relojería (f) *watchmaker's shop*
remar *to row*
REMEDIO (m) *remedy*
  No hay más remedio = *there's
nothing else for it* (= *it can't
be helped*)
  No me queda remedio = *I can't
do anything about it*
remendar *to mend, repair, patch*
remitente (m & f) *sender* [of letter,
parcel, etc.]
remolacha (f) *beetroot*
rendición (f) *surrender; yield,
profit*
RENDIR *to subdue, conquer; to
yield* [of industry]; *to render*
[account(s)]
  rendirse = *to surrender, give in*
  rendirse de fatiga = *to give in
from fatigue*
renovar *to renew, renovate*
renta (f) *income, rental*
  a renta = *at a rent*
reparación (f) *repair; amends*
reparar *to repair; to make amends*

REPENTE (m) *sudden movement*
  de repente = *suddenly*
repentino (adj) *sudden*
repetición (f) *repetition*
REPETIR *to repeat*
reposado (adj & pp) *quiet, peaceful; calm*
REPOSAR *to rest, take a rest
(nap); to lie on*
representación (f) *act of representing performance* [in
theatre]
representante (inv n) *representative*
representar *to represent* [a firm,
etc.]; *to present* [at a theatre]
representativo (adj) *representative*
REPÚBLICA (f) *republic*
republicano (adj) *republican*
RESERVA (f) *reserve; reticence,
prudence*
  de reserva = *extra, in store, spare*
[of parts]
  sin reserva = *openly*
  en reserva = *confidentially*
reservar *to reserve; to keep in store*
RESFRIADO (m) *common cold;
chill*
RESFRIARSE *to catch a cold; to
grow cold, indifferent*
residencia (f) *residence (place);
act of residing, staying;
official residence*
residir *to reside; to live*
respecto (m) *respect; aspect*
  (con) respecto (a, de) = *in regard
to*
  en este respecto = *in this connection*
RESPETAR *to respect*
RESPETO (m) *respect; regard*
respetuoso (adj) *respectful*
respirar *to breathe*
RESPONDER *to answer, reply; to
respond; to be responsible for*

responder a una pregunta = *to reply to a question*

responder por una persona = *to answer for a person*

responsabilidad (f) *responsibility*

responsable (adj) *responsible; reliable*

RESPUESTA (f) *reply, answer*

RESTAR *to remain, to be left over*

RESTAURANTE (m) *restaurant*

RESTO (m) *what remains; rest*

RESULTA (f) *effect, consequence*

RESULTADO (m) *result, what follows*

RESULTAR *to result, turn out (to be)*

   Resulta que . . . = *It turns out that* . . . . .

resumen (m) *summary, abstract*

en resumen = *in short, to sum up*

resumir *to sum up, summarise*

retirar *to retire; to withdraw money*

   retirar dinero del banco = *to withdraw money from the bank*

retiro (m) *retirement*

RETORNAR *to turn back, go back*

retrasar *to delay*

   retrasarse = *to linger*

RETRASO (m) *delay; slowness*

   (con) una hora de retraso = *(with) an hour's delay* (= *an hour late*)

REUNIÓN (f) *meeting; reunion*

reunir *to unite; to reconcile*

   reunirse = *to get together*

reventar *to burst; to blow up*

— de risa = *to burst out laughing*

reventón (m) *burst*

reverso (m) *reverse side*

REVÉS (m) *wrong side; set-back*

   al revés = *upside down; on the contrary*

revisar *to revise, re-examine*

   revisar las cuentas = *to audit the accounts*

revisor (m) *reviser; auditor;* also *ticket-collector*

REVISTA (f) *review; magazine* [periodical]

   pasar revista = *to inspect*

revolución (f) *revolution; turn*

REVOLVER *to turn (over); to stir (up)*

revuelto (adj) *restless; difficult, intricate*

   huevos revueltos = *scrambled eggs*

REY (m) *king*

   los reyes = *the monarchs*

rezar *to pray*

rezo (m) *prayer*

RICO (adj & noun) *rich; rich person; exquisite* [of sth]

ridículo (adj) *ridiculous*

RIESGO (m) *risk; danger*

   correr riesgo (de) = *to run the risk (of)*

rincón (m) *corner; book*

RÍO (m) *river*

riqueza (f) *riches; wealth*

RISA (f) *laughter*

   morirse de risa = *to die with laughter*

rival (inv n) *rival; competitor*

rivalizar *to rival; to compete*

rizar *to curl* [hair]

rizo (m) *curl*

ROBAR *to rob; to steal*

ROBO (m) *robbery; theft*

rodar *to rotate; to roll. Also to run on wheels* [of a car]

rodear *to make a detour; to surround*

rodeo (m) *roundabout way; detour; round up, rodeo*

rodilla (f) *knee*

   de rodillas = *on one's knees*

ROGAR *to beg; to entreat, request* (pres) **ruego**

ROJO (adj) *red*

romería (f) *pilgrimage; picnic; excursion*

ROMPER *to break*
  romper las amistades = *to quarrel*
ron (m) *rum*
ronda (f) *round* [of duty]; *round* [of drinks, cigarettes, etc.]
ROPA (f) *clothes, garments; fabric, dry goods*
  ropa blanca = *linen*
  ropa sucia = *soiled clothes* [for the laundry]
  ropa hecha = *ready made clothing*
  ropa de cámara = *morning gown*
  ropa vieja = *cast off clothes*
ROSA (f) *rose*
rosbif (m) *roast beef*
rostro (m) *(human) face; countenance*
  rostro a rostro = *face to face*
rotundo (adj) *round, rotund; sonorous* [of the voice]
RUEDA (f) *wheel; round, slice; turn*
ruego (m) *request; entreaty*
ruido (m) *noise*
  hacer ruido = *to kick up a shindy*
ruidoso (adj) *noisy*
ruina (f) *ruin; destruction*
rumbo (m) *course* [of ship]; *direction*
  con rumbo a = *in the direction of*
ruptura (f) *rupture; breaking (off)*
rural (adj) *rural*

S

sábana (f) *bed sheet*
SABER *to know* (*sth*); *to be able to.* See p. 46
  a saber = *namely*
  saber cuántos son cinco = *to know what's what*
  saber a = *to taste of*
  ¿Sabe? = *You know, don't you?*
  ¿Quién sabe? = *Who knows?* (= *perhaps*)
  saber de = *to be familiar with sth*

sabio (adj) *learned; wise*
saborear *to taste; to relish*
sabroso (adj) *tasty, pleasant (to taste)*
sacacorchos (m) *corkscrew*
SACAR *to take out; to withdraw; to extract*
  sacar un corcho = *to draw a cork*
  sacar la cuenta = *to make up the account(s)*
  sacar partido de = *to profit by*
  sacar en claro = *to reach a conclusion*
sacerdote (m) *cleric; priest*
SACO (m) *sack, bag; sackful, bagful*
  saco de noche = *hand-bag, valise*
  saco de viaje = *travelling bag*
sacudir *to shake, jolt, jerk*
saeta (f) *arrow; hand* [of timepiece]; *song to the Virgin in Holy Week processions*
sagrado (adj) *sacred*
SAL (f) *salt*
SALA (f) *drawing room; hall; large room; lounge*
  sala de espera = *waiting-room*
salado (adj) *salted, salty; witty*
salario (m) *wages; salary*
salchicha (f) *sausage*
salchichería (f) *sausage shop; delicatessen shop*
SALIDA (f) *exit; departure* [of trains, planes, ships, etc.]
  horas de salida = *hours of departure*
  salida del sol = *rising of the sun*
SALIR *to go or come out; to depart, leave*
  salir a = *to come to so much* [of a bill, account]; *to go out into*
  salir al encuentro de = *to go to meet sb*
  salir bien = *to come out well* (= *be successful*)

salirse = *to leak; to overflow*

salirse con la suya = *to have one's own way*

salmón (m) *salmon*

salón (m) *lounge; hall; drawingroom*

salsa (f) *sauce; gravy*

SALTAR *to leap, jump, spring; to skip* [in reading, writing]

SALTO (m) *leap, jump, bound; skip*

SALUD (f) *health*

beber a la salud de = *to drink sb's health*

¡Salud! used as greeting for *Hello! How goes it? Cheerio!*

saludable (adj) *wholesome* [of food, drink]; *salutary* [of action]

SALUDAR *to greet; to salute; to bow to; to wave (to)*

SALUDO (m) *greeting; salutation*

saludos a ... = *greetings to ...*

SALVAR *to save, rescue; to avoid* [a difficulty]

salvarse = *to be saved; to escape from danger*

salvavidas (m) *life-belt; life preserver*

bote salvavidas = *life-boat*

SALVO (adj) *safe; unhurt*

(adv) = *except, save*

san short for **santo** before m proper nouns except **Tomás, Tomé, Toribio** and **Domingo**

sanatorio (m) *nursing home*

sangrar *to bleed*

SANGRE (f) *blood*

sangre fría = *presence of mind; sang froid*

sangriento (adj) *blood-stained; bloody*

sanidad (f) *soundness; health*

Servicio de Sanidad = *Health Service(s)*

SANO (adj) *sound, healthy*

sano y salvo = *safe and sound*

santo (adj) *holy.* See **san**

santo -a (m & f) *saint; saint's day*

sardina (f) *sardine*

sartén (f) *frying-pan*

SASTRE (m) *tailor*

un sastre remendón = *tailor who does repairs*

sastrería (f) *tailor's shop; tailoring*

satisfacción (f) *satisfaction*

satisfacer *to satisfy; to pay in full*

satisfacer una deuda = *to pay a debt*

SATISFECHO (adj & pp) *satisfied*

SE (pers pron) *-self, -selves.* See pp. 22–25 and pp. 37–38, Reflexives

se dice = *it is said; they say*

se habla español = *Spanish spoken*

secar *to dry*

secarse = *to dry oneself*

sección (f) *section, division; department* [in office]

SECO (adj) *dry, dried up; withered*

en seco = *high and dry*

secretario, -a (m & f) *secretary*

SECRETO (adj & noun m) *secret*

SED (f) *thirst*

tener sed = *to be thirsty*

matar la sed = *to quench the thirst*

tener sed de = *to hunger after*

seda (f) *silk*

segar *to mow; to reap*

seguido (adj) *continued; successive* (adv) **DE SEGUIDA** = *consecutively; in succession*

EN SEGUIDA = *forthwith*

seguir *to follow, come after; to go on, continue*

como sigue = *as follows*

SEGÚN (prp) *according to, as; depending*

Juan irá o no, según = *he will go or he won't, it all depends.* See p. 59

SEGUNDO (adj) *second, 2nd*
  de segunda mano = *secondhand*
segundo (m) *second* [of time]
seguridad (f) *security; certainty; safety*
  con (toda) seguridad = *with (absolute) certainty*
SEGURO (adj) *sure, certain, safe*
  ¡Seguro! *For certain! Of course!*
seguro (m) *security; insurance*
  seguro contra accidentes = *accident insurance*
  en seguro = *in safety*
  Su Seguro Servidor (S.S.S.) = *yours faithfully* [end to a letter]
selección (f) *selection*
seleccionar *to select*
selecto (adj) *select*
SELLO (m) *seal; stamp (postage)*
  poner los sellos = *to stamp (a) letter(s)*
SEMANA (f) *week; week's work or pay*
  Semana Santa = *Holy Week (Easter)*
semanal (adj) *weekly*
semanario (m) *weekly publication*
sembrar *to sow a field*
SEMEJANTE (adj) *similar, like*
semejanza (f) *similarity*
sencillez (f) *simplicity; candor*
SENCILLO (adj) *simple; mere; ingenuous*
senda (f) *path; footpath; way*
sensato (adj) *sensible; prudent*
sensible (adj) *sensitive*
SENTAR *to place in a seat; to suit*
  SENTARSE = *to sit down*
  el vestido no le sienta = *the dress does not suit you*
  la comida no me sentó = *the dinner did not agree with me*
  sentarse a la mesa = *to sit at table*

SENTIDO (m) *sense; meaning*
  Eso no tiene sentido = *That has no meaning*
  sentido común = *common sense*
sentimiento (m) *feeling; sentiment*
SENTIR *to feel; to grieve, regret*
  sin sentir = *without noticing; inadvertently*
  Lo siento mucho = *I'm very sorry (about it)*
  sentirse bien, mal = *to feel well, bad*
SEÑA (f) *sign; mark; gesture*
  señas personales = *personal description*
  mis señas son = *my address is*
  por señas = *by signs*
señal (f) *indication; trace; signal*
SEÑALAR *to point out*
SEÑOR (m) *gentleman; owner (master) of a place; Mr; Sir;*
  El Señor = *The Lord (God)*
  Señor Don . . . See pp. 69–70
SEÑORA (f) *lady; lady of the house; owner; wife* [respectful term]. See pp. 69–70
SEÑORITA (f) *young lady; Miss.* See pp. 69–70
SEÑORITO (m) *young gentleman; young master.* See p. 70
separación (f) *separation*
separar *to separate*
  separarse = *to part company*
septentrional (adj) *northern; northerly*
sepultura (f) *grave; tomb*
  dar sepultura = *to bury*
SER *to be.* See pp. 39–40
  Soy yo = *It is I*
  Son ellos = *It is they*
  ser de (1) *to belong to* (2) *to be from, of London* etc.
  ser verdad = *to be true*
  llegar a ser = *to become*
serenidad (f) *calmness; tranquillity*

sereno (adj & m noun) *clear, fair, cloudless* [of the weather]; *calm, unruffled* [of a person]
el sereno = *night watchman*
serie (f) *series*
fabricación en serie = *mass production*
SERIO (adj) *serious*; *earnest*; *sincere*
servicial (adj) *obliging*; *serviceable*
SERVICIO (f) *service*; *servants*
estar de servicio = *to be on duty*
prestar un servicio = *to render a service*
s. de mesa = *table service*
un servicio flaco = *an ill turn*
servidor, -a (m & f) *servant*; *waiter, waitress*
servidor de Vd. = *at your service* (m & f)
servilleta (f) *table napkin*
SERVIR *to serve*; *to wait on*; *to look after*
servir de = *to act as*
servir la mesa = *to wait at table*
no servir = *to be of no use*
no sirve para nada = *it's no use for anything*
servirse = *to make use of*
SÍRVASE + inf = *please* + verb:
Sírvase venir temprano = *Please come early*
severo (adj) *strict, severe, rigorous*
sexo (m) *sex*
SI (conj) *if*; *whether.* See p. 60
SÍ (adv) *yes.* Also used as emphatic: **él no irá, pero yo sí** = *he won't go, but I will.* **yo sí hablo español** = *I do speak Sp.*
dar el sí = *to say yes*; *to accept a proposal*
por sí o por no = *in any case*
sí used for 3rd pers sing & pl reflexive pers pron = *himself, herself, itself, oneself, themselves.*

After prepositions note:
de sí = *of oneself, of itself*
de por sí = *apart, separately, of itself*
SIEMPRE (adv) *always*
para siempre = *for always* (= *for ever*)
siempre que = *provided that*
sierra (f) *ridge of mountains*; *saw*
siesta (f) *siesta*; *nap*
dormir la siesta = *to have a siesta* (*nap*)
SIGLO (m) *century*; *age*; *period*
Hace un siglo que no le veo = *It's ages since I saw him*
significado (m & pp) ⎫
significación (f)　　 ⎬ *meaning*
significar *to signify, mean*
signo (m) *sign*
SIGUIENTE (adj) *following*
el, la, lo siguiente ⎫ *the following*
los, las siguientes ⎭
el día siguiente = *the next day*
SILENCIO (m) *silence*
silencioso (adj) *silent*
SILLA (f) *chair*; *saddle*
silla de tijera = *folding* (*deck*) *chair*
sillón (m) (*arm*)*chair*; *easy chair*
simpatía (f) *sympathy*; *understanding*
tener simpatía por = *to like sb*
SIMPÁTICO (adj) *likeable*; *nice*; *charming*; *attractive*
simpatizar *to have a liking for*; *to be attracted to*
simple (adj) *simple*; *mere*
SIN (prp) *without.* Often used with noun to make equivalent to *-less*:
sin duda = *doubtless*
sin nombre = *nameless*
sin valor = *worthless*
sin hilos = *wireless*
sincero (adj) *sincere*
sindicato (m) *trade union*; *syndicate*

SINGULAR (adj) *singular; unique; unusual*

SINO (conj) *but; only; except, besides*

Nadie ha venido sino Juan = *Nobody has come but (except) John*

sinvergüenza (inv n) *shameless person; rascal*

SIQUIERA (adv & conj) *at least; even*

ni siquiera = *not even*

SISTEMA (m) *system*

el sistema métrico = *metric (decimal) system*

sistemático (adj) *systematic*

SITIO (m) *place, site; spot*

SITUACIÓN (f) *situation, locality; state of affairs*

la situación política = *the political situation*

SITUAR *to place; to put*

situarse = *to put oneself* [in a place]

smoking (m) *dinner jacket*

soberano (adj & m noun) *sovereign*

soberbia (f) *arrogance; haughtiness; pride*

soberbio (adj) *arrogant, haughty; superb, magnificent*

sobornar *to bribe*

soborno (m) *bribe; bribery*

SOBRE (m) *envelope* [for letter]

SOBRE (prp) *on, upon; above, over; about, near* [of time]

sobre todo = *above all; especially*

sobre la mesa = *on the table*

sobre 20 años = *about 20 years*

sobre la una = *about one o'clock*

sobremanera (adv) *excessively*

sobretodo (m) *overcoat*

sobrevivir *to survive*

sobrino, -a (m & f) *nephew; niece*

sociabilidad (f) *sociability*

sociable (adj) *sociable*

12—B.E.S.

social (adj) *social*

la razón social = *trading name*

socialismo (m) *socialism*

SOCIEDAD (f) *society; association; partnership*

sociedad anónima = *limited (stock) company* abbr **S.A.**

la buena sociedad = *better (class) society*

socio, -a (m & f) *member of a society; partner* [in business]

sofá (m) *sofa; divan*

SOL (m) *sun; sunshine*

hacer sol = *to be sunny* [weather]

rayo de sol = *ray of sunshine*

tomar el sol = *to bask in the sun; to sunbathe*

SOLDADO (m) *soldier (private)*

soledad (f) *loneliness; solitude*

solemne (adj) *solemn*

soler *to be in the habit of*

solidaridad (f) *solidarity; unity*

sólido (adj) *solid; firm; massive*

solitario (adj) *solitary; lonely; desolate* [place]

SOLO (adj) *sole, alone; single; lone*

a solas = *alone*

SÓLO (adv) *only*

SOLTAR *to unfasten, untie; to loosen, release; to let go, set free*

soltar la cuerda = *to unfasten the string*

soltar el agua = *to run off the water*

soltarse a + inf = *to begin to (do sth)*

SOLTERO, -A (m & f) *single (unmarried) person; bachelor, spinster*

soluble (adj) *soluble; solvable*

solución (f) *solution*

solucionar *to solve*

SOMBRA (f) *shade; shadow; ghost*

a la sombra = *in the shade*

hacer sombra = *to shade; cast a shadow*

sombra = *shady side of the bullring* [in contrast to **SOL** = the sunny side]

SOMBRERO (m) *hat*

sombrero cordobés (= s. de ala ancha) = *broad-brimmed* Sp *hat*

sombrero flexible = *soft (felt) hat*

quitarse el s. = *to take off one's hat*

SON (m) *sound, noise; news*

¿A qué son? = *For what reason? on what pretext?*

a son de = *at the sound of*

SONAR *to sound; to cause a sound; to ring* [a bell]

sonarse = *to be rumoured* (impers)

se suena que = *It is said (rumoured) that . . .*

sonarse las narices = *to blow one's nose*

SONIDO (m) *noise; sound; report*

sonreir *to smile*

sonrisa (f) *smile*

SOÑAR *to dream*

soñar con = *to dream of*

soñar despierto = *to daydream*

SOPA (f) *soup*

sorbo (m) *sip*

soporte (m) *support; prop*

SORDO (adj) *deaf*

sorprendente (adj) *surprising*

sorprender *to surprise*

sorprenderse = *to wonder*

sorprendido (adj) *surprised*

sorpresa (f) *surprise*

de sorpresa = *by surprise*

sortija (f) *(finger) ring*

sosiego (m) *quiet; tranquillity*

sospecha (f) *suspicion*

sospechoso (adj) *suspicious*

sostener *to sustain; to uphold*

SU, SUS (poss adj) *his, her, its, your, their.* See pp. 27–28

SUAVE (adj) *soft, delicate; smooth; suave, gentle, mild*

de genio suave = *mild tempered*

suavidad (f) *softness; gentleness*

SUBIR *to go up, come up; to climb*

subir las escaleras = *to go up the stairs* (= *upstairs*)

el vino sube a la cabeza = *wine goes to the head*

los precios han subido = *prices have risen*

substancia (f) *substance; stuff*

substancial (adj) *substantial; essential*

substituir *to substitute; to take the place of*

substituto (m) *substitute*

substraer *to subtract; to deduct*

SUCEDER *to succeed, to follow;* (impers) = *to happen*

suceda lo que suceda = *whatever may happen*

sucedió que = *it happened that*

sucesivo (adj) *consecutive; successive*

SUCESO (m) *event*

suciedad (f) *dirt; dirtiness*

SUCIO (adj) *dirty; soiled*

sucursal (f) *branch* [of firm]; *branch office*

SUD (m) *south; south wind*

sudar *to perspire*

sudeste (m) *south-east*

sudoeste (m) *south-west*

suegro, -a (m & f) *father-in-law; mother-in-law*

SUELDO (m) *salary*

SUELO (m) *soil; ground; floor* [of room]

suelo natal = *native country*

SUEÑO (m) *sleep; also dream*

tener sueño = *to be sleepy*

sueño pesado = *heavy sleep*

entre sueños = *in dreamland*
ni por sueño = *not a bit of it*; *by no means*
SUERTE (f) *fate*; *luck*; *good luck*; *chance*
  por suerte = *by chance*; *luckily*
  tener mala suerte = *to be unlucky*
  de todas suertes = *in any case*
  echar suertes = *to draw lots*
SUFICIENTE (adj) *sufficient*; *able*; *competent*
sufrido (pp & adj) *long-suffering*; *enduring* [of colours]
SUFRIR *to suffer*; *to tolerate*; *to endure*
sugerir *to suggest*; *to propose*; *to hint*
sugestión (f) *suggestion*
SUJETO (m) *subject, topic*; *fellow, individual*
  (adj) = *liable*; *subject (to)*
SUMA (f) *sum*; *addition*
sumar *to add up*; *to amount to*
suministro (m) *supply*
  (pl) = *supplies*
sumo (adj) *high*; *great*; *supreme*
  a lo sumo = *at most*
  de sumo = *fully*
  suma necedad = *utter nonsense*
superar *to excel, surpass*; *to defeat*
superficial (adj) *superficial, shallow*
superficie (f) *surface*
SUPERIOR (adj) *superior*; *higher*; *upper*
  parte superior = *top part*
  lado superior = *upper side*
  labio superior = *upper lip*
superioridad (f) *superiority*
superviviente (adj & inv noun) *surviving*; *survivor*
SUPONER *to suppose*; *to assume*; *to take for granted*
suposición (f) *supposition*; *assumption*
supremo (adj) *supreme*; *highest*

tribunal supremo = *supreme (highest) court*
SUPUESTO (m) *assumption*; *hypothesis*
  (adj) *supposed, assumed*
  supuesto que = *granting that*
  esto supuesto = *this being understood*
  por supuesto = *of course*; *naturally*
SUR (m) *south*
  América del Sur = *South America*
surtido (m) *choice, variety*; *supply*
suspirar *to sigh*
suspiro (m) *sigh*
SUSTO (m) *fright*
  dar un susto = *to cause fright*; *to frighten, scare*
SUYO, SUYA } (poss adj & pron)
SUYOS, -AS } *his, her(s), its*; *your(s), their(s)*
  (pron) el suyo, la suya, los suyos, las suyas.
See pp. 27–28

T

TABACO (m) *tobacco*
— de pipa = *pipe tobacco*
TABERNA (f) *tavern*; *public house*
tabernero, -a (m & f) *tavern keeper*; *tavern keeper's wife*
tabla (f) *plank, board*; *table*
  hacer tablas = *to be undecided*
TAL, TALES (adj) *such (a)*; *so, as*; *similar*
  Jamás he visto tal cosa = *I've never seen such a thing*
  No conozco a tal hombre = *I don't know such a man*
  tal cual = *such as it is*; *so-so*
  el tal hombre = *such a man*
  la tal mujer = *such a woman*
  un tal López = *one, a certain López*

TAL (pron) *such, such a one, such a thing*

  No hay tal = *there's no such thing, person*

  otro que tal = *another of the same kind, ilk*

  ¿Qué tal? = *Hello!* or *How goes it?*

  con tal que = *provided that*

  tal vez = *maybe; perhaps*

talento (m) *talent*

talonario (m) *cheque book; book with stubs*

talle (m) *form, figure; waist; bodice*

taller (m) *workshop; studio*

  taller de reparaciones = *service station* [for cars]; *repair shop*

TAMAÑO (m) *size; bulk*

TAMBIÉN (adv) *also*

TAMPOCO (adv) *neither*

  ni yo tampoco = *nor I either*

TAN (adv) *as, so; so much; as well, as much*

  TAN pobre COMO = *as poor as* See p. 16

  Juan es tan pobre = *John is so poor*

TANTO, -A, -OS, -AS (adj) *as, so much; so many*

  (adv) **TANTO** = *so much, so greatly.* (pron) = *that much*

  por tanto, por lo tanto = *for that reason; therefore*

  cinco y tantos = *five and a little more* (= *five-odd*)

  él sabe tanto como yo = *he knows as much as I* (*do*)

  Vd. no debe beber tanto = *you must not drink so much*

  tanto mejor (peor) = *so much the better* (*worse*)

  entre tanto = *meanwhile*

TAPA (f) *lid, cover* [of boxes]

tapiz (m) *tapestry*

taquigrafía (f) *shorthand*

taquígrafo, -a *shorthand-writer* (m & f)

TAQUILLA (f) *ticket office; booking-office*

tardanza (f) *delay; slowness; tardiness*

TARDAR *to delay; to put off; to dally*

  a más tardar = *at latest*

  tardar en + inf = *to delay in* [doing sth]

  el tren tarda una hora en llegar a Madrid = *the train takes 2 hours to reach Madrid*

TARDE (adv) *late; too late*

  hacerse tarde = *to grow late*

  tarde o temprano = *sooner or later*

TARDE (f) *afternoon; evening*

  buenas tardes = *good afternoon; good evening*

  por la tarde = *in the afternoon; evening*

TAREA (f) *task, toil; day's work*

TARJETA (f) *card; label*

  tarjeta postal = *postcard*

  tarjeta de visita = *visiting card*

taxímetro (m)⎫
TAXI (m)   ⎬ *taxi-cab; taximeter*

TAZA (f) *cup; cupful*

  una taza DE té = *a cup of tea*

  una taza PARA té = *a tea-cup*

TÉ (m) *tea*

te (pron) *thou (you).* See pp. 22–23

TEATRO (m) *theatre; stage* [profession]

técnica (f) *technique*

TÉCNICO (adj) *technical*

techo (m) *ceiling*

técnico (m) *technician*

tejado (m) *roof*

tejer *to weave*

tejido (m) *woven material; fabric*

tela (f) *cloth; stuff*

TELEFONEAR *to telephone*

TELEFONEMA (m) *phone message*

telefónico (adj) *telephonic*

telefonista (inv n) *phone operator*

TELÉFONO (m) *telephone*
  por t. = *by phone*

TELEGRAFIAR *to telegraph; to send a telegram*

telegráfico (adj) *telegraphic*

TELÉGRAFO (m) *telegraph*
  por telégrafo = *by telegraph*

telegrama (m) *telegram*

televisión (f) *television*

TEMA (m) *theme; subject*

temblar *to shake; tremble*
  temblar de frío = *to shiver with cold*

tembloroso (adj) *trembling; shaking*

TEMER *to fear; to be afraid*

temerario (adj) *rash; imprudent*

temor (m) = *fear, dread*

temperamento (m) *temperament*

temperatura (f) *temperature*

TEMPESTAD (f) *storm; tempest*

tempestuoso (adj) *stormy*

templado (adj) *lukewarm*

temporada (f) *season; spell* [of weather]
  — de lluvias = *spell of rain*
  — de nieves = *spell of snow*

TEMPRANO (adj & adv) *early; soon*

tenaz (adj) *tenacious; persevering; stubborn*

tendencia (f) *tendency*

tender *to unfold, spread out; to tend*
  tender la ropa = *to hang out* (*wet*) *clothes*

TENDERO, -A *shopkeeper; retailer* (m & f)

tenedor (m) *table-fork; holder*
  — de libros = *bookkeeper*

TENER *to have; to possess; to hold, grasp*
  See pp. 45, 51, 68–9.

tener cuidado = *to take care*
  — éxito = *to be successful*
  — tener ganas de + inf = *to feel like* [doing sth]
  — hambre = *to be hungry*
  — sed = *to be thirsty*
  — sueño = *to be sleepy*
  — necesidad de = *to need*
  — noticias de = *to hear about* or *from*
  — la ocasión = *to have the opportunity*
  — que = *to have to; must*

tenerse = *to hold fast; to stop*
  — en pie = *to stand; to keep standing*

teniente (m) *lieutenant* [army]

TENIS (m) *tennis*

tentación (f) *temptation*

tentar *to try, attempt, endeavour; to grope; to examine by touch*

tentativa (f) *attempt*

teñir *to dye*
  teñir de negro = *to dye black*

teoría (f) *theory*

teórico (adj) *theoretical*

terminación (f) *end; ending* [act of]

TERMINAR *to end, finish*

TÉRMINO (m) *end, completion; term, word; boundary; terminus*
  (por) término medio = (*on*) *an average*
  poner término a = *to put an end to; to stop*
  estar en buenos términos (con) = *to be on good terms* (*with*)

termómetro (m) *thermometer*

ternero, -a *calf* (m & f). (f) = *veal*

tenura (f) *tenderness; fondness*

terraza (f) *terrace; border* [in garden]

TERRENO (m) *piece of land, lot, plot; sphere of action*
  terreno abierto = *open ground*

terrestre (adj) *terrestrial; earthly*

TERRIBLE (adj) *terrible; dreadful; huge*

territorio (m) *territory*

terrón (m) *clod; lump of earth*

    terrón de azúcar = *lump of sugar*

terror (m) *terror; dread*

tesorería (f) *treasurer's office; treasury*

tesorero, -a *treasurer* (m & f)

testamento (m) *will; last testament*

testar *to make a will or testament*

TESTIGO (m) *witness; testifier; testimony, evidence*

    testigo de vista = *eyewitness*

tetera (f) *tea-pot*

texto (m) *text*

TÍA (f) *aunt*

    cuéntaselo a tu tía = *tell it (that) to the marines* (coll)

TIEMPO (m) *time; weather*

    a su tiempo = *in good time, in due course*

    en tiempo de = *in the time of*

    tiempo atrás = *some time ago*

    tiempo ha = *a long time ago*

    a tiempo = *on time; at the proper time*

    a tiempos = *at times*

    hace mucho tiempo = *a long time ago*

    no hay tiempo = *there's no time*

    hacer buen tiempo = *the weather is fine*

    hace mal tiempo = *the weather is bad*

    matar el tiempo = *to kill time*

    tomarse el tiempo = *to take one's time*

TIENDA (f) *shop, store; tent; awning*

tiento (m) *touch; feeling*

    dar un tiento = *to have a try; to try*

    por el tiento = *by touch*

tierno (adj) *tender, soft; affectionate; amiable*

TIERRA (f) *earth; land; plot of soil; native land*

    tierra adentro = *inland*

    por tierra = *overland, by land*

    ver tierras = *to see the world*

    tierra alta = *highland*

    tierra baja = *lowland*

tieso (adj) *stiff, rigid*

tijeras (pl f) *scissors*

timbre (m) *door bell*

    tocar el timbre = *to ring the bell*

timidez (f) *timidity, fear*

tímido (adj) *shy; timid*

tinieblas (pl f) *darkness*

TINTA (f) *ink*

tinte (m) *dye; dyeing; dyer's shop*

tinto (adj) (1) *red* [of wine] (2) *dyed, tinted*

    vino tinto = *red wine*

TÍO, -A (m & f) *uncle; aunt*

típico (adj) *typical; characteristic*

TIPO (m) *type, pattern; standard; fellow, guy*

    un buen tipo = *a good fellow*

tirantes (pl m) *suspenders; braces*

TIRAR *to pull, drag, draw; to shoot, fire* [a weapon]; *to throw*

    tirar una cosa = *to throw sth*

    tirar una piedra = *to throw a stone*

    tirar una línea = *to draw a line*

    tirar a la derecha (izquierda) = *to turn right, left*

    tirar una fortuna = *to squander a fortune*

tirarse — *to abandon oneself; to be printed, published*

    'El Diario' se tira en una aldea = *'El Diario' is printed in a village*

TIRO (m) *cast, throw, shot; shooting*

tiro al blanco = *target shooting*
de tiros largos = *in full dress; in full regalia*
a un tiro de piedra = *within a stone's throw*
TÍTULO (m) *title; degree; heading; caption*
título al portador = *payable to bearer*
toalla (f) *towel*
TOCAR *to touch; to play an instrument*
tocar el timbre = *to ring the bell*
tocar a la puerta = *to rap (knock) at the door*
¿A quién le toca? = *Whose turn is it?*
Me toca a mí = *It's my turn*
El vapor toca en Lisboa = *The steamer calls at Lisbon*
tocar la guitarra = *to play the guitar*
tocina (m) *bacon; salt pork*
tocino gordo = *fat pork*
TODAVÍA (adv) *still, yet*
todavía no = *not yet*
TODO (adj) *all; every; whole*
en todas partes = *everywhere*
de todos modos = *in any case; anyhow*
todo el día = *the whole day; all day*
todos los días = *every day*
todas las noches = *every night*
todo el mundo = *everybody*
en todo el mundo = *everywhere*
(adv) **ante todo** = *before everything; first of all*
en todo caso = *in any case*
sobre todo = *especially*
todo lo posible = *everything possible*
tolerable (adj) *tolerable; bearable*
tolerar *to tolerate; to bear*
TOMAR *to take; to eat or drink*

tomar el desayuno = *to have breakfast, etc.*
tomar una bebida = *to have a drink*
tomar un cuarto = *to rent a room*
tomar medidas = *to take steps*
tomar precauciones = *to take precautions*
tomar en serio = *to take seriously*
tomar a broma = *to take as a joke*
tomar por la derecha (izquierda) = *to take the right (left)*
tomate (m) *tomato*
tonelada (f) *ton*
tónico (m) *tonic*
tono (m) *tone; tune*
gente del buen tono = *smart set*
darse tono = *to put on airs*
tontería (f) *foolishness; nonsense*
¡Qué tontería! = *What rubbish!*
tonto, -a (adj & m & f) *stupid, silly stupid person*
topar *to collide with; to run into*
torcedura (f) *sprain; twisting*
TORCER *to twist; to bend; to curve; to sprain [a foot, etc.]*
torcido (adj) *twisted; crooked; bent*
torear *to fight bulls*
torero (m) *bullfighter [applies to any member of a cuadrilla]*
torneo (m) *contest; tournament*
TORO (m) *bull*
correr toros = *to fight bulls*
la corrida de toros = *bullfight*
(pl) **los toros** = *bullfighting*
torpe (adj) *heavy; awkward; dull*
torpeza (f) *stupidity, dullness*
torre (f) *tower; church belfry*
tortilla (f) (1) *omelette* [Sp] (2) *pancake* [Mexico]
tos (f) *cough*
toser *to cough*
tostada (f) *toast; toasted bread*
dar una tostada = *to cheat; to disappoint*

tostar *to toast; to brown*
TOTAL (adj & noun m) *total; whole*
trabajador, -a (adj & noun) *industrious, working*
  un t. = *a worker*
TRABAJAR *to work; to labour*
  trabajar a destajo = *to do piece work*
TRABAJO (m) *work, labour; piece of work*
  (pl) **trabajos** = *hardship, want*
  pasar trabajos = *to have a hard time; to meet with difficulties*
tradición (f) *tradition*
tradicional (adj) *traditional*
traducción (f) *translation*
traducir *to translate*
  (pres) **traduzco**
traductor, -a *translator* (m & f)
TRAER *to bring, fetch; to lead* [a person]; *to wear* [a garment]
  traer consigo = *to bring with one*
  traer a la mano = *to carry* or *fetch*
  traer un vestido verde = *to wear a green dress*
TRÁFICO (m) *traffic*
tragar *to swallow*
  no poder tragar = *not to be able to swallow* (= *believe*) *sth*
tragedia (f) *tragedy*
trágico (adj) *tragic*
TRAGO (m) *draught of liquid; swallow; drink*
  un trago de vino = *a drink of wine*
  tomar un trago = *to have a drink*
  un traguito = *a little drink*
traición (f) *treason; betrayal; treachery*
traicionar = *to betray; to let down*
TRAJE (m) *costume, suit; dress, gown*
  traje de etiqueta = *full dress; evening dress*
  traje de luces = *bullfighter's dress*

tranquilidad (f) *peace, quiet; calmness*
TRANQUILO (adj) *tranquil, calm, quiet*
transatlántico (adj) *transatlantic* (noun m) = *liner*
transferir *to transfer*
transición (f) *transition*
transigir *to compromise; to settle*
transparente (adj) *transparent*
transportar *to transport*
transporte (m) *transport; transportation; conveyance; carriage*
tranvía (m) *tram; tramway*
tras (prp) *after, behind, at the back of*
trasladar *to move (shift) from one place to another*
traslado (m) *transfer; move; copy, transcript*
trastornar *to upset; to turn upside down, disarrange; to perturb, perplex*
trastorno (m) *disarrangement; disorder; confusion*
tratado (m) *treaty; treatise*
TRATAR *to treat* [but not to a drink, meal, etc.]; *to discuss* [a subject]; *to deal* [trade, business]
  tratar de = *to treat* (or *address as*)
  tratar de tonto = *to treat us a fool, an ass*
  tratar en = *to deal in*
  tratar de + inf = *to try to*
  tratar de hablar = *to try to speak*
TRATO (m) *deal; transaction; bargain*
TRAVÉS (m) *slant, slope; reverse; traverse*
  de través ⎫ = *across*
  al través ⎭
  a través de = *through*

TRAVESÍA (f) *sea voyage; sea crossing; passage; crossroad; short cut*

travesura (f) *prank, caper; bright conversation*

travieso (adj) *mischievous; frolicsome*

trazo (m) *outline, plan*

TREN (m) *train* [railway]; *retinue, show, pomp*

  tren ascendente = *up train*

  — **descendente** = *down train*

  tren expreso = *express train*

  tren de pasajeros = *passenger train*

  tren correo = *mail train*

  tren de recreo = *excursion train*

tremendo (adj) *tremendous; terrific*

  ¡Es tremendo! = *That's terrific, marvellous*

trepar *to climb, mount, clamber*

TRIBUNAL (m) *tribunal; court of justice*

TRIGO (m) *wheat*

trimestral (adj) *quarterly*

trimestre (m) *quarter* [of year]; *quarterly payment*

trinchar *to carve*

tripulación (f) *crew*

TRISTE (adj) *sad; sorrowful*

tristeza (f) *sorrow; gloom*

triunfo (m) *triumph; victory; success*

tronar *to thunder*

  truena = *there's thunder; it's thundering*

tropa (f) *crowd, multitude*

  (*pl*) **tropas** = *troops, military force(s)*

tropezar *to stumble*

  tropezar con = *to strike against; to stumble on*

  tropezar con una persona = *to run into, meet by chance*

  tropezar con una piedra = *to trip on (over) a stone*

tropical (adj) *tropical*

trópico (m) *tropic*

TROZO (m) *fragment, piece; bit, scrap*

truco (m) *trick*

trueno (m) *thunder; detonation*

  trueno gordo = *loud detonation; big piece of scandal*

TÚ (familiar pers pron). *you.* See p. 22

TU (poss adj & pron.) *your.* See pp. 27–28

TUBO (m) *tube, pipe, duct*

tuerto (adj) *blind in one eye*

tumba (f) *tomb; grave*

túnel (m) *tunnel*

turismo (m) *tourism; travel*

turista (inv n) *tourist*

TURNO (m) *turn; order*

  al turno = *by turns*

  por su turno = *in one's turn*

  Es mi turno = *It's my turn*

turrón (m) *nougat; almond paste*

  comer del turrón = *to have a nice (public) job*

tutear *to address by* **TÚ** *and* **TE**; *to use the familiar pers prons*

TUYO, -A; EL TUYO, LA TUYA *your*

TUYOS, -A; LAS TUYOS, LAS TUYAS *yours*

(Poss adjs & prons). See pp. 27–28

U

U (conj) = *or*, is used in place of **O** *before words beginning* **O** *or* **HO**:

  diez u once = *10 or 11*

ÚLTIMO (adj) *last, latest; farthest*

  a última hora = *at the 11th hour*

  a la última = *in the latest fashion*

  por último = *finally*

últimamente (adv) = *of late, recently*

ultramar (m) *across the sea; overseas*

UN, UNA (indef art) *a, an*

UN, UNO, UNOS, UNAS (adj) *one; some, few*
  unos días = *some days; a few days*
  unas noches = *some nights*
  unos cinco días = *about 5 days*

UNO (indef pron) *(the) one*
  cada uno = *each one*
  el uno o el otro = *one or the other; either*
  ni el uno ni el otro = *neither one nor the other; neither*

ungüento (m) *ointment*
  ungüento bórico = *boric (boracic) ointment*

uña (f) *nail* [of finger or toe]

urgencia (f) *urgency*

URGENTE (adj) *urgent*

usado (adj) *worn, worn out; second-hand*

USAR *to use, make use of; to wear*

uso (m) *use; usage*

USTED, USTEDES (pers pron) *you.* See p. 22

usual (adj) *usual; customary*
  no usual = *unusual*

ÚTIL (adj) *useful; effective*
  (Noun m pl) **ÚTILES** = *tools, utensils*

utilizar *to utilise*
  utilizarse = *to profit; to turn to advantage*

uva (f) *grape*
  un racimo de uvas = *bunch of grapes*

V

vaca (f) *cow*
  carne de vaca = *beef*

vacaciones (pl f) *holidays; vacation*

vacante (adj) *vacant, unoccupied*
  (noun f) = *vacant job*

vaciar *to empty*

VACÍO (adj) *empty*

vado (m) *ford*

vagabundo (m) *tramp; vagabond*

vagar *to wander; to hike*

vago (adj) *vague*

VAGÓN (m) *railway carriage; wagon*
  vagón de pasajeros = *passenger coach*
  vagón-restaurante = *dining car*
  vagón de mercancías = *goods truck*

vaivén (m) *oscillation, vibration, sway*

VALER *to be worth; to be valued at; to be equal to*
  valer tres pesetas (pesos) = *to be worth 3 pts (ps)*
  ¿Cuánto vale esto? = *How much does this cost?*
  no vale nada = *it's not worth anything; no use*
  valer la pena = *to be worth the trouble*
  valerse de = *to make use of; to avail oneself of*

valiente (adj) *brave; courageous; gallant*

VALOR (m) *value; valor, courage*
  sin valor = *valueless*
  (pl) **valores** = *securities, stocks and shares*

valorar *to set a price on*

valla (f) *fence; railing*

valle (m) *valley*

VAPOR (m) *vapour, steam; steamship*
  un vapor correo = *mail boat*

vara (f) Sp measurement = *2.8 inches; rod, stick*

variable (adj) *variable; changeable*

variación (f) *change; variation*

variar *to change, alter*; *to vary*
variedad (f) *variety*; *diversity*
VARIO (adj) (1) *different* (2) *various, diverse*
  (pl) = *several, some*
  varias personas = *several people*
varón (m) *male*
vasto (adj) *vast*; *huge*
vecindad (f) *neighbourhood*; *vicinity*
VECINO (adj) *neighbouring*
  la casa vecina = *the house next door*
VECINO, -A *neighbour* (m & f)
vega (f) *fertile plain* [Sp]; *tobacco plantation* [Cuba]; *swamp* [Chile]
vegetal (adj & noun m) *vegetable*
vehículo (m) *vehicle*
vejez (f) *old age*
vela (f) *wax candle*; *night work*
  en vela = *without sleep*
velar *to watch, be vigilant*; *to work at night*
velocidad (f) *speed*; *velocity*
velocímetro (m) *speedometer*
veloz (adj) *fast, swift*; *rapid*
vencedor (m & f) *victor*; *winner*
VENCER *to conquer, vanquish, defeat*
  vencer las dificultades = *to overcome the difficulties*
vencido (adj) *overcome, defeated*
VENDEDOR, -A (m & f) *seller*
  vendedor por mayor = *wholesaler*
  — por menor = *retailer*
VENDER *to sell*
veneno (m) *poison*
venenoso (adj) *poisonous*
vengar *to revenge, avenge*
  vengarse = *to take revenge*
VENIDA (f) *coming*; *arrival*; *return*
venidero (adj) *coming, future*
VENIR *to come*; *to arise, result*; *to be becoming*; *to suit, fit*

la semana que viene = *next week*
el año que viene = *next year*
El vestido no me viene bien = *The suit does not fit me*
¿A qué viene eso? = *What has that to do with it (the matter)?*
venir de Bilbao = *to come from Bilbao*
venir el deseo de = *to feel the desire for . . .*
VENTA (f) *roadside inn*; *sale*
VENTAJA (f) *advantage*
  llevar ventaja a = *to have advantage over*
ventajoso (adj) *advantageous*
VENTANA (f) *window*; *window frame*; *window shutter*
ventilación (f) *ventilation*
ventilador (m) *ventilator*
ventilar *to ventilate*
VER *to see*; *to look into, examine*
  ver de = *to try to*
  ver venir = *to see coming*
  hacer ver = *to show*
  estar por ver = *to remain to be seen*
  no poder ver a = *to detest sb*
  estoy viendo que = *I have a feeling that . . .*
  ver tierras = *to see the world*
  verse con = *to interview, have a talk with*
veranear *to pass the summer*
VERANO (m) *summer*
ver (m) *seeing*; *aspect, appearance*
veras (noun f pl) *truth, earnestness*
  DE VERAS = *truly, really*
verbena (f) *night festival on the eve of a saint's day*
verbal (adj) *verbal*
VERDAD (f) *truth*
  en verdad = *truly*
  ser verdad = *to be true*
  ¿No es verdad? = *Isn't it true? (= so)*

Es verdad = *It's true* (= *so*)
la pura verdad = *the simple* (= *real*) *truth*
decir verdad = *to speak the truth*
verdadero (adj) *true; sincere; truthful*
VERDE (adj) *green*
(noun m) *green colour*
verduras (pl f) *greens; vegetables*
vergonzoso (adj) *causing shame; shameful; shy*
vergüenza (f) *shame; bashfulness*
tener vergüenza = *to be ashamed*
¡QUÉ VERGÜENZA! = *How shameful!*
sin vergüenza = *shameless*
verso (m) *verse*
verter *to pour out; to spill*
vertical (adj) *upright; vertical*
VESTIDO (m) *garment; dress*
vestir *to dress sb*
VESTIRSE = *to dress oneself; to put one's clothes on*
veterinario (m) *veterinary surgeon; vet*
VEZ (f) *time* (= *occasion*)
a la vez = *simultaneously*
una vez = *once*
dos (etc.) **veces** = *twice* (etc.). See p. 20
a veces = *at times*
alguna vez = *occasionally*
algunas veces = *sometimes*
cada vez = *each time*
otra vez = *another time*
muchas veces = *many times*
varias veces = *several times*
a su vez = *in his* (*her*) *turn*
por primera vez = *for the first time*
rara vez = *seldom*
de vez en cuando = *from time to time*
tal vez = *perhaps; maybe*
VÍA (f) *way, road, route; via; railway track*

vía pública = *highway; public thoroughfare*
por la vía de = *by* (*route*); *via*
VIAJANTE (m) *commercial traveller*
VIAJAR *to travel*
VIAJE (m) *journey, voyage, trip*
viaje de ida y vuelta = *return journey*
viaje redondo = *round trip*
viaje por mar = *sea journey*
viaje por avión = *aeroplane journey* (*trip*)
¡Buen viaje! = (*May you*) *have a good journey*
VIAJERO, -A *traveller* (m & f)
vicio (m) *vice; bad habit; fraud*
de vicio = *by* (*bad*) *habit*
quejarse de vicio = *to be habitually complaining*
vicioso (adj) *vicious, given to vice; spoiled* [child]
víctima (f) *victim*
victoria (f) *victory*
victorioso (adj) *victorious*
VIDA (f) *life; lifetime; livelihood; human being*
vida ancha = *good living; gay living*
darse buena vida = *to live well*
seguro sobre la vida = *life insurance*
llevar una vida = *to lead a life*
vidriera (f) *glass window; glass door*
vidrio (m) *glass* [for pane, etc.]
VIEJO (adj & noun) *old*
un viejo = *an old man*
una vieja = *an old woman*
ir para viejo = *to be getting on* (*in years*)
VIENTO (m) *wind*
viento fresco = *fresh breeze*
molino de viento = *windmill*
hacer viento = *to be windy*

vigilante (adj & noun) *watchful*; *watchman*

vigilar *to be watchful*; *to keep an eye on*

vigor (m) *vigour*

VIL (adj) *vile, mean, base*

villa (f) *town*; *country seat*; *villa*

vinagre (m) *vinegar*

VINO (m) *wine*
— **blanco** = *white wine*
— **tinto** = *red wine*
— **de pasto** (**mesa**) = *table wine*
— **de Jerez** = *sherry*
— **de Oporto** = *port*
— **de Málaga** = *Málaga*
— **añejo** = *old wine*
— **seco** = *dry wine*
  tomarse del vino = *to get drunk* (*on wine*)

violento (adj) *violent*

violín (m) *violin*

visar *to mark with a visa*; *to visé*

virgen (adj & inv n) *virgin*
  la Virgen = *the* (*Blessed*) *Virgin*

visión (f) *sight*; *vision*; *dream*; *fantasy*; *phantom*
  ver visiones = *to build castles* (*in the air*)

VISITA (f) *visit, social call*; *visitor*; *caller*
  hacer una visita = *to pay a visit*
  pagar una visita = *to return a visit*

VISITAR *to visit, pay a visit*; *to examine, inspect*
  visitarse = *to visit one another*

VISTA (f) *sight, view*; *eyesight*
  a vista de = *in sight of*; *in the presence of*
  en vista de = *in view of, considering*
  conocer a uno de vista = *to know sb by sight*
  perder de vista = *to lose sight of*
  tener vista corta = *to be short-sighted*

¡Hasta la vista! = *au revoir* (= *until we meet again*)

una vista de Londres = *a view of London*

visto (adj) *obvious, evident*
  bien visto = *approved*
  mal visto = *disapproved*
  visto bueno = *correct, O.K.* (abbr V°.B°)
  visto que . . . = *considering that . . .*

vital (adj) *vital*; *necessary*; *essential*

vitalidad (f) *vitality*

VIUDO, -A (adj & noun) *widower, widow*

¡viva! (excl) *hurrah!*
  ¡VIVA EL REY! = *Long live the King!*

víveres (pl m) *provisions, victuals*; *stores*

vivienda (f) *dwelling*; *lodging*

VIVIR *to live*; *to last, endure*
  ¿Quién vive? = *Who goes there?*
  el mal vivir = *riotous living*

VIVO (adj) *alive, living*; *lively*
  de viva voz = *by word of mouth*
  tocar en lo vivo = *to hurt to the quick*
  los vivos = *the living*

VOLAR *to fly* [of birds and aeroplanes]

volumen (m) *volume, size*; *bulk*

voluntario (adj) *voluntary*

VOLVER *to return*

vosotros, -as (pers pron) *you*; *ye*. See p. 22

votación (f) *voting*; *ballot*

votar *to vote*

VOZ (f) *voice*; *vote*
  (pl) *outcry, clamour*
  en voz alta = *aloud*; *in a loud voice*
  en voz baja = *in a low voice*
  a voz en grito = *at the top of one's voice*; *yelling*

ser voz común = *to be a common rumour*

a voces = *loudly, shouting*

VUELO (m) *flight; flying; distance of a flight*

VUELTA (f) *turn, turning; revolution (of wheel); bend; return (= coming back); change [of money]*

de vuelta = *on returning*

a la vuelta = *carried forward*

de la vuelta = *brought forward*

la vuelta de un duro = *the change of a duro*

dar una vuelta = *to take a stroll*

a vuelta de = *in the course of, in (time)*

vuestro, -a ⎫ (poss adj & pron)
vuestros, -as ⎭ *your(s)*. See p. 27

W

W not in the Sp alphabet

X

X no words beginning with X are of frequent occurrence

Y

Y (conj) *and*. See also E

ya ... ya ... (conj) *either ... or ...*

ya que = *seeing that, since ...*

YA (adv) *already; now; at once*
Often used as emphatic, as in:

ya entiendo = *I do understand*

ya veo = *I do see*

ya lo creo = *I do believe it* (= *of course*, or *naturally*)

ya se ve = *it's easily seen* (= *it certainly is so*)

ya no = *no longer*

ya voy = *coming* [at once]

¡Pues ya! = *Why, certainly*

¡Ya está! = *That's it! Now it's right!*

yanqui (adj & inv noun) *Yankee; American* [U.S.]

yarda (f) *yard* [measure]

yate (m) *yacht*

yerba (= hierba) (f) *herb; grass; weed*

yerba de mar = *seaweed*

yerba mate = *maté tea* [S.A.]

yerno (n) *son-in-law*

YO (pers pron) *I*

yo mismo = *I myself*

Z

zapatería (f) *shoe(maker's) shop*

zapatero, -a *shoemaker* (m & f)

zapatilla (f) *light (indoor) slipper*

ZAPATO (m) *shoe* [for human foot]

zona (f) *zone*

zona templada = *temperate zone*

zona tórrida = *torrid zone*

zoológico (adj) *zoological*. See PARQUE

zorro, -a *fox; cunning person* (m & f)

zumo (m) *juice* [of fruits]

zumo de naranja = *orange juice*

WEIGHTS AND MEASURES: MONEY

Linear measure: Medida de longitud

1 centímetro = *0.393 inches, or slightly less than* ⅓ *of 1 inch;* abbr **cm(s)**.
1 metro = *39.37 inches or 1 yard and 3¾ inches;* abbr. **m(s)**.
1 kilómetro = *1093.61 yards, or about* ⅔ *of 1 mile* (*English*); abbr **Km**
10 kilómetros = *about 6¼ miles.* **100 Km.** = *about 62 miles.*

Weight measures: Peso

1 gramo = *15.432 grains, or about 0.035 oz. Avoirdupois;* abbr **gr(s)**.
100 gramos = *3 oz. 8½ drs. Av.*
1 kilogramo = *2.204 lb. Av.;* abbr **Kg(s)**.
50 kilogramos = *110 lb. Av.*

Liquid measures: Medida de capacidad para líquidos

1 litro = *1.749 English pints, or about 1¾ pts.,* abbr **l, ls.**
5 litros = *1 gallon +* ¾ *of 1 pint.*
10 litros = *2 gallons + 1½ pints.*
50 litros = *11 gallons, approximately.*

Square measure: Medida de superficie

1 metro cuadrado = *10.76 sq. feet, or just over 1 sq. yard,* abbr. **m.c.**
5 metros cuadrados = *5.98 sq. yards* = *just under 6 sq. yards;* abbr. **ms. cs.**
1 hectárea = *2.47 acres* (= **10,000 metros cuadrados**); abbr. **hect.**

Money

The monetary unit in Spain is the peseta, in most of Spanish-America the peso.

Spain:

1 duro = **5 pesetas** (abbr **pts.**).
10 céntimos (abbr **cs.**), *copper coin.* **100 céntimos** = **1 peseta.**

Spanish paper money:

Billetes (de Banco) de 25, 50, 100, 500 *and* **1,000 pesetas.**

In Spanish-American countries the centavo (abbr c., cs.) is the smallest unit.

100 centavos = **1 peso** (abbr. **p., ps.**).

Some Spanish-American countries give a special name to their monetary unit: in Venezuela, it is called the bolívar.

☞ As most of these currencies tend to fluctuate, some of them from day to day, it is always advisable to consult a bank for the current rate of exchange for any one of them.

WEIGHTS AND MEASURES; MONEY

Linear measures: Medida de longitud

Weight measures: Peso

Liquid measures: Medida de capacidad para líquidos

Square measures: Medida de superficie